USEFUL KNOWLEDGE

THE AMERICAN
PHILOSOPHICAL SOCIETY
MILLENNIUM
PROGRAM

USEFUL KNOWLEDGE

THE AMERICAN PHILOSOPHICAL SOCIETY MILLENNIUM PROGRAM

ALEXANDER G. BEARN

Editor

AMERICAN PHILOSOPHICAL SOCIETY
Independence Square • Philadelphia

1999

Memoirs
of the American Philosophical Society
Held at Philadelphia
For Promoting Useful Knowledge
Volume 234

Copyright © 1999 by
the American Philosophical Society for its
Memoirs series, volume 234.

Publication of this volume has been made possible by the generous contributions of:
Mr. Edmund N. Carpenter II, Mr. Lewis Van Dusen, Jr. and Dr. Ruth Patrick,
Mr. and Mrs. A. Bruce Mainwaring, Mr. and Mrs. Morton Sand,
and Dr. John M. Templeton, Jr.

ISBN: 0-87169-234-1
US ISSN: 0065-9738

Library of Congress Cataloging-in-Publication Data

Useful knowledge : the American Philosophical Society millennium program /
Alexander G. Bearn, editor
p. cm. — (Memoirs of the American Philosophical Society, ISSN 0065-9738; v. 234)
Includes bibliographical references and index.
ISBN 0-87169-234-1 (hardbound)
1. Learning and scholarship — Congresses.   2. Twenty-first century — Congress.
3. American Philosophical Society — Congresses.   I. Bearn, Alexander G., 1923 –
II. American Philosophical Society.   III. Series
Q11.P612 vol. 234
[AZ221]
081 s—dc21
[001.2]   99-039406

Contents

Wiring the Brain: Dynamic Interplay Between Nature and Nurture

CLASS V: THE PROFESSIONS, ARTS AND AFFAIRS

Preface

ANOTHER BOOK summarizing an academic symposium? How many prefaces in how many disciplines have tried to avoid the sting of this question by preemptively posing it to themselves? But there is really only one answer to this question: novel insight. It may be fine-grained insight or, with good fortune, it may be the broader vision that can come with age and experience, the broader, farther vision that is called wisdom.

In the past, new unpublished data were often presented at academic and scientific meetings and publication of such papers represented a milestone in the acquisition of new knowledge. Sadly, this is now seldom the case. Too often today the publication of scientific meetings re-present already-published work, many times without even the benefit of a thoughtful bibliography: stale insights hastily sketched by authors who know full well that their time would be more valuably spent seeking new knowledge.

We hope that these Millennial proceedings of the American Philosophical Society live up to the best of our traditions and present not only fine-grained insights but, with more daring, the current wisdom of our membership. The symposium was not designed so that already-acquired knowledge could reappear in new wrappers. It was, rather, designed to turn the accident of a new millennium into an opportunity for scholars in this country and overseas, all members of the Society, to reflect critically about the accomplishments of the past and to project the future trajectories of their disciplines.

It is my happy responsibility, on the part of all members of the Society and distinguished guests, to thank our accomplished Editor, Carole LeFaivre-Rochester, whose attentions to the myriad details of this project shepherded the papers into this book. Special thanks to Andrea Nicotera, who expertly transcribed many of the papers, and to Annie Westcott, who was instrumental in obtaining generous donations to help with its publication. Indeed our thanks are owed to the entire Society staff, all of whom worked indefatigably to make the meeting a success. We are all fortunate to have their professional support.

Our greatest debt, of course, is to the participants who provided one of the most memorable meetings of the Society for many decades and who graciously provided manuscripts of such quality that they will remind us for all time that scholars in different fields can create a symposium of permanent value. Its publication now ensures that others unable to attend the Millennium Meeting will be able to enjoy its rich fabric of speculation and wisdom.

A.G.B.

PRELIMINARY REMARKS

After Dinner Remarks*

PAUL A. VOLCKER

Former Chairman
Board of Governors of the Federal Reserve System

I STAND BEFORE you this evening in awe and trepidation. It is a unique occasion when my signature can be joined with that of Benjamin Franklin—as well as with so many other distinguished contributors to the sum of useful knowledge over the years. I cannot claim to have discovered electricity, to be a master of the epigram, to have contributed to either science or literature—or even to have mastered the Internet.

Yet somehow here I am, responding to Alexander Bearn's invitation to say a few words at this opening event of the American Philosophical Society's Millennium Program.

What I do know—what we all know—is that we are in the midst of enormous change in the way the world runs. It is changing inexorably precisely because of advances in practical technology, the very objective this Society has sought to promote from its start.

The changes are pervasive. The speed and economy of communication, of data transmission, of information exchange boggles a mind that is 70 years old. More significantly—it is all taken for granted by my grandchildren. But if I understand at all what the experts are saying, we (and the grandchildren) "ain't seen nothing yet."

The point I want to linger on for a few minutes this evening, is to explore some of the implications.

I realize that I'm more spectator than participant with respect to modern technology. But, as my favorite American philosopher, Yogi Berra, once said, "You can observe quite a lot just by watching." What I have been observing is the remarkable increase in international business and more par-

---

*21 April 1999.

ticularly the explosion in international finance in recent years. The change encompasses the developing as well as the industrial world.

Technology has made it all possible. But something less tangible has been at work as well.

Alongside the computer revolution has been the intellectual triumph of the ideas of open markets and democratic capitalism. The analytic case for private property, for the free movement of goods, and for competition is not new. It has been a mainstay of classical economics for almost the entire lifetime of the Philosophical Society, dating back to Adam Smith's *Wealth of Nations* in 1776.

As a practical matter, the application of those ideas has been uneven, to understate the point. A great deal of progress had been made in freeing trade among the industrialized countries in the decades after World War II. But it has only been since the end of the Cold War and the intellectual and practical breakdown of Communism that the ideology of democratic capitalism has swept the world. It is essentially a phenomenon of the late 1980s and 1990s that controls on capital moving across national borders have been dropped by almost all countries, small and poor as well as large and rich. A convincing case has been made that the implications are far broader than the purely economic, specifically that the free flow of money, protected by property rights, will powerfully reinforce individual initiative and democracy.

On the face of it, the current performance of the world economy hardly bears out the bright promise that the free flow of money internationally will speed economic growth. The United States excepted, almost all of the industrialized world has found itself in an economic rut as the Twentieth Century draws to a close. Unemployment is at historically high levels and global economic expansion has slowed to a trickle, below the rate of population growth.

Economic history provides ample evidence of the potential volatility of free financial markets. What we have seen in these past few years is how that volatility can impact forcibly on economically small countries in Asia and Latin America that have only recently emerged into full participation in the global economy. In stark contrast to earlier sustained strong economic performance, they were at mid-decade plunged into deep recession with so far only feeble signs of recovery.

What does it all mean for the new millennium? Well, I take seriously Yogi Berra's famous warning that "it's hard to make predictions, particularly about the future." But we can start by getting a little perspective.

It's not commonly recalled, but it's nonetheless a fact, that the net transfer of capital over national borders took place in relative terms on a larger scale at the beginning of the Twentieth Century than at the end. The peak came on the eve of World War I, when England was exporting capital equivalent to 10 percent of its gross domestic product. That ratio has not been approached by any major country in the second half of the century.

The decades before World War I were also marked by unprecedented economic growth. No doubt the large flow of savings from the industrializing core of Europe to the rapidly emerging North America and to the colonized areas of Asia and Africa played a large role. There was price stability in the framework of the gold standard, which in effect provided a kind of world currency.

Financial crises were not unknown, particularly in Latin America. The United States had its share as well. But generally the effects were short-lived, not severely damaging in the context of the whole. On balance, open markets for trade and international finance provided strong support for the sense of peace, economic prosperity and confidence about the future.

Of course, the structure of the world economy was very different then. Neither money nor information could move quickly. Investing decisions required commitments over a long period of time, supporting continuing business objectives. Much of the investing and lending was to colonial dependencies that neither had nor anticipated political sovereignty and policy autonomy. But it was also true that among the main countries there were growing political and commercial rivalries, rivalries that contributed to the outbreak of the first World War in, of all places, the Balkans.

As it turned out, the internationalization of commerce and finance and Victorian visions of one world prosperity didn't last long. The World War and the subsequent inflations and the depression changed the rules of the game and thinking. Economic policy and doctrine and policy turned inward. Controls on trade and finance proliferated. John Maynard Keynes great opus written in 1935, *The General Theory of Employment, Interest and Money*, had a profound influence on a generation of economists and policy makers, and it made only passing reference to foreign trade and almost none to international finance. That omission would have been unthinkable in 1910 or in 1990!

A lot of sad experience with protectionism and hard thinking—partly inspired by Keynes—helped restore a more outward looking international framework for international trade after World War II. It took more than a decade for tariffs and other barriers to fall appreciably, but once they did, trade again became a driving force for economic expansion in the industrialized world. But it was only in the 1990s that the developing world really entered into the world financial markets in force.

Those financial markets were much larger and more fluid than anything seen before. Some of the flows resembled those of a century earlier. Direct investment in infrastructure and in manufacturing industry revived, speeding growth as much by bringing industrial technology and management experience as by bringing money. There has been a burgeoning of bond financing as well.

But in contrast to the earlier period the flows became increasingly dominated by short-term credits. The lenders, instead of being impelled by long-term relationships, are institutions looking to maximize immediate returns in highly competitive markets.

Today it is easy and cheap—a few blips on a computer to move money around fast, back and forth, in response to changes in market circumstances, perceived and real. The current estimates are that foreign exchange trading amounts to 1½ trillion dollars in a single day, or about a fifth of the entire annual GNP of the United States. That daily churning—way, way above the amount of trade and long-term investing—suggests the potential volatility.

The perceptions are as important as the so-called fundamentals, and it is demonstrable that the mood of those who man the computers and make the decisions can swing sharply and unexpectedly. At the same time, the typical emerging nation has small and poorly developed financial markets.

When the money flows in they prosper, but it also brings the risk that healthy expansion becomes an unmanageable bubble. When sentiment changes, the money flows out faster than it comes in for fear of devaluations and defaults. Interest rates soar. The viability of local financial institutions is undermined. What starts out as a financial crisis becomes an economic debacle.

The interesting question, of course, is where we go from here: What does the next century hold in store? The basic economic pressures seem clear enough. The pace of globalization is being forced even faster. For instance:

- In sharp contrast to earlier policies, foreign influence and ownership of financial institutions in emerging economies is not only tolerated but encouraged. There is a strong instinct—a correct instinct—that stability requires size and diversification. Size and diversification for financial institutions operating in small countries means they must be international.
- The speeding of economic integration is also clear in the non-financial world. Large and strong multi-national companies perceive in the crisis opportunities for enhancing their penetration in developing markets. They see that as a key to sustaining their future growth. Potentially, the economic benefits will extend to host countries as well.
- Most surprising of all, running right against the grain of most economists advice, a number of emerging countries are exploring ways to attach their domestic currencies more tightly to much bigger and more stable currencies. Some of them are considering the extreme of abandoning their own currencies in favor of use of the dollar. We have already had the example of the nations of the European Union joining together to form the Euro, as the single common currency.

Yogi Berra's advice on coming to a fork in the road is to take it. And the interesting fact is that, so far at least, emerging countries have responded to the financial crisis by taking the fork in the direction of integration. For one thing the potential benefits from participating in world markets are not lightly abandoned. Moreover, the practical complexity and difficulty of maintaining bureaucratic controls on the movement of money are so daunting that efforts in that direction are deemed counter-productive.

So the pattern for the Twenty-first Century—the economic logic— seems set. Technology combines with ideology to produce one economic world. Small currencies will tend to disappear. Over time, many of those currencies could be merged into a dominant world currency perhaps built on the dollar.

Without currency crises, capital will flow more consistently toward the highest economic returns. Large businesses and financial institutions will rationalize their production and services on an international scale. And presumably, economic productivity and growth will be enhanced.

That vision bears an almost eerie resemblance to the economic world 100 years ago: a stable world currency, a liberal trading order, a dominant economic power, rapid growth. Colonialism at the economic periphery is long since gone. But in the world I describe the scope for national economic policies for small countries would be limited; monetary conditions would be set by international markets and fiscal flexibility would be circumscribed.

Will all that really happen, and happen so smoothly? Is it an economist's conceptual dream of "one world" but a practical illusion in a world where civilizations still clash and ancient enmities persist? Or more prosaically, will commercial rivalries, political differences, and simple shortsightedness challenge it all, as it did in the middle decades of the present century "deja vu all over again"?

One possible outcome will be not one economic world but several. It's easier to imagine the Americas, Europe, and Asia each with regional monetary arrangements and currencies, each with a high degree of economic integration, but each maintaining distinctive political and cultural traditions. But that avenue would run the risk of commercial restrictions and currency instability between the regions, undermining global cooperation. And the implications of regional rivalries would run far beyond the economic.

I'd place my bet on the optimistic view—that the force of technology will break down tendencies toward inward-looking regionalism, just as it has led small emerging countries to reject economic isolation. But that benign outcome is hardly assured. Technology doesn't rule human nature and human passions.

I cannot be fully optimistic without strong leadership rising to the challenge. For the time being that leadership must lie in the United States. Arguably, we have the wealth and the power. Will we maintain the spirit as well, a spirit that can look outward, taking full account of the international implications of what we do?

We can, I think, be proud of our record in that respect since World War II. Right now, with the dissolution of the USSR, the opportunities are greater than ever. The benefits of an open economic order seem demonstrable. Technology drives us in the direction of one economic world.

But there are temptations to turn inwards as well, and our unique position as an island of prosperity and the only superpower won't last forever. Technical achievement, however brilliant, is no substitute for citizen understanding and political wisdom.

Nations lost their way in the middle years of the Twentieth Century. We don't need to look beyond our morning papers to realize there are tensions, hate, and violent conflicts today.

There are still those who believe George Santayana ranks with Yogi Berra as a wise philosopher. His words that "those who cannot remember the past are condemned to repeat it" still resonate with this simple economist!

I trust the long and proud heritage of the American Philosophical Society can in some small way help to innoculate us against that danger.

Champagne Toast*

Jonathan E. Rhoads

Professor of Surgery and Provost Emeritus, University of Pennsylvania
President of the American Philosophical Society, 1976–1984

Ladies and Gentlemen

I HAVE BEEN accorded the privilege of proposing a toast to our society on this unusual occasion. As we open the final annual meeting of the society for the Twentieth Century, it behooves us to look back a bit and to thank some of our benefactors. We are indeed grateful to Arlin Adams for his exceptional service as our president during the past six years in which capacity he has been aided very much by his two executive officers, Herman Goldstine and Aleck Bearn. Our gratitude goes to our librarian, Edward Carter, and historian and former librarian and executive officer, Whitfield J. Bell and to every member of the staff.

To Paul Volcker, we are indebted not only for a wonderful address tonight but for the role he and his successor have played in maintaining an economic climate in which the society's resources have multiplied.

To Herman Goldstine, we are indebted for initiating and gaining acceptance for modifications in our election procedure designed to facilitate the election of talented persons from new disciplines and for a modest increase in our membership limits, reflecting the great increase in the number of scholars in the United States and abroad. To Aleck Bearn, for strengthening the annual giving program and for assuring the Society of future space for expansion by the acquisition of 431 Chestnut Street.

While it may seem premature to welcome our presidential nominee, Dr. Frank Rhodes, I would remind our members that it has not only been decades but I believe over two centuries since anyone nominated for the presidency has failed election.

---

*21 April 1999.

I feel therefore safe in addressing our toast to him and his administration for the inception of the Twenty-first Century.

And so to all to whom we are in the past and the present, let us drink to the continuing and expanding success of the American Philosophical Society held in Philadelphia for Promoting Useful Knowledge.

Opening Remarks[*]

ALEXANDER G. BEARN

Executive Officer, American Philosophical Society

CONFIDENT OF the general irrelevance of round-numbered dates, and in perverse disregard for the popular celebration of the next millennium, the American Philosophical Society, 'midst the drizzles of April, and in the heart of 1999, welcomes you to our Millennium meeting with boundless enthusiasm.

Let me say at the outset that the structure of this meeting departs from long-standing tradition. All the speakers today are members of the Society, and it is a particular joy for us to have among our speakers Sir John Elliott, Marc Fumaroli, Hermann Hunger, Max Perutz and Sir Martin Rees from overseas. Our numbers have also been enriched by the presence of special guests of great academic distinction. It is my privilege, on behalf of the Society, to welcome all of you, and I do so with volcanic enthusiasm: we are deeply honored that you are here and hope that you will enjoy the meeting. We keenly anticipate your active participation in the discussion.

Each class of the Society elected a chairman to help design the program. Herbert Friedman chaired Class I, encompassing the mathematical and physical sciences; Purnell Choppin chaired Class II, the biological sciences; Class III, the social sciences, was chaired by Lawrence Klein; Class IV, comprising the humanities, had as chairman Glen Bowersock; and Class V, the arts, professions, and affairs, was chaired by Robert Goheen.

Inevitably we are concerned with the future, but unwilling to join the Olympian orgy of prediction overtaking common sense; our speakers today have been asked, in a spirit of optimism, to identify some of the trends and peaks in their field during the last one hundred years, reflect on where we are today, and boldly look at prospects for the future. No scholar likes to be

---

[*] 22 April 1999.

told, however genteelly, what he or she should discuss. Their justifiable disquiet at my impudence at suggesting a theme may have been soothed by the opportunity they will have to reflect on the past and perhaps sketch the shape of the unknown. We are enormously grateful for their willingness to adhere to an unappreciative and unforgiving time constraint of 20 minutes.

A hundred years ago the Secretary and Treasurer of the Society was I. Minis Hays, to whom we express biannually in our program our gratitude for realizing that even an intellectual feast such as ours requires regular refueling at the luncheon buffet. Whether it was I. Minis Hays who first introduced oyster stew for lunch, I do not know, but in his honor we shall be offering it again today.

Throughout this meeting you will be reminded of the highest achievements of our century, but it may well be worth reminding ourselves, before we begin, that 1900 was not an entirely undistinguished year. It was in 1900 that Mendel's work in his garden of peas was rediscovered, setting in motion the genetical revolution that has changed the way we think about life, health, and disease, throughout the natural world. Moreover, it was in 1900 that Max Planck fired the quantum shot still echoing 'round the world. Puccini was busy putting his last touches to *Tosca,* Marconi was getting ready to send wireless signals from Cornwall to Newfoundland, and nobody yet realized the downward path that was to be the disastrous fate of the recently-launched Zeppelin.

One last word: there are two dangers we all face when speculating about the future—the twin dangers of sanguinity and cynicism. In our different moods, we can all succumb to the one or the other, but knowing as we do how the rack of circumstance can crack the most glorious plans, cynicism often seems the safer bet. And it is against the danger of creeping cynicism that I want to remind us all as we begin our meetings today, that the joy and energy of our lives, personal, intellectual, poetical and professional, are, in every case, a function of our rising imaginations and our delight in adventure. There can be no contentment but in proceeding.

An intellectual feast awaits us and I will delay no longer. But we do want you to know how enormously welcome you are, and how proud and honored the APS is to have you here today.

May the meeting to celebrate the millennium begin.

CLASS I

MATHEMATICAL AND PHYSICAL SCIENCES

The Laws of Nature

Steven Weinberg

Josey Regental Professor of Science, University of Texas

A T THE END of the nineteenth century the American physicist, Albert Michelson, looking forward to the coming twentieth century in a talk at the University of Chicago, made the following prediction: "While it is never safe to affirm that the future of physical science has no marvels in store even more astonishing than those of the past, it seems probable that most of the grand, underlying principles have been firmly established and that further advances are to be sought chiefly in the rigorous applications of these principles to all the phenomena which come under our notice. An eminent physicist has remarked that the future truths of physical science are to be looked for in the sixth place of decimals." Despite this prediction, Michelson was elected a few years later to this Society.

It may seem that Michelson's statement provides a good example of what Dr. Bearn referred to as the danger of sanguinity, of overconfidence. In fact I think it represents rather the reverse. Michelson was no fool, after all. He could not have thought that physics had succeeded in explaining the principles of chemistry, or the behavior of metals, for example. His statement that most of the grand, underlying principles of physics had been discovered reflected a narrow view of what physics is capable of accomplishing. Physics to him represented what it still represents in our high school courses: mechanics, electricity, heat and light. Michelson would not have dreamed that it was part of the task of physics to explain the principles of chemistry. The peculiar accomplishment of this century, one not anticipated by Michelson, has been to show how all the laws of the physical sciences can be knit together in a unified, logical structure, resting on a set of fundamental laws of nature. This goal has not yet been reached, but during this century we have come much closer.

I think that by far the most important step toward this goal in the twentieth century was the discovery in the mid 1920s of quantum mechanics. Compared to this, all other discoveries of physical science pale into insignificance. Quantum mechanics is nothing less than the language of physics. Among many other applications, quantum mechanics opened up the possibility of explaining all the phenomena of chemistry in terms of physics. Indeed, Paul Dirac, one of the founders of the new quantum mechanics, proclaimed triumphantly in 1929 that "the underlying physical laws necessary for the mathematical theory of the larger part of physics and the whole of chemistry are thus completely known and the difficulty is only that the application of these laws leads to equations much too complicated to be soluble." And he was not being too sanguine.

Twenty minutes is not quite enough to explain quantum mechanics. I will just present a six-sentence introduction to quantum mechanics, so that the rest of my talk will not be incomprehensible. The essential principle of quantum mechanics is that physical states are identified as directions in a space, a space named after the German mathematician David Hilbert, and known as Hilbert space. The number of dimensions of this space is equal to the number of possible results of any complete set of experiments. So, for example, if the experiment is just to flip a coin and the only possible results are heads or tails, then Hilbert space will be a two-dimensional space, and the state of the coin will be encoded as a direction in this two-dimensional space. There are two perpendicular directions in this space, called "heads" and "tails" instead of "north" and "east." If the state of a coin corresponds to the heads or tails direction then the coin is defi-nitely in the heads state or the tails state, respectively. The weird new thing about quantum mechanics is that typically the state of the coin is not in the heads or tails directions but in some intermediate direction. If one looks to see if a coin in such a state is head or tails, then you may get either result; the probability of your finding the coin in the heads or tails state will be given by the square of the component of the direction that represents the state along the heads or tails directions, respectively.

Now you understand quantum mechanics. Well, at least I think you will be able to recognize some of the key points I want to make about quantum mechanics.

One point already mentioned is that quantum mechanics is really weird. We are used to things having definite values, to particles having definite positions, to coins being definitely heads or tails. In quantum mechanics that can't be counted on. Any system is always in some definite state, corresponding to a definite direction in Hilbert space, but until you make a measurement the system will not have a definite value for classical quantities, like headsness or tailsness. This weirdness of quantum mechanics has led to an increasingly esoteric quality in our physics, which I think has made a chasm between the kind of work that goes on every day in physics and the general culture. I know that Lionel Trilling for one was always disappointed that he was not able to read work on quantum mechanics and relativity the way that Voltaire, for instance, was able to understand the work of Newton.

Second, although I said that quantum mechanics is the language of physics, that is not quite right; quantum mechanics is only a grammar—it gives us no semantics. The general rules of quantum mechanics themselves do not tell you what are the possible physical systems, or what experiments may be performed on these systems, and they don't tell you how fast the direction that represents a state of a system rotates.

Third, despite what you often read, quantum mechanics is a deterministic theory. Whatever the system may be, its state changes in a completely well defined way: given the state at one instant and knowing the details of the system, you can predict without any uncertainty at all what it is at any future instant. It is only when you interfere in your crude, classical way with the system and make a measurement, that an uncertainty enters. This often leads to confusion. Last week in Washington I heard a speaker explain that quantum mechanics was deeply satisfying to him as a Buddhist, because by bringing the observer into the picture along with particles or whatever it was that were being studied, quantum mechanics had showed the interconnectedness of all reality. I don't think that's true. The state of a system has an objective reality that is quite independent of any observer, and the direction corresponding to this state rotates in a completely deterministic way, though of course, if you ask questions about what observers find, you have to bring the observer into the picture. In this sense quantum mechanics does not represent a departure from the style of physics in the previous century.

The last point about quantum mechanics (and the one that is most relevant to my talk) is that quantum mechanics is extremely fragile, and leads to very fragile theories. In quantum mechanics, if you try to change the general rules that tell us how to calculate probabilities or how the direction of the state rotates, you quickly find that you get nonsense, For instance, the probabilities that you calculate may turn out to be negative, or may not add up to 100 percent. No one has ever found any way of changing the rules of quantum mechanics by a small amount that would lead to logically satisfactory theories. Of course, you can abandon quantum mechanics altogether and go back to Newtonian mechanics. I don't mean to say that quantum mechanics is logically inevitable, but only that it seems to be impossible to find any other logically consistent theory that is close to quantum mechanics. Furthermore, when you add dynamics to the picture, when you introduce a particular theory of forces or particles or whatever it is you are interested in, you find that these quantum mechanical theories are themselves very fragile. Small changes are likely to lead to logical disasters. For instance, the actual number of outcomes of a complete set of experiments is usually not just two, but infinite. As a result when you do calculations in quantum mechanics, you typically find yourself summing up infinite numbers of terms, and if you are not very careful with the theory you've constructed, you are likely to get an infinite answer—which is not profound but simply absurd. Therefore quantum mechanics does not allow you to write down theories ad libidum— there are only certain special theories that can lead to sensible results in a quantum setting. This is particularly true when you combine quantum mechanics with the other great revolution in physical theory of this century— the theory of relativity. Quantum mechanics and relativity together seem to require forces to act at a point rather than over an extended volume, which can lead to infinitely strong forces because most forces increase in strength as particles get closer and closer. It has been a great problem in this century to make relativistic quantum theories that did not lead to infinities. To avoid other paradoxes, for example to avoid effects preceding causes, relativistic quantum theories also require new particles: for every kind of particle there must be an anti-particle, with the same mass but opposite electric charge.

For a long time it seemed that the only way of combining relativity and quantum mechanics is in what are called quantum field theories. These are theories in which the fundamental constituents of nature are understood not to be not particles but fields, like the magnetic field or the gravitational field; particles are just little bundles of the energy and momentum of these fields. The modern theory that encompasses all the phenomena that we can study in our present elementary particle laboratories is a quantum field theory known as the Standard Model. It represents a remarkably comprehensive understanding of physical phenomena, although one that as yet is not complete.

The quality I have emphasized here of the fragility of quantum mechanics and of the theories that are formulated within quantum mechanics is really quite wonderful. Fragility is a quality that you don't hope for in furniture or automobiles, but it is something that is highly desirable in fundamental physical theories. After all, we are not trying to develop a set of theories that is capable of describing any conceivable universe, but one that to the greatest degree possible explains to us why our universe is the way it is. If we find that we can't vary the rules that govern our world without encountering logical absurdities, then we are entitled to some satisfaction that we understand why our world is the way it is.

Our present theory of particles and forces, the Standard Model, accounts for the weak interactions that are responsible for certain kinds of radioactivity and nuclear processes in stars, for the strong interactions that hold together the quarks inside the protons and neutrons inside the atomic nucleus, and for the electromagnetic interactions that are responsible for the phenomena of atomic physics, chemistry, solid-state physics, and, of course, light. It is not a complete theory; it represents the best that we have been able to do in this century. One sign of its incompleteness is that there are 18 numerical constants (like the electric charge of the electron) that have to be specified in order to make the theory fit experiment. Of course, the theory fits a vast number of experiments, so 18 parameters is not that bad, but it is certainly not something that we want to be left with indefinitely into the future.

In a sense our situation now is a little bit like the situation of physics at the beginning of this century. At the beginning of the century, physicists had measured a vast number of frequencies of the lines in the spectrum of atoms, frequencies at which light is preferentially emitted and absorbed. These frequencies filled large books, but no one knew how to calculate them from fundamental principles, or what they meant. The first great breakthrough in the development of quantum mechanics was in learning how to calculate these frequencies from a theory of the atom—a breakthrough that was begun by Niels Bohr in 1913 and was triumphantly brought to fruition in the discovery of modern quantum mechanics in the mid-1920s. Now we are not faced with millions of mysterious measured numbers; we are faced with 18. But just as happened with quantum mechanics, a theory that succeeded in explaining these 18 constants would be identified immediately as a success and as a great step toward a final theory.

The other thing that's missing in our present theories is that gravitation has not been brought into the same quantum field theoretic framework as the weak, strong, and electromagnetic forces. There are indications that the unification of gravitation with the other forces will be found in a theory that is not a field theory at all, and whose fundamental structures are not characterized by energies like those in our present accelerator laboratories, energies of the order of 100 billion volts, but energies that are larger than this by a factor of 100 trillion. Apparently we must look to a scale of energies that are experimentally inaccessible in order to try to formulate our final theory of physics. I don't know if this task will be accomplished in the next century. One way we will recognize that it has been done is that this theory will allow us to calculate the 18 mysterious parameters of the Standard Model. We can hope that in the meeting of the American Philosophical Society a century from now we will be able to look back at the formulation of a final theory, but it would be rash now to predict that this will happen. One thing we do know with reasonable certainty is that the final theory will not be logically unique, because we can already conceive of other logical possibilities. The best we can hope for is that it may have a very high degree of the fragility I have described; it may be that, although we cannot explain logically why this final theory is what it is, we will be able to explain logically why it is not something slightly different. That may be the best we will ever be able to do. So I anticipate that not only in the next century but in centuries to come we will be left with irreducible mysteries in our understanding of nature.

DISCUSSANT

WOLFGANG K. H. PANOFSKY

Stanford Linear Accelerator Center

WE HAVE heard from Professor Weinberg his views about the laws that the laws of physics should obey. And indeed he reminds us that the general framework of those laws is sometimes more important than their actual detailed nature. On the other hand, as an experimentalist, we make measurements and observations which have to be compared with specific calculations.

So in some respects, generalities notwithstanding, the experimentalists today are at a very frustrating point. They are frustrated because we are between successes and failures. Professor Weinberg indicated that four basic forces of nature are recognized: the strong, weak, electromagnetic, and gravitational and he has made key contributions in the quest to unify the electromagnetic and weak forces. And Professor Weinberg also mentioned the Standard Model, which at this point in time correctly describes the first three of these forces, but at this time attempts to unify the fourth remain speculative. The other thing, and this speaker is an experimentalist, the experimental basis of the Standard Model rests largely on observations of the subatomic and even subnuclear level that is on a distance scale of 10^{-10} to 10^{-18} meters. But there is no observational basis at all of gravitational phenomena at distances below a few millimeters. So there's no overlap whatsoever of the region of observation of gravitational forces and the other three forces of nature. That's an enormous empirical gap in these forces, if these are to be joined. Theoretically, the gap appears even larger since the theoretical point of unification of these forces if one takes current vast extrapolation into account, should be in the 10^{-40} meter or so region. Thus we are in a very frustrating situation. The standard model has met, to quote Pauli's expression, the "not even wrong standard," that is, it agrees fully with observation, but it does not meet the standard of simplicity as Professor Weinberg has indicated. There are too many free parameters that have to be plugged into the theory, those that measure the masses of the particles involved and the strength of the forces that connect them. To simplify this discordant situation and make the laws of nature meet Professor Weinberg's standards is a formidable challenge for physical scientists in the future. Whether there can be experimental results with physical apparatus we can construct in the future depends crucially on whether the gulf between current observation and the unification scale is really as large as it seems. Several theoretical speculations have been made that indicate that gravity starts behaving completely differently at scales smaller than a few millimeters. If nature is actually so kind for that to be true, then, indeed, our gravity may be more accessible to physical observation than currently meets the eye. Let me note that, historically, our resolving power at which we can discern nature in the laboratory has grown by about one order of magnitude per decade. But that pace cannot possibly be maintained through the next century through the construction of larger and larger colliding-beam machines. Rather, the progress must increasingly rest on joining cosmological to subnuclear observations.

Our Concepts of the Cosmos: Progress, Prospects, and Mysteries

SIR MARTIN J. REES

Royal Society Professor; Cambridge University

Introduction

AT FIRST sight, any attempt to understand the cosmos may seem over-ambitious. Cosmologists would claim, nonetheless, to have transformed their subject into a genuine empirical science, especially in the last three decades. This progress has proved possible because the universe possesses a surprising degree of overall symmetry and uniformity. It is *complexity* and not sheer size, that makes a phenomenon baffling. In the fierce heat of a star and (even more surely) in the early universe, everything has been broken down into its simplest constituents. So cosmology need not be the most intractable science. Our biological colleagues—studying the intricate multi-layered structure of trees, butterflies and brains—face challenges that may be even tougher.

Stars, Atoms and Planets

A century ago, the Sun presented a mystery. Darwin and the geologists had already inferred that the Earth's age was measured in billions of years. On the other hand, Lord Kelvin had done a real calculation: he'd shown the Sun's age to be little more than 10 million years. That was the timescale on which the Sun would deflate, owing to gravity, as its energy leaked away. Kelvin saw no way round this limit unless—to quote him—there were "some other power source laid up in the storehouse of creation." We have learnt during the twentieth century that there was such a source, within the atomic nucleus. The paradox was resolved, and we now have a convincing picture of the Sun's evolution.

The proto-Sun condensed from a gas cloud. Gravity pulled it together until its center was squeezed hot enough to trigger nuclear fusion. This energy source supplies power at just the rate needed to balance the heat shining from its surface. Less than half the Sun's central hydrogen has so far been used up, even though it's already 4.5 billion years old. The Sun will keep shining for a further 5 billion years. It will then swell up to become a red giant, large and bright enough to engulf the inner planets, and to vaporize all life on Earth. After this "red giant" phase, some outer layers are blown off, leaving a white dwarf—a dense star no larger than the Earth, which will shine with a dull glow, no brighter than the full moon today, on whatever remains of the Solar System.

Stars are simple enough, in their gross structure, that one can compute their structure and life cycles, for any assumed initial mass and composition. But how can we check such calculations? Stars live so long compared to astronomers that we're granted just a single "snapshot" of each one's life. But just as it wouldn't take a newly landed Martian long to infer the life cycle of trees or people, astronomers can test their theories, by surveying whole populations of stars.

The best "test beds" are the globular clusters—swarms of a hundred thousand stars, of different sizes, held together by their mutual gravity, which formed at the same time. Stars seem still to be forming in, for instance, the spectacular Eagle Nebula, about 7,000 light years away. Clouds like these harbor bright young stars and newly-condensing protostars that haven't yet got hot enough to ignite their nuclear fuel.

Not everything in the cosmos happens slowly, however. Stars that are more than ten times as heavy as the Sun end their lives violently by exploding as supernovae. The closest supernova of the twentieth century, about 150 thousand light years distant, was observed to flare up on 23–24 February 1987. Theorists were given a chance to check their elaborate computer calculations, and the supernova remnant's gradual fading has been studied using all the techniques of modern astronomy. In about 1,000 years it will resemble the Crab Nebula, the expanding debris from an explosion recorded by Chinese astronomers in 1054 AD.

Supernovae fascinate astronomers. But out of very 10,000 people taken at random, only one is an astronomer. (In most parts of the world, they are out-numbered by astrologers!). Why should the other 9,999 care about stellar explosions thousands of light years away? One answer is that they are an essential part of our environment; without them, the Earth could not have formed.

On Earth, for every 10 atoms of carbon, there are about 20 of oxygen and 5 each of nitrogen and iron. But gold is a million times rarer than oxygen; platinum and mercury are rarer still. What determines this mix? Did the creator have to turn 92 different knobs? These exploding stars offer a less "ad hoc" explanation.

Stars more than ten times heavier than the Sun use up their central hydrogen hundreds of times quicker than the Sun does—they shine much brighter in consequence. Gravity then squeezes them further, and the centers get still hotter, until helium atoms can themselves stick together to make the nuclei of heavier atoms. A kind of "onion skin" structure develops: a layer of carbon surrounds one of oxygen, which in turn surrounds a layer of silicon. The hotter inner layers have been transmuted further up the periodic table and surround a core that is mainly iron. When their fuel has all been consumed, big stars face a crisis. A catastrophic infall compresses the stellar core to neutron densities, triggering a colossal explosion. This explosion manifests itself as a supernova.

The outer layers of a star, by the time a supernova explosion blows them off, contain the outcome of all the nuclear alchemy that kept it shining over its entire lifetime. There is a lot of oxygen and carbon in this mixture, plus traces of many other elements. The calculated "mix" is gratifyingly close to the proportions now observed in our Solar System.

Astronomers have for a long time suspected planetary systems to be common, because protostars, as they contract from rotating clouds, spin off around them discs of dusty gas. In these discs, dust grains would stick together to make rocky "planetesmals," which can in turn merge to make planets.

Protostellar discs have been observed by their infrared emission, but actual planets orbiting other stars have proved more elusive. We have learnt only quite recently that other stars besides our Sun have retinues of planets on which intricate complexities might develop. In 1995 two Swiss astronomers, Didier Quelez and Michael Mayor, found that the Doppler shift of 51 Pegasi, a nearby star resembling our Sun, was wobbling sinusoidally by

50 m/sec—they inferred that a planet weighing a thousandth as much was circling it at 50 km/sec$_1$ causing the star to pivot around the combined center of mass.

Marcy and Butler, in California, have now discovered that several more stars display similar motions. But the planets inferred so far are all big ones—like Jupiter. These may be the largest members of other planetary systems like our own—individual Earth-like planets would a hundred times harder to detect.

Beyond Our Galaxy

Our galaxy, and its neighbor Andromeda, are "ecosystems": before our Sun formed, pristine gas had already been cycled through fast-burning heavy stars. We're stardust—or, less romantically, the "nuclear waste" from the fuel that makes stars shine.

The nearest few thousand galaxies—those closer than about 300 million light years—have been mapped out in depth. They're irregularly distributed—into clusters, and superclusters. Are there, one wonders, clusters of clusters of clusters ad infinitum? There don't seem to be. Deeper surveys show a smoother distribution: our Universe isn't a fractal. If it were, we'd see equally conspicuous clumps, on ever-larger scales, however deep into space we probed. Even the biggest superclusters are still small in comparison with the horizon that powerful telescopes can reach. So we can define the average "smoothed-out" properties of our observable universe.

But what set the stage for the first stars and the first galaxies? To answer this question, we must look back in time to the era when galaxies were young. Telescopes are now powerful enough to do this. The longest-exposure pictures taken with the Hubble Space Telescope show several hundred galaxies, even in a patch of sky less than a hundredth of the area covered by a full moon. The light registered on these images set out ten billion years ago—before these galaxies had settled down into steadily-spinning "pinwheels" like Andromeda. They're imaged when they're mainly still glowing gas, before their stars have had time to transmute the chemical elements. They'd not yet harbor planets, and presumably no life.

(Technical advances are now accumulating immense amounts of digitized data about the distant universe, as in other subjects. These are a valuable resource. It is one of the benign byproducts of modern information technology that isolated scientists will soon be able to access or download these vast data sets and pursue their own studies anywhere in the world).

Astronomers can actually *see* the remote past. But what about still more remote epochs, before any galaxies had formed? The term "big bang" was introduced into cosmology by Fred Hoyle, as a derisive description of a theory he didn't like. The undignified name has stuck, and there is now firm evidence that it connotes an actual event. Weak microwaves, first detected by Penzias and Wilson in 1965, pervade all of space, making it slightly warm. Their intensity has now been measured, at many different wavelengths to a precision of a part in 10,000. The spectrum is a precise fit to a black body, characteristic of thermal equilibrium—the errors are smaller than the thickness of the line of the graph. The only credible interpretation is that these microwaves are an "afterglow" of a pregalactic era when the entire Universe was hot, dense, and opaque. The expansion has cooled and diluted the radiation, and stretched its wavelength. But this primordial heat is still around—it fills the Universe and has nowhere else to go!

And there is another "fossil" of the hot beginning: if the universe had once been briefly, cooked hotter than a star, one can calculate what nuclear reactions could have occurred. The proportion of helium in the universe, which can be measured with one percent precision, agrees with the amount that, according to calculation, would have been made in the hot initial instants.

Futurology

In about 5 billion years the Sun will die; and the Earth with it. At about the same time (give or take a billion years) the Andromeda Galaxy which is in the same cluster as us and is actually falling towards us, will crash into our own Milky Way. But will the universe go on expanding *forever*? Or will the entire firmament eventually collapse into a "big crunch"?

The answer depends on how much the cosmic expansion is being decelerated by the gravitational pull that everything in the Universe exerts on everything else. It is straightforward to calculate that the expansion can eventually be reversed if there is, on average, more than about 5 atoms in each cubic meter. That doesn't sound like much. But if all the galaxies were dismantled, and their constituent stars and gas spread uniformly through space, they'd make 50 times less—1 atom in every 10 cubic meters—like one snowflake in the entire volume of the Earth.

Cosmologists use the term omega for the ratio of the actual density to the critical density. At first sight this seems to imply that omega is only 1/50—and hence perpetual expansion, by a wide margin. But it's not so straight-forward. Astronomers have discovered that the internal motions within galaxies, and even within entire clusters of galaxies, are so rapid that these systems would fly apart unless they were held together by the gravitational pull of 10 times more material than we actually see.

Compelling corroboration of "dark matter" comes from pictures of big clusters of galaxies. The brighter-seeming galaxies in such pictures belong to the cluster. But the picture also contains a lot of faint streaks and arcs: each of these is a remote galaxy, several times further away than the cluster itself, whose image is, as it were, viewed through a distorting lens. It is be-ing gravitationally lensed by the cluster. These drastic distortions require ten times more mass than we see in the galaxies themselves.

It seems that the early universe contained not just atoms and radiation, but other particles, of uncertain nature, that make up the dark matter. Our Copernican modesty must be carried a stage further; even "particle chau-vinism" has to go. We, the stars, and the galaxies seem almost an afterthought in a cosmos whose large-scale structure is dominated by quite different stuff. But there's still only 30 percent of what's needed to halt the expansion of the universe,—in cosmologist's jargon, omega is 0.3.

The odds favoring perpetual expansion have recently strengthened. There is evidence for an extra long-range repulsion force—what Einstein called the cosmological constant, lambda. The expansion may actually ac-celerate. If it does—and the jury's still out—the forecast is an even darker and emptier universe.

Back to the Beginning

People sometimes wonder how our universe can have started off as a hot, amorphous fireball and ended up intricately differentiated. This may seem contrary to the second law of thermodynamics. But it's no mystery: the *workings of gravity* render the expanding universe unstable to the growth of structure. Theorists can now follow a "virtual universe" in a computer. The calculations clearly portray the emergence of incipient galaxies and larger structures as the density contrasts grow. Overdense regions condense into protogalaxies, each an arena for the emergence of stars, planets, and life.

Such calculations need to specify, at some early time like one second, a few numbers:

(i) The cosmic expansion rate

(ii) The proportions of ordinary atoms, dark matter and radiation in the universe

(iii) The character of the fluctuations—large enough to evolve into structures, but not to invalidate the overall uniformity; and, of course,

(iv) The basic constants of microphysics.

Any explanation for these numbers must lie *still earlier* in cosmic history—not just the first second, but the first tiny fraction of a second. What's the chance, then of pushing the barrier back still further?

The extrapolation back to the stage when the Universe had been expanding for *a few seconds* (when the helium formed) deserves to be taken as seriously as, for instance, what geologists or paleontologists tell us about the early history of our Earth. The matter was no denser than air; our extrapolation is vindicated by well-measured "fossils" from that era—background radiation, helium and deuterium. But for the first trillionth of a second every particle would have more energy than even CERN's new accelerator will reach. So we lose our foothold in experiment.

Emphasizing that the ground is now less firm, I'll press on backwards into the first tiny fraction of a second. One mystery is the seemingly "fine tuned" balance between kinetic energy and gravity. Our 12 billion year old universe is still expanding: a universe that re-collapsed sooner would not have allowed time for stars to evolve, or even to form. But the initial expansion wasn't *too* fast; otherwise kinetic energy would have so overwhelmed gravity that galaxies would have been unable to condense out. The initial potential and kinetic energies were very closely matched. How did this come about? Cosmologists have developed serious (though still, of course, tentative) theories to account for this, and for the related mystery of why our Universe is so large. Under extreme densities, it's argued, an extra force of "cosmic repulsion" would have exponentially accelerated the expansion, inflating and homogenizing a microscopic embryo universe. This idea is compellingly attractive, especially as the fluctuations that evolved into galaxies may then have evolved from microscopic vibrations or ripples implied by quantum physics. With luck, this idea, which refers to the first 10^{-36} sec of cosmic history, will soon be confronted with observational tests, just as the first few seconds already have been.

The inflation concept looks like "something for nothing," but it isn't really. That's because our present vast universe may, in a sense, have zero net energy. Every atom has an energy because of its mass—Einstein's Mc^2. But it has a negative energy due to gravity—we, for instance, are in a state of lower energy on the Earth's surface than if we were up in space. And if we added up the negative potential energy we possess due to the gravitational field of everything else, it could cancel out our rest mass energy. Thus it doesn't, as it were, cost anything, to expand the mass and energy in our universe.

Cosmologists sometimes loosely assert that the universe can essentially arise "from nothing." But they should watch their language, especially when talking to philosophers. The physicist's vacuum is latent with particles and forces—it's a far richer construct than the philosopher's "nothing." Physicists may, some day, discover a final theory governing physical reality. But they'll never tell us what "breathes fire" into their equations, and actualizes them in a real cosmos.

There are intimate connections between the cosmos and the microworld. Our everyday world is determined by chemistry: the properties of atoms. Stars shine because of reactions of atomic nuclei. Galaxies are held together by the gravity of a huge swarm of subnuclear particles. The ultimate synthesis that still eludes us is between the very largest and smallest scales of all—between gravity, the main cosmic force, and the quantum principle that governs the microworld.

The two great foundations of twentieth-century physics are Einstein's theory of gravity, and the quantum theory. Normally, there's no overlap between their domains of relevance—quantum effects are crucial on the microscopic scale, but gravity is only important for large objects, where quantum uncertainty can be ignored. But back at the beginning, everything would have been squeezed so densely that quantum effects could shake the entire universe. This happens at the Planck time, 10^{-44} sec. In the beginning of our universe, and deep inside black holes, conditions are so extreme that we know for sure that we don't yet know the relevant physics. Perhaps current ideas on "superstrings" will offer an answer.

Some Conjectures

I'm uneasy about how cosmology is sometimes presented. The distinction is often blurred between what's well established and what's still speculative. Back to one second, cosmology has as firm a base as other historical sciences. But the ultra-early universe, as already emphasized, is more speculative, and I must offer a special "health warning" for the following brief comments.

In our universe, intricate complexity has unfolded from simple laws— we wouldn't be here if it hadn't. But simple laws don't *necessarily* permit complex consequences. To take an analogue from mathematics, the Mandelbrot set, with its infinite depth of structure, is encoded by a short algorithm; but other algorithms, superficially similar, yield very boring patterns.

As we have seen, our universe couldn't have become structured if it weren't expanding at a special rate. And there are other prerequisites for complexity. If nuclear forces were a few percent weaker, only hydrogen would be stable: there'd be no periodic table, no chemistry. Nor would stars and galaxies form if the residue of the big bang were entirely dark matter, with no ordinary atoms at all. If gravity were too strong, any large organisms would get crushed. Or the number of dimensions might even be different.

This apparent "tuning" could be just a brute fact. But there's another interpretation. It's that many "universes" actually exist. Only some would allow creatures like us to emerge. And we obviously find ourselves in one of that subset. The seemingly "designed" features of our universe need then occasion no surprise.

Perhaps, then, our big bang wasn't the only one. This speculation, dramatically enlarges our concept of reality. The entire history of our universe would just be an episode, one facet, of an infinite multiverse. Some universes may resemble ours; most would be "stillborn" because they re-collapse after a brief existence, or because the laws governing them don't permit complex consequences.

The status of this speculation depends on the answers to two questions:

1. Will a deeper understanding of the inflationary universe firm up the concept—espoused by Linde and Vilenkin and others—that our big bang wasn't the only one?
2. Does the final theory governing the entire multiverse allow different variants of low energy physics?

This might seem arcane stuff. But it affects how we should place our bets in current controversies. I mentioned the debate about the density of the universe, and about whether there is an extra repulsive force, the cosmological constant lambda. Some theorists have a strong "prior preference" in favor of the simplest model, with omega exactly 1: they're unhappy that observations suggest that omega is closer to 0.3,; even more so by extra complications, like a non-zero lambda. But I'm relaxed about this, because I draw a lesson from Kepler and Galileo. They were upset to find that planetary orbits were elliptical. Circles were more beautiful—and simpler, with one parameter not two. But Newton later explained all orbits in terms of a universal law with just one parameter, the gravitational constant G. Had Galileo still been alive then, he'd surely have been joyfully reconciled to ellipses.

The parallel is obvious. If a universe with low omega, non-zero lambda, and so forth seems ugly, this maybe shows our limited vision. Just as Earth follows one of the Keplerian orbits around the Sun that allow it to be habitable—but the orbit is no more special than that—so our universe may be just one anthropically-allowed member of a grander ensemble. So perhaps we should go easy with Occam's razor and be wary of arguments that omega = 1 and lambda = 0 are less ad hoc.

Conclusions

Edwin Hubble's famous book *The Realm of the Nebulae* concludes, "Only when empirical resources are exhausted do we reach the dreamy realm of speculation." We still dream and speculate, but there has been a crescendo of empirical progress since Hubble's time. This is owed to large telescopes on the ground, to the great instrument in space that bears Hubble's name, and to the advent of novel observational techniques in all bands of electromagnetic spectrum.

There are three great frontiers in science: the very big, the very small and the very complex. Cosmology involves them all.

Cosmologists must pin down the basic numbers like omega, and find what the dark matter is—this could happen within 10 years.

Second, theorists must elucidate the exotic physics of the very earliest stages—I wouldn't presume to second-guess Steven Weinberg on the prospects here.

But cosmology is also the grandest environmental science, and its third aim is to understand how a simple fireball evolved, over 12 billion years, into the complex cosmic habitat we find around us—how, on at least one planet around at least one star, conscious creatures evolved who are starting to see patterns in nature. And this is surely one of the greatest intellectual challenges of all for the next millennium.

DISCUSSANT

FREEMAN J. DYSON

I THINK there is something to be learned from the history of mathematics in the nineteenth century which might apply to the twenty-first. In the nineteenth century there were three solitary individuals who produced ideas that were about 100 years ahead of their time. The first of those was Carl Friedrich Gauss, who invented differential geometry simply as a device for mapping a spherical Earth onto a flat piece of paper. Being a very creative mathematician, he went way beyond what was required for that mundane task and invented differential geometry, which was then followed up a little later by Bernhard Riemann. But it remained isolated from the rest of mathematics and the rest of physics. Nobody imagined in the nineteenth century that this was really important. There was another even more individual character, Hermann Grassmann, a high school teacher in Stettin, who invented something he called *Die Ausdehnungslehre,* the calculus of extension, a marvelous mathematical construction which involved vector spaces and non-commuting algebraic quantities, wonderful mathematical apparatus which he believed was the key to the understanding of nature. Nobody took him seriously; in fact, he was resourceful enough to give up his career as a mathematician and become an expert in Sanskrit for which he's much better known. He translated the Sanskrit classics into German. The third solitary individual is Sophus Lie, a Norwegian mathematician, who started a huge enterprise which he called "continuous groups," which now everybody calls Lie Groups, with which he hoped to simplify classical dynamics. He did nothing of the kind; he made classical dynamics look so much more complicated that nobody took him seriously either.

Those three mathematical creations in the nineteenth century turned out to be key to the physics of the twentieth. Differential geometry was the foundation for Einstein's general relativity. Grassmann's algebra was the foundation for super-symmetry, the symmetry of the two basic types of particles that we see in the universe—the bosons and the fermions. And Lie groups became the working tool of particle physics for the second half of the century. The whole of particle physics is based on classification of particles by their symmetries under different types of Lie Groups. So let's hope that something similar may happen with string theory, which is, to my mind, a marvelous enterprise (I'm not a practitioner myself, but I'm surrounded in Princeton by practitioners and they're doing wonderful, beautiful mathematics). Nobody has the faintest idea how to relate it to physics. But it will probably come in somehow, as these other things did, unexpectedly. It will be the answer to some great question that we haven't yet asked. That at least is my dream.

Mathematics and Computing*

PETER D. LAX

Professor of Mathematics, Courant Institute of New York University

I T IS A DAUNTING task to talk about mathematics to an audience of non-mathematicians, even more daunting if the audience includes scientists from other fields. A remark of Einstein's is pertinent here: "I didn't become a mathematician, because the field was so full of beautiful and difficult problems that one might waste one's powers in pursuing them without finding the central question." Indeed, if you look at mathematics today, you do not see a central question, but you see a hundred—or at any rate several dozen—flowers bloom; no doubt another dozen or so will bloom in the coming century.

That does not mean that mathematics is falling apart into separate branches; on the contrary, astonishing connections between seemingly distant parts are discovered all the time. Nor should one think of mathematics as developing entirely on its own steam; as von Neumann observed, [35], "It is undeniable that some of the best inspirations in mathematics—in those parts of it which are as pure mathematics as one can imagine—have come from the natural sciences." No doubt the same will be true in the future; whereas in the past inspiration came mostly from geometry and physics, in the future they will come also from chemistry, biology, and the information sciences.

Although there is no common theme at the frontiers of mathematics, there is one overarching methodology for a large part of it: computing. This is not surprising; computers are a part of almost all aspects of our lives and have altered the way we look at the world. Computing is edging closer to cen-

---

*Read 22 April 1999. To the memory of Gian-Carlo Rota; the world is a duller place without him.

ter stage in the sciences; Nobel prizes have been awarded for work whose main methodology is computational. Thus in the sixties the mathematical physicist Alan Cormack shared the prize given to honor computerized tomography; his contribution was a practical method to determine a function from its integrals along straight lines. In 1986 Herbert Hauptman and Jerome Karle were honored for their work in X-ray crystallography; a crucial key to their success was a numerical implementation of Toeplitz's characterization of the Fourier transform of positive mass distributions. And last year Walter Kohn and John Pople shared the Nobel prize in chemistry given for the computational study of large molecules. It is safe to predict that computational science, fueled by new mathematical ideas, will grow in the next century, and that computing will be an integral part of many branches of mathematics.

This paper is an overview, necessarily selective, of the rise of computing in mathematics in the last half of this century, and the infusion of mathematical ideas into computing.

1. Introduction

During World War II, when von Neumann was working on the design of nuclear weapons, he came to the conclusion that analytical methods were inadequate for the task, and that the only way to deal with equations of continuum mechanics is to discretize them and solve the resulting system of equations numerically. The tools needed to carry out such calculations effectively are high speed, programmable electronic computers, large capacity storage devices, programming languages, a theory of stable discretization of differential equations, and a variety of algorithms for solving rapidly the discretized equations. It is to these tasks that von Neumann had devoted his energies after the war. He was keenly aware that computational methodology is crucial not only for designing weapons, but also for an enormous variety of scientific and engineering problems; understanding the weather and climate particularly intrigued him. But he also realized that computing can do more than grind out by brute force the answer to a concrete question. In a lecture delivered in Montreal in 1945, he concluded that "really efficient high speed computing devices, in the field of nonlinear partial differential equations as well as many other fields which are now difficult or entirely denied of access, provide us with those heuristic hints which are needed in all parts of mathematics for genuine progress." Computing is a tool for the theorist, wielded in the manner of the experimentalist; here are a few examples:

2. Experimental computing

In the fifties Fermi, Pasta, and Ulam (FTU) [10] studied numerically solutions of a discretized version of a nonlinearly perturbed wave equation. The initial configuration was the lowest mode of the linearized equation. Instead of meandering all over phase space, as taught by ergodic theory, the system returned to a small neighborhood of the initial state after a time far too short to be accounted for by Poincaré's recurrence. This greatly surprised the authors, especially Ulam, who jointly with Oxtoby [40] had proved earlier that generically volume preserving flows are ergodic. The explanation had to await the KAM theory, according to which smooth flows that lie near a completely integrable flow stay on low dimensional tori for a very long time.

In the sixties Kruskal and Zabusky [24] tackled the FPU flow by approximating it with solutions of the Korteweg-de Vries equation. The KdV equation was introduced at the end of the nineteenth century as a model of waves in shallow water in a channel; Gardner and Morikawa showed in 1960 that the KdV equation governs the oscillation of cold plasmas. The KdV equation reads as follows:

$$u_t + uu_{xxx} = 0;$$

here u denotes amplitude, x and t space and time, and the subscripts signify partial derivatives. I realize that the majority of this audience does not understand the language of partial differential equations, and therefore I am providing a translation into a more familiar, but equally concentrated literary form, a *haiku:*

> Speed depends on size,
> Balanced by dispersion,
> Oh solitary splendor.

The numerical experiments carried out by Kruskal and Zabusky showed, among others, that solutions of the KdV equation on the real line which tend to 0 fast as $|x|$ tends to infinity emit, after a while, solitary waves, dubbed *solitons,* each traveling at a constant speed. Solitons preserve their identity after repeated collisions, see Figure 1; nothing remotely like this had ever been seen in solutions of nonlinear equations. The explanation, found by Kruskal, Gardner, Greene, and Miura [16], as well as Faddeev and Zakharov [7], lies in the complete integrability of the KdV equation, an even bigger surprise.

When mathematicians claim to have solved a problem, they usually don't use the word "solve" in its ordinary sense; they mean that they have proved that a solution exists. Therein lies the significance of completely integrable systems: they can be solved exactly; this is not just a mathematical curiosity, but makes it possible to extract, not without a major effort, the kind of detail about solutions that a scientific theory needs to make predictions. Examples abound:

(a) The integrability of the motion of two gravitating bodies enabled Newton to verify Kepler's laws quantitatively.

(b) In the old quantum theory, completely integrable systems served as quantized models.

(c) Onsager used the complete integrability of the Ising model to demonstrate the existence of a critical temperature in magnetization.

Another example of a system of differential equations that a series of calculations revealed to be completely integrable is the *Toda Chain* [47]. A series of numerical calculations by Joe Ford [13] of the Poincaré map for a short Toda chain indicated that, in addition to the Hamiltonian, there is another conserved quantity. Subsequently Hermann Flaschka [11] succeeded in constructing a full set of conserved quantities for Toda chains of arbitrary length.

These discoveries opened the flood gates; more than a dozen ordinary and partial differential operators were shown to be integrable. We refer to Moser's monograph [34] and to the conference proceedings edited by Fokas and Zakharov [12]. These new completely integrable systems are more than curiosities; they rear their heads in the most unlikely contexts, some in physics, some purely mathematical. Witten conjectured, and Kontsevich proved, that the generating function for the intersection number on the moduli spaces of algebraic curves satisfies the KdV equation.

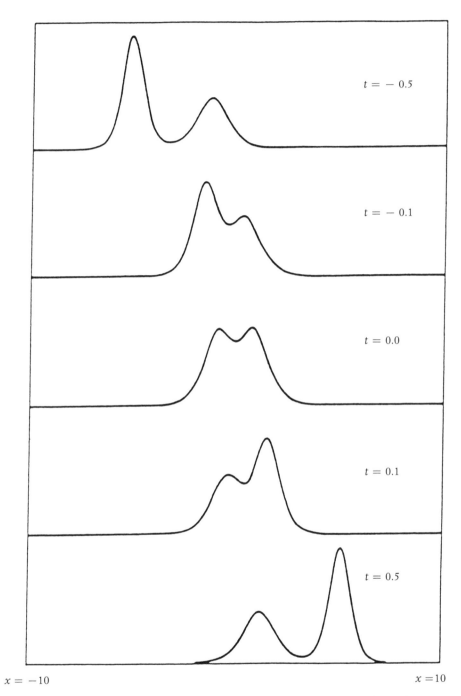

$t = -0.5$

$t = -0.1$

$t = 0.0$

$t = 0.1$

$t = 0.5$

$x = -10$

$x = 10$

FIGURE 1. Interaction of two solitons in which single peak is not formed.

The Kadomtsev-Petviashvili equations, introduced to model two-dimensional water waves and shown to be completely integrable, turned out to play an important role in their solution of Schottky's classical conjecture about Riemann matrices, see [1] and [44]; this is one of those astonishing connections between distant parts of mathematics.

An application of solitons that is of great practical significance is to the transmission of signals in optical fibers. The formation and stability of solitons is due to a balance between a nonlinear effect—the dependence of signal speed on intensity—and the dispersion of different frequencies. Both are present in light propagating in glass: the index of refraction is an increasing function of the intensity of light, and waves of shorter wave lengths travel faster than longer ones in the relevant range. These facts led Akira Hasegawa to make the mathematical prediction that solitons would propagate through optical fibres. This was demonstrated convincingly by Linn F. Mollenauer in a series of brilliant engineering studies. For a fuller discussion, see [20] and [33].

No subject relies more on computing for insight and for its popular appeal than chaos theory, see for instance [43] and [45]. There are many roads to chaos; here are a few examples:

(a) Mitchell Feigenbaum, see [4] and [9], has investigated a very simple class of dynamical systems, described by a single variable, and discrete in time. The dynamics in this case is

$$x_{n+1} = Tf(x_n).$$

Here f is a unimodal map of the interval $[0,1]$ into itself, $f(0) = f(1) = 0$, and T is a parameter, typically temperature. Through numerical experiments Feigenbaum found, and then proved mathematically, the following scenario for a wide class of functions f.

Since $f(0) = 0$, zero is a *fixed point* of the dynamics, that is, if x_n is zero, so is $x_n + 1$. When T is less than a critical value T_1, $x = 0$ is the only fixed point, and it is *attracting* in the sense that, for arbitrary starting point x_0, x_n tends to zero. For $T > T_1$, a second fixed point appears which is attracting until T reaches a second critical value T_2. As T passes beyond T_2, a periodic orbit of period 2 appears, and it is attracting until T reaches a third critical

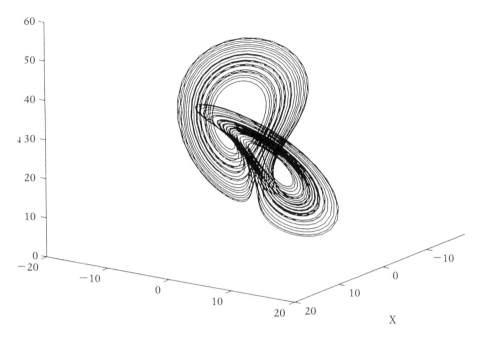

FIGURE 2. The Lorenz attractor: trajectories wind around
the two centers alternatingly.

value, T_3, beyond which a periodic orbit of period 4 appears and is attracting until T reaches the next critical value. There is altogether an infinitude of critical values T_n, each signaling a period doubling; they tend to a limit T_∞, which is the threshold of chaotic behavior, see Figure 2. T_n approaches T_∞ at an exponential rate:

$$\frac{T_m - T_{m-1}}{T_{m+1} - T_m} \to d$$

The value of d, 4.6692016 . . . , is *independent* of the details of the dynamics.

One-dimensional dynamics is rather special. Yet, numerical and laboratory experiments have disclosed period doubling as a road to chaos even in infinite-dimensional systems.

(b) The meteorologist Edward Lorenz has discovered a different route to chaos by studying numerically the long term behavior of a system of three ordinary differential equations. For large times, solutions were attracted to a set having a very weird geometrical structure. Such sets are called *strange attractors,* see Figure 2.

(c) To understand turbulence in fluid flow is one of the biggest challenges to science. The basic phenomenon is utterly intriguing: smooth flow of liquid becomes irregular when a parameter, typically Reynolds number, exceeds a threshold value. The theorist's task is to explain why smoothness is lost, and to calculate some kind of average value of the flow quantities in the turbulent region. The difficulty of both these tasks can be traced to the nonlinear character of the equations of fluid dynamics. In spite of recent advances in our understanding of turbulence [3], and the practical usefulness of modeling it empirically we are still far from a complete theory. Curiously, attempts at numerical simulation often yield ambiguous results.

(d) Smale's horseshoe.

(e) Last but not least, there are the fascinating fractal sets of Benoit Mandelbrot, [31].

PERHAPS THE most astonishing discovery through numerical experimentation concerns the distribution of the zeros of the Riemann zeta function. Riemann surmised that all these zeros in the complex plane have real part 1/2. Why is the Riemann hypothesis so intriguing? Because it stands astride so many mathematical problems about prime numbers. It is like the mysterious bog in *Peer Gynt* that bars him whichever way he turns. Most mathematicians who have thought about the Riemann hypothesis believe that its solution will reveal something very deep.

Let $\frac{1}{2} + ig_j$ be the jth zero of zeta; renormalize the g_j by defining

$$\bar{g}_j = \frac{g_j \log g_j}{2\pi}$$

Hugh Montgomery has determined the pair correlation of the renormalized zeros, and Freeman Dyson observed that it is the same as the correlation of the eigenvalues of random unitary matrices. Odlyzko [39] em-

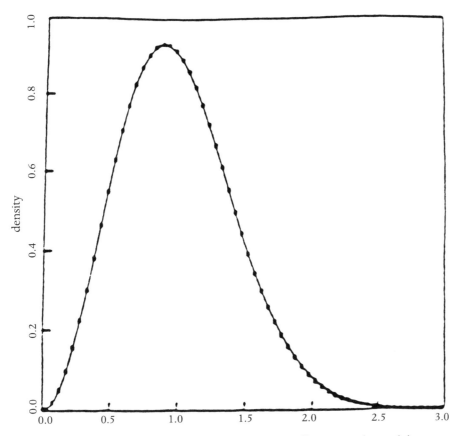

FIGURE 3. Nearest neighbor spacings among 70 million zeroes beyond the $10^{20^{\text{th}}}$ zero of zeta, versus μ_1 (*GUE*)

barked on a detailed numerical study of the spacing of the renormalized ze-ros. Figures 3 and 4 show the histogram of the differences of consecutive renormalized $\bar{g}_j$'s and their pair correlation in the range

$$10^{20} < j < 10^{20} + 7 \cdot 10^6$$

the agreement with the Gaussian unitary ensemble is well nigh perfect. For further results and discussion we refer to the paper of Katz and Sar-nak [23].

The above data show, incidentally, that an enormous number of the ze-

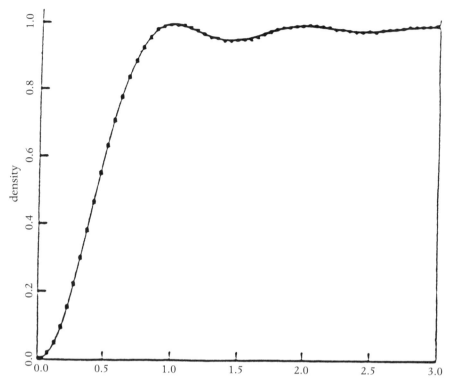

FIGURE 4. Pair correlation for zeros of zeta based on 8×10^6 zeros
near the $10^{20\text{th}}$ zero, versus the GUE conjectured density

$$1 - \left(\frac{\sin \pi x}{\pi x}\right)^2.$$

ros of the zeta function are known, and all of them have real part 1/2; isn't this overwhelming evidence for the truth of Riemann's hypothesis? One must be careful about jumping to conclusions and recall another conjecture in number theory, that the number (x) of primes less than x never exceeds the logarithmic integral $li(x)$. The numerical evidence for this also was overwhelming; yet Littlewood proved that $(x) > li(x)$ for infinitely many x. His proof, being indirect, gave no indication where the first reversal would occur; his student Skewes showed that it must occur for x less than ten raised to the power of 10 four times. Later proofs whittled this number down to about 10^{300}, still way out of the range of x for which (x) could be effectively computed.

3. How much confidence can one place in a calculation?

There are many kinds of computations and many kinds of confidence. Some computations are an integral part of the logical structure of a proof. An example is Lanford's demonstration [25] of Feigenbaum's conjecture about the iterates of smooth unimodal maps of an interval into itself: when suitably re-scaled these iterates approximate a universal shape f characterized by a functional equation of form $F(f) = f$. Lanford computed, by re-scaled iterations, a very good numerical approximation to a fixed point of F; then he showed, using computer calculations, the contractive character of F in a neighborhood of the approximate fixed point. The arithmetic calculations had to have iron clad error bounds; one technique for obtaining such bounds is so-called interval arithmetic.

The most famous proof relying on massive computer calculations is Haken's and Appel's demonstration of the four-color theorem. Here the calculations are with discrete objects and can be carried out exactly. Many have criticized this proof for giving no insight into why the result is true; others have criticized it because no single reader can verify all the steps. Both objections are on valid grounds; they will come up much more frequently as computer assisted proofs proliferate. Of course, such criticism can be leveled equally against proofs that use no computers but are indirect, or extremely long.

Enthusiasts among the artificial intelligentsia like to predict that soon computers will be able to prove on their own interesting mathematical theorems, with little or no human assistance. I believe that day is very far off; mathematics is an enormously deeper mental activity than what computers have been able to do so far, say play chess.

Most calculations are carried out to provide quantitative information for solutions of problems whose theory is well understood. In such cases we are looking for realistic error bounds, not ironclad ones. Alas, these are not easy to come by. In many cases theoretical estimates show that, for sufficiently small values of some discretization parameter h, the error is proportional to a known power of h. By carrying out the calculations for three or four values of h, one can verify this power law dependence. But in the future we shall need more sophisticated methods for estimating the error, possibly by doing a fair amount of à posteriori estimates.

There is a large class of calculations whose significance is only statistical, such as in the Monte Carlo methodology. It is a challenge to probabilists and dynamical systems people to give guidance to numerical analysts in these matters.

4. Three-dimensional fluid flow

In the design of the last generation of civilian aircraft, computing has played as important a role as wind tunnel testing. The equations governing the flow of air are discretized and flow velocity, pressure, and air density are calculated at millions of points in the exterior of the aircraft. Figure 5, taken from [21], shows the numerically calculated pressure distribution on the surface of an aircraft. This approach works very well for studying the performance of aircraft in the cruising regime, less well in off-design situations, such as during take-off and landing. The economics of aircraft operations are such that modest improvements in efficiency can substantially reduce operating costs. In the future there will be efforts to optimize the shape of aircraft by reducing drag; this is much more easily accomplished computationally than in wind tunnel tests.

The equations governing the flow of air are the laws of conservation of mass, momentum and energy. They have the form of a first order symmetrizable hyperbolic system of quasilinear partial differential equations. The theory of smooth solutions of such systems for small time has been worked out some time ago; in the hands of Paul Garabedian, this has led to the design of shockless airfoils. However, even with very smooth initial data, solutions may lose smoothness after a finite time due to the formation of shocks. They can nevertheless be continued as generalized solutions of the conservation laws in the sense of physics. A basic result of James Glimm [17] shows that for one space dimension the initial value problem has a weak solution for all time, for a fairly wide class of initial data. *No comparable result is known in more than one dimension.*

Experience with calculations of compressible flows in two and three space dimensions holds out hope that solutions exist for all time. However,

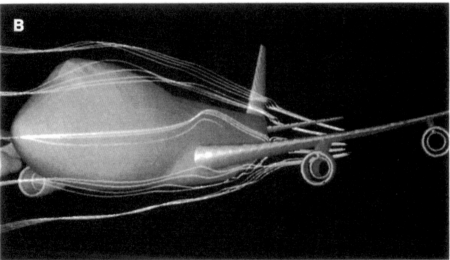

FIGURE 5. Flow past a Boeing 747-200 at Mach number 0.84 and 2.73 degrees angle of attack. (A) The color contours represent the surface pressure, with red indicating low pressure in the supersonic zone. (B) Another view showing streamlines around aircraft. (Calculated by A. Jameson and T. J. Baker.)

Density T=0.23

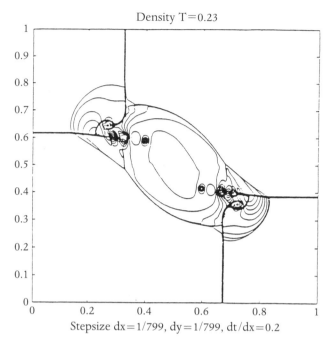

Stepsize dx=1/799, dy=1/799, dt/dx=0.2

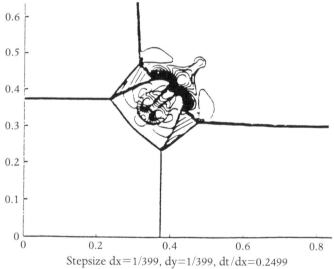

Stepsize dx=1/399, dy=1/399, dt/dx=0.2499

FIGURE 6

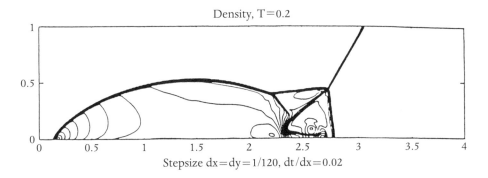

Density, T=0.2

Stepsize dx=dy=1/120, dt/dx=0.02

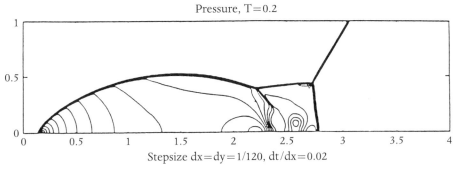

Pressure, T=0.2

Stepsize dx=dy=1/120, dt/dx=0.02

FIGURE 7

these calculations show that even for very simple initial data the structure of the solution is far from simple. Figures 6a and 6b depict the density contour lines of solutions of so-called Riemann problems, whose initial values are constant in each of the four quadrants, [27], and Figure 7 shows the density and pressure contour lines of a flow resulting from the diffraction of a strong shock by a wedge. In these cases very simple initial configurations lead instantaneously to flows of bewildering complexity.

5. Incompressible fluid flow

It is an old truism that the heart is only a pump. The studies of Charles Peskin [41] in the last two decades brilliantly justify this adage. His model of the flow of blood in the heart of a slightly viscous incompressible fluid, moving under the influence of forces exerted by the heart muscle, substantiated all

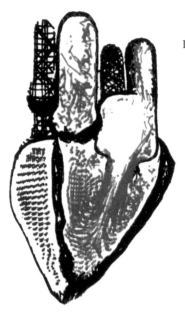

DIASTOLE

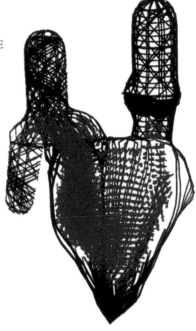

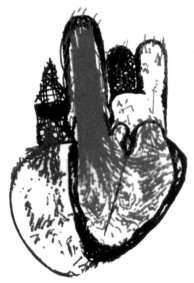
SYSTOLE

FIGURE 8

we knew about the circulation of blood in the heart chambers and revealed much that was not known, see Figure 8. In particular, Peskin found that *aerodynamic lift* exerted by the flow of blood on the leaves of the valves is a crucial part of the mechanism of closing, in a timely fashion, the heart valves, normal, pathological, or artificial. Thus Peskin was able to use his model as a test chamber for the design of new artificial valves.

6. The challenge of scientific computing

Everybody is aware of the striking increase over the last 50 years in the speed and storage capacity of computer hardware, and of improvements in software and graphics capabilities. As a result, problems that in the past have strained the capabilities of computers can now be done routinely, much faster and at much less cost, and problems of enormous complexity can be tackled confidently. What many people are unaware of is how much of this progress has been due not only to improvements in computer hardware and software, but *in equal measure to new mathematical ideas* about how to solve efficiently the computational problems that arise. Here are some striking examples.

Shock capturing: The difficulty in calculating flows with shocks is that it is very hard to predict, even in the course of a flow calculation, when and where new shocks arise; tracking the shocks, specially their interactions, is burdensome. Von Neumann and Richtmyer [38] had the ingenious idea of adding to the hydrodynamic equations a viscous term of the same size as the truncation error. The discontinuities turn into very rapid transitions which don't have to be tracked separately. The shock conditions are satisfied provided the equations of gas dynamics are discretized in conservation form.

Multigrid: After discretizing a partial differential equation—the Laplace equation is typical—one is faced with the problem of solving numerically the resulting system of linear algebraic equations. An extremely efficient iterative method for performing this task, called the multigrid method, had been proposed in the sixties by Federenko [8] and analyzed be Bakhvalov; it was further developed and implemented by Achi Brandt, see [2] and [49]. The idea, crudely put, is to obtain large scale information about the solution from calculating on a coarse grid, and finer scale information from calculations on increasingly finer grids.

39

Image reconstruction: New mathematical techniques give vastly more rapid, more accurate methods for reconstructing images scanned by X-rays, magnetic resonance or positron emission.

Fast Fourier transform: To evaluate approximately the Fourier coefficients of a function on the unit circle and to express the function in terms of its Fourier series requires the calculation of the finite Fourier transform

$$a_j = \frac{1}{n}\sum_1^n w^{jk} f_k, \qquad w = e^{2\pi i/n}$$

The straightforward evaluation of these sums requires n^2 multiplications. Using the special structure of the matrix w^{jk}, Tukey and Cooley [5] devised an algorithm that requires only $n \log n$ multiplications. This discovery made the Fourier transform a practical numerical tool; in particular, it opened the way for spectral methods to solve partial differential equations numerically. For a history of this subject, see [6].

Fast matrix multiplication: The straightforward multiplication of two n by n matrices requires n^3 scalar multiplications. In the sixties, Volker Strassen [46] has devised, to everyone's astonishment, a method of matrix multiplication that requires only $O(n^{2.807\ldots})$ scalar multiplications, where the exponent is the logarithm of 7 in base 2. This exponent has been whittled down further. The Strassen method is a time saver for operations on large, unstructured matrices.

Multi-resolution is a numerical version of the microlocal point of view; it is a representation of functions that takes both scale and location into account. The most successful forms are the various versions of wavelet representation. These are extremely useful in mathematics (approximation of solutions of differential equations), electrical engineering (signal processing), physics, and linguistics (representation of speech), see [19] and [30].

Cryptosystems: Some methods of encryption, such as the RSA system, see [42] and [28], are based on number theoretic results. In this system the encryption algorithm is public knowledge, yet does not endanger security, because decoding is an extremely laborious and time consuming process. Except, of course, for the intended recipient of the message, who has a secret key that makes rapid decoding possible. The mathematician's role here is to make sure that rapid decoding without the secret key is not possible, and that reconstruction of the secret key is also extremely time consuming. A branch of mathematics/computer science, called *computational complexity,* is devoted to such issues.

These are but a few examples of unexpected mathematical shortcuts; many others have been thought of in the past, such as combinatorial algorithms, fast function evaluations, and efficient algorithms in linear algebra, see for instance [18] and [48]. No doubt, many more remain to be discovered in the future, to fuel further advances in the art of computing.

Bibliography

[1] Arbarello, E. and De Concini, C., *Geometrical Aspects of the Kadomtsev-Petviashvili Equation.* Lecture Notes in Math., 1451, Springer Verlag, Berlin, 1990.

[2] Brandt, A., Multi-level Adaptive Solutions to Boundary Value Problems, *Math. of Comp.* 31 (1977): 333.

[3] Chorin, A. J. *Turbulence as a Near-Equilibrium Process,* 235–249. Lectures in Applied Mathematics 31 Amer. Math. Soc., 1996.

[4] Collet, P. and Eckmann, J. P., *Iterated A Maps of the Interval as Dynamical Systems,* Birkhäuser, Boston, 1980.

[5] Cooley, J. W. and Tukey, J. W., "An Algorithm for Machine Calculation of Complex Fourier Series," *Math. Comp.* 19 (1965): 297–301.

[6] Cooley, J. W., Garvin, I., et al. The 1968 Arden House Workshop on Fast Fourier Transform Processing, IEEE, Transactions on Audio-and Electro Acoustics, AU-17, (1969).

[7] Faddeev, L. and Zakharov, V. E., The KdV equation: A Completely Integrable Hamiltonian System, *Funct. Anal. Appl.* 5 (1971): 280–287.

[8] Federenko, R. E., The Speed of Convergence of an Iterative Process, *USSR Comp. Math. Phys.* 4 (1964).

[9] Feigenbaum, M. "Quantitative Universality for a Class of Nonlinear Transformations," *J. Stat. Phys.* 19 (1978): 25–52.

[10] Fermi, E., Pasta, J. and Ulam, S., Studies in Nonlinear Problems I, Los Alamos Report #1940 (1956), reprinted in *Nonlinear Wave Motion,* Lectures in Appl. Math. 15, AMS 1974.

[11] Flaschka, H., On the Toda Lattice I, *Phys. Rev. B* 9 (1974): 1924–1925; II, *Prog. Theor. Phys.* 51 (1974): 703–716.

[12] Fokas, A. S. and Zakharov, V. E., *Important Developments in Soliton Theory,* Springer Verlag, New York, 1993.

[13] Ford, J., *Adv. Chem. Phys.* 24 (1973): 155.

[14] Garabedian, P. R. Bauer, F., Korn, D. G., Jameson A., *Supercritical Wing Sections II,* Lecture Notes in Economics and Math. Systems 108, Springer-Verlag, 1975.

41

[15] Gardner, C.S., The KdV Equation and Generalizations VI: The KdV Equation as a Hamiltonian System, *J. Math. Phys,* 12 (1971):1548–1551.

[16] Gardner, C. S., Greene, J. M., Kruskal, M. D. and Miura, R. M., A Method for Solving the KdV Equation, *Phys. Rev. Lett.* 19 (1967): 1095–1097.

[17] Glimm, J., *Solutions in the Large for Nonlinear Hyperbolic Systems of Equations,* CPAM 18 (1965), 697–715.

[18] Greengard, L. and Rokhlin, V., "A Fast Algorithm for Particle Simulation," *J. Comp. Phys.* 73 (1987): 325.

[19] Harten, A., Discrete Multiresolution Analysis and Generalized Wavelets, *J. Appl. Num. Math.* 12 (1993): 153–193.

[20] Haus, H. A., Molding light into solitons, *IEEE Spectrum* (1993): 48–53.

[21] Jameson, A., Computational Aerodynamics for Aircraft Design, 245 (1989): 361–371.

[22] Jimbo, M. and Miwa, T., Algebraic Analysis of Solvable Lattice Models, *CBMS Regional Conference Series in Math.* 85, AMS, Providence, 1995.

[23] Katz, N. M. and Sarnak, P., Zeros of Zeta functions and Symmetry, *Bull. AMS* (new series) 36 (1999): 1–26.

[24] Kruskal, M. D. and Zabusky, N., Interactions of Solitons in a Collisionless Plasma, and the Recurrence of Initial States, *Phys. Rev. Lett,* 15 (1965): 240–243; 19 (1967): 1095–1098.

[25] Lanford, O. E., A Computer-assisted Proof of the Feigenbaum Conjectures, *Bull. AMS* (new series) 6 (1982): 427–434.

[26] Lax, P. D., The beginning of applied mathematics after the second World War, *Quarterly Appl. Math.* 56 (1999): 607–613.

[27] Lax, P. D. and Liu, X. D., Solution of Two-dimensional Riemann Problems of Gas Dynamics by Positive Schemes, *SIAM J. of Sc. Comp.* 19 (1998): 319–340.

[28] Lenstra, A. K. and Lenstra, H. W., Algorithms in Number Theory, *Handbook of Theoretical Computer Science* A, Algorithms and Complexity, Ch. 12, 673–715. Elsevier and MIT Press, 1990.

[29] Lorenz, E., Deterministic nonperiodic flow. *J. Atmos. Sci.* 26 (1973): 130–141.

[30] Mallat, S. *A Wavelet Tour of Signal Processing,* Academic Press, San Diego, 1998.

[31] Mandelbrot, B. B., *The Fractal Geometry of Nature,* W. H. Freeman, New York, 1983.

[32] McQueen, D. M., Peskin, C. S. and Yellin, E. L., Fluid Dynamics of the Mitral Valve: Physiological Aspects of a mathematical Model, *Amer. J. Physiology,* 242, (1982): H1095-H1110.

[33] Mollenauer, L. F., Lichtman, E., Harvey, G. T., Neubelt, M. J. and Nyan, B. M., Demonstration of Error-Free Soliton Transmission over more than 15000km. *Electron. Lett* 27(1992): 792–794.

[34] Moser, J., Three Integrable Systems Connected with Isospectral Deformations, *Adv. in Math.* 16 (1975): 107–220.

[35] von Neumann, J., *The Mathematician,* reprinted in J. R. Newman, *The World of Mathematics,* 4, 2053–63, Simon and Schuster, 1956.

[36] von Neumann, J., *Proposal and Analysis of a New Numerical Method in the Treatment of Hydrodynamical Shocks*, (1944), Collected Works VI, Pergamon Press, New York 1963.

[37] von Neumann, J. and Goldstine, H. H., *On the Principles of Large Scale Computing Machines*, 1945, Collected Works V, Pergamon Press, New York, 1961.

[38] von Neumann, J. and Richtmyer, R., A Method for the Numerical Calculation of Hydrodynamic Shocks, *J. Appl. Phys.* 21 (1950): 232–237.

[39] Odlyczko, A., *The 10^{20}-th Zero of the Riemann Zeta Function and 70 Million of its Neighbors*, 1989 AT&T Bell. Lab. Preprint.

[40] Oxtoby, J. C. and Ulam, S., Measure.-preserving Homeomorphisms and Metric Transitivity, *Ann. Math.* 42 (1941): 874–920.

[41] Peskin, C. S. and McQueen, D. M., *Fluid Dynamics of the Heart and its Valves, Case Studies in Mathematical Modeling—Ecology, Physiology, and Cell Biology*, Prentice Hall, Englewood Cliffs, NJ

[42] Rivest, R. L., Shamir, A., and Adleman, L., A Method for Obtaining Digital Signature and Public Key Cryptosystems, *Comm. ACM* 21, (1978): 120–126.

[43] Ruelle, D. *Chaotic Evolution of Strange Attractors, the statistical analysis of time series for deterministic nonlinear systems*, Cambridge Univ. Press, 1989.

[44] Shiota, T., Characterisation of Jacobian Varieties in Terms of Soliton Equations, *Invent. Math.* 83 (1986): 333–382.

[45] Stewart, I. *Does God Play Dice ?* Blackwell, Cambridge, 1989.

[46] Strassen, V., Gaussian Elimination is Not Optimal, *Num. Math.* 13 (1969): 354–356.

[47] Toda M., *Theory of Nonlinear Lattices*, Series in Solid State Sciences 20, Springer Verlag, New York, 1988.

[48] Trefethen, L. N. and Bau, D., Numerical Linear Algebra, *SIAM*, Philadelphia, 1997.

[49] Wesseling, P., *An Introduction to Multigrid Methods, Pure & Appl. Math.*, Wiley & Sons, 1992.

DISCUSSANT

CHARLES L. FEFFERMAN

Princeton University

WHEREAS OTHER discussants have had the disadvantage that they haven't seen what they are supposed to comment on beforehand, I have the disadvantage that I have seen it beforehand and I find that it states very well, very wisely, very sensibly my own views. And now I am supposed to put forth wisdom. Let me just ask the speaker two questions: The first is to invite you, Peter, to speculate on the role of symbolic computation. The other is to speculate on the relationship of mathematics to important alternate forms of computation such as DNA and quantum computing.

Peter Lax responds:

Certainly after having denigrated computers as being not that good at mathematics, let me say that they are wonderful at symbolic calculations: much better than us poor humans who have developed through the coincidence of certain cosmic constants. Computers don't get tired, they don't make careless mistakes. They already are used and I'm sure the tendency will accelerate. As to other forms of computing: DNA computing is a very interesting idea and I think there is great future in it. I am more skeptical about quantum computing; it has yet to be demonstrated whether it is even theoretically feasible, though certainly all the demonstrations we have seen were not only baby problems but were embryonic problems.

Global Warming: Does Science Matter?[*]

RICHARD M. GOODY

Professor Emeritus, Harvard University

A Grave International Problem

THE GLOBAL warming debate is more than one hundred years old, but it has risen to the top of the federal agenda only during the past decade. It is concerned with the effect of industrial emissions, principally carbon dioxide, on the global climate. It is only one of many environmental issues arising from human activities, but global warming has raised the political stakes of the environmental debate because mitigation measures involve power generation, a matter that is crucial to the emergence of countries from poverty, and that involves significant fractions of the world GNP.

In recognition of these international political considerations, the United Nations created the Intergovernmental Panel on Climate Change (IPCC) to assess the science, the impacts, and possible response strategies for global warming. IPCC has produced a number of publications[1] which were source documents for the 1997 Kyoto Summit. Of these, *Climate Change 1995* is the most important scientific document. It contains a "Summary for Policymakers," the headings of which give the logical flow of their argument:

- Greenhouse gas concentrations have continued to increase
- Anthropogenic aerosols tend to produce negative radiative forcing

---

[*]Read 22 April 1999.

1. The two important scientific contributions are: *Climate Change: The IPCC Scientific Assessment*, Eds. J. T. Houghton et al,. Cambridge University Press, 1990, 365 pp. *Climate Change 1995: The Science of Climate Change*, Eds. J. T. Houghton et al. Cambridge University Press, 1996, 572 pp.

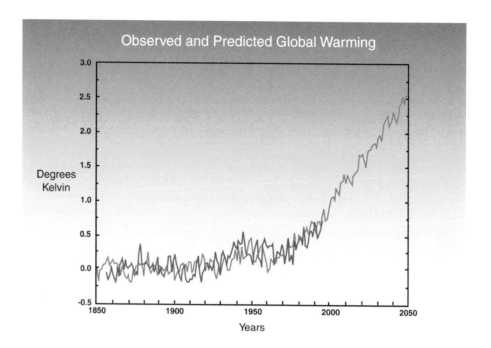

FIGURE 1. Global average surface air temperature from 1850 C.E. (deviations from the mean for 1880 to 1920 C.E.). The blue line shows measured temperatures up to the present time. The red line is a model calculation extending to 2050 C.E. By permission from S. Manabe, 1998, *Ambio* 27: 184.

- Climate has changed over the past century
- The balance of evidence suggests a discernible human influence on global climate
- Climate is expected to continue to change in the future
- There are still many uncertainties

In the remainder of this paper I shall examine these headings, one at a time.

The essence of the argument is illustrated in figure 1. The blue line represents the course of global average surface temperature over this century. It appears to increase with time, but not steadily. The red line represents the results of a theory based on the effect of increasing quantities of anthropogenic gases (principally carbon dioxide). These appear to agree quite well up to 2000 C.E.[2] and the question is whether we are willing to accept an extrapolation of the theory to the middle of the next century when the temperature is predicted to rise by 2.5°C—a very significant change in the climate.

Greenhouse gas concentrations have continued to increase

Carbon dioxide is not the only greenhouse gas, but it is the most important of the industrial gases (natural water vapor is the most important greenhouse gas overall). That the concentration of carbon dioxide increases with time has long been known but was dramatically illustrated by the observations of Keeling on Mauna Laua, Hawaii (figure 2). These data show an inexorable increase in the carbon-dioxide concentration together with annual changes associated with the cycle of northern hemisphere vegetation. Latest figures give an increase in 1995 of 25 percent from a nineteenth century "pre-industrial" level. Although some details can be debated the consensus view is that the observed increase of carbon dioxide is attributable to industrial activity. The increase of carbon dioxide in the atmosphere is approximately half of the total industrial emission during the same period; the other half has plausibly been taken up by the oceans and the biosphere. If this is correct, the upward trend will continue as long as industrial activity increases, with a doubling of the concentration predicted for 2050 C.E.

There is also no reasonable doubt that this increase in carbon dioxide will have significant thermal consequences for the climate. This statement rests on very simple ideas. The temperature of the Earth's surface is the result of a balance which involves heating by absorbed radiation and cooling by convection and low-temperature thermal radiation emitted from the surface (figure 3, wide red arrow). Heat emitted by the surface is dependent on the temperature: the higher the temperature the more rapid the loss of heat, and *vice versa*. The heating, to which the surface must respond, is

---

2. This agreement is less significant than it may seem to be. The theory contains adjustable parameters that can be chosen to give a good fit for 1850 to 2000 C.E.

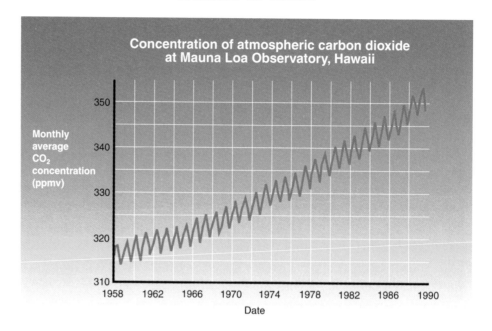

FIGURE 2. The concentration of carbon dioxide in the atmosphere in parts per million by volume (ppmv) for 1958–1990 C.E. By permission from T. E. Graedel, and P. J. Crutzen, 1995: *Atmosphere, Climate , and Change.* Scientific American Library.

caused by solar radiation (yellow arrow) and downward directed, low-temperature radiation from the atmosphere itself (narrow red arrow).

This downward-directed thermal radiation is the key. It comes from small concentrations of atmospheric gases, principally water vapor, but including also carbon dioxide and some other gases that result from industrial activity. Heat transport from the surface must increase to compensate this downward radiation, so that the presence of water vapor and industrial gases leads to an increase of surface temperature. In fact, the surface of the Earth is about 33°C warmer than it would be in the absence of all atmospheric gases. This is the "greenhouse effect." Its existence is not in question. Nor is the statement that increases in greenhouse gas concentrations will cause the downward radiation to increase and, hence, almost certainly, the surface temperature to increase. A temperature rise of a degree or two

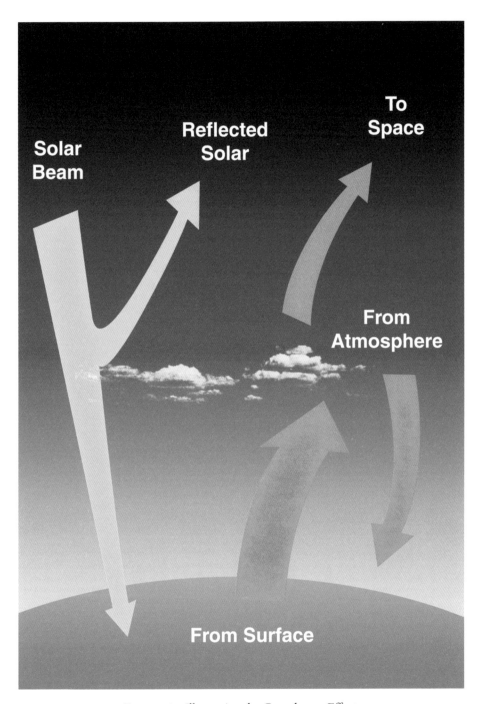

FIGURE 3. Illustrating the Greenhouse Effect.

as a result of doubling the carbon dioxide concentration is, certainly, plausible. But a believable answer to the question: How much warming? can only be given in terms of very complex calculations by general circulation climate models.

Anthropogenic aerosols tend to produce negative radiative forcing

As climate research has progressed it has become clear that carbon dioxide is not the only anthropogenic forcing that can affect the climate. There are negative forcings, that can bring about cooling (blue blocks in figure 4), in addition to positive forcings, or heating (red blocks in figure 4). The former arise from industrial dust, haze or smog that reflect sunlight and decrease the surface solar heating. These negative forcings cannot only be large, they are also very uncertain (see the black error bars). If we add together the extreme error limits in figure 4, both positive and negative, it is

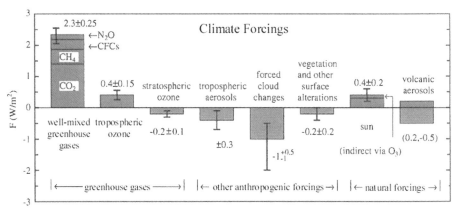

Estimated radiative forcings between 1850 and the present.

FIGURE 4. Estimated radiative forcing from 1850 C.E. to the present. Forcing (F) is the stress that causes temperature change. To a first approximation the two are proportional. By permission from J. Hansen, et al., 1998, *Proc. Natl. Acad. Scis.* USA 95 : 12754.

possible to conclude that zero net effect of industrial activity is a theoretical possibility.

Climate has changed over the past century

We have already seen that, over the past 100 years, the global mean surface temperature has risen by 0.3 to 0.6°C (see figure 1). It has been argued, based on measurements from satellites and from meteorological balloons, that this increase does not take place in the atmosphere itself,[3] to which theoretical calculations refer. It is possible, by making selections from the data, to reach a variety of conclusions, but I shall proceed on the assumption that figure 1 does, in fact, apply to the free atmosphere. However, as shown in figure 5, this increase is far from uniform; even in the United States there are unexplained variations between strong heating ($+3$°C for large red spots) and equally strong cooling (-3°C for large blue spots) during the past century. It is interesting to note that the strong heating occurs in the Boston/Washington corridor of the Northeast, where it will receive maximum political attention. And I am tempted to speculate that I might not have been asked to give this paper if the National Capital were in the Deep South.

But before we go on we must satisfy ourselves that there is something here that really needs to be explained. Some climate variation is "natural" meaning that it would occur with or without the intervention of man. "Natural variations" are caused by slow changes in the oceans and the polar ice sheets over periods from 1 to 10,000 years. They are slowly-acting analogies to terrestrial weather and, until they can be predicted, which we cannot do at present, we can only note their approximate magnitudes on the basis of the historical and the geological record. Figure 6 shows our best guess at the temperature record in middle latitudes on four expanding time-scales out to 150,000 years ago, which takes us past the last great Ice Age.

---

3. J. Hansen, et al., 1995:"Satellite and Surface Temperature Data at Odds," *Climate Change* 30: 103–117.

Temperature Trends in the 20th Century

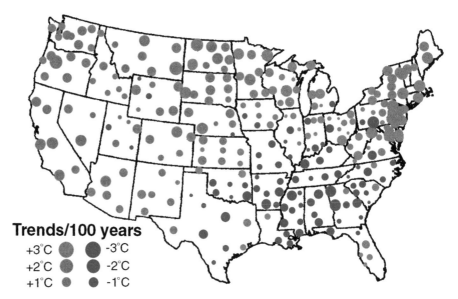

FIGURE 5. Change of mean temperature for the period 1900 to 1994 C.E. By permission from T. Karl, et al., 1996, *Bull. Am. Met. Soc.* 77:279.

Even if we set aside the large temperature changes during the ice ages we note that historical records (second panel) indicate a "little ice age" in the fourteenth to eighteenth centuries when northern Europe was very cold indeed, and oxen were roasted at winter ice fairs held on the river Thames in London. During the same period European glaciers advanced rapidly to an extent from which they are still retreating. Before the Little Ice Age, there may have been a Medieval Warm Period with good weather in the North Atlantic that allowed the Vikings to colonize Greenland and to farm there, digging graves deep in what is now permanently frozen soil.

In the context of these "natural" climate variations it is reasonable to ask whether the observed changes of the last century are so exceptional that they demand an explanation. Experts offer different opinions on this point, but it is not possible by rigorous statistical argument to rule out the possibility that, in 50 years time, the global mean temperature will be decreasing, even if no steps are taken to mitigate Global Warming.

AVERAGE MIDLATITUDE AIR TEMPERATURE

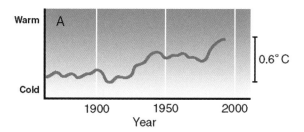

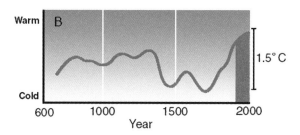

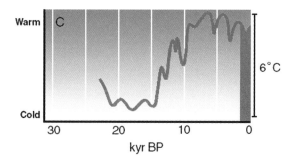

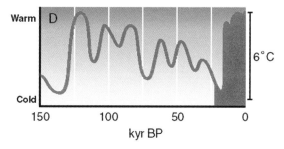

FIGURE 6. A representation of the average temperature in middle latitudes on
four expanding time scales. The third and fourth panels are based on geological data,
the second on historical accounts, and the first on conventional thermometry.
By permission from T. E. Graedel, and P. J. Crutzen, 1995: *Atmosphere, Climate
and Change.* Scientific American Library.

The balance of evidence suggests a discernible human influence on global climate

This is the crucial assertion from *Climate Change 1995,* upon which international decisions will be based. It depends upon two debatable propositions: that the climate is warming in a way that cannot be explained naturally and that, therefore, requires an external cause; and that warming due to greenhouse gases can account for this warming. If both propositions could be demonstrated they would reinforce one another, and it would be possible to claim that anthropogenic warming is now taking place; but that is not exactly where matters stand.

We have just discussed the evidence for detection of an external, unnatural forcing. With regard to the predicted greenhouse warming: models examined by *Climate Change 1995* vary in their response to greenhouse gas increases by a factor of three; alterations to the cloud and ocean components of models can lead to even greater changes; and the debatable role of industrial aerosols could drive these predictions into negative territory. Existing theoretical models do not, therefore, afford a useful, objective prediction of the size of global warming, without the use of adjustable parameters.

To associate these two arguable propositions as cause and effect, and to conclude that each confirms the other is, at the very least, open to question, and no scientist in the field should be entirely surprised, on the present evidence, to find a view significantly different from that of *Climate Change 1995,* prevailing 10 years from now.

This is not quite the whole story. Efforts are being made to find an unmistakable "fingerprint" of anthropogenic warming, the detection of which in the climate record would carry real conviction. However, this work has its own difficulties and I do not believe that it has yet added to conclusions to be drawn from a simple comparison between observed and predicted amplitudes of mean global warming.

Climate is expected to continue to change in the future

We can be reasonably confident that anthropogenic greenhouse gases will increase to the year 2050 if no steps are taken to prevent that from happening. On this basis, and using the available model calculations, *Climate Change*

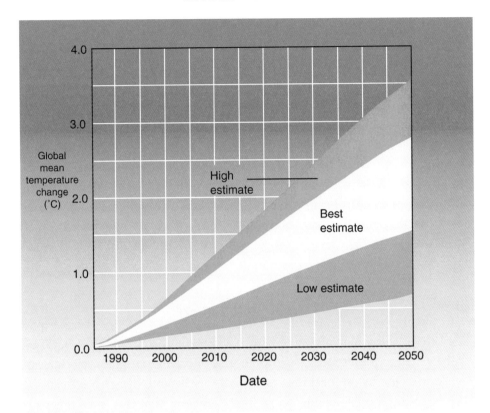

FIGURE 7. Estimates of Global Warming to the year 2050 C.E. By permission
from T. E. Graedel, and P. J. Crutzen, 1995: *Atmosphere, Climate and Change.*
Scientific American Library.

1995 created the data in figure 7. The "best estimate" is an honest opinion
based on the available data, but the uncertainties are subjective and are, in
my opinion, underestimated.

There are still many uncertainties

Climate Change 1995 was candid to admit to many uncertainties; these have
been studied carefully and are fully appreciated by the petroleum industry.[4]

---

4. B. P. Flannery, 1991: "Climate change: science and environmental impacts," *Global
Climate Change: A Petroleum Industry Perspective.* The International Petroleum Industry Environmental Conservation Association, pp.1–22.

From the scientific point of view the important question is: Can we improve the quality of, and our confidence in, decadal climate predictions to a degree that they are useful for policy decisions? I see no hope of greater confidence simply by working on and increasing the complexity of predictive models. Whatever the improvements, these models will always be approximations, and there is no way of knowing *a priori* that a model's forecasts will be satisfactory: performance must be demonstrated by means of comparisons between model behavior and reliable observations. This requires better climate observations than we now have, and the development of objective and appropriate statistical tests. At the present time, a program of systematic, objective tests of models is not a part of the official US program (the US Global Change Research Program), but ideas for doing so are beginning to make an appearance in the literature.[5]

Does science matter?

The title of this paper was taken from a session at the 1997 international Global Change conference at Kyoto.[6] It may be taken to suggest that science has done its job by establishing a potential threat[7] and that global warming then becomes a political and social issue. I believe that this is a dangerous idea for two reasons. First, the uncertainties in the science are so great that they offer legitimate handles for opposing views.[8] To judge by recent experience with health care and tobacco legislation, the present case could easily be destroyed on a political level and, with it, immediate hopes for a rational environmental policy.

Second, one undeniable feature of this discussion is the immense cost involved in mitigation. Sooner or later it will be necessary to develop cost trade-offs and, when that happens, we need *credible and quantitative* forecasts of the extent of environmental damage.

---

5. "Testing Climate models: An Approach", by R. Goody, J. Anderson and G. North, 1998: *Bull. Am. Met. Soc* 79: 1541–1549.

6. S. Schneider, 1997: *Climate Change* 39: 1.

7. Whatever the outcome of the Global Warming debate, a "potential threat" is established beyond reasonable doubt.

8. S. F. Singer, 1997: *Hot Talk Cold Science: Global Warming's Unfinished Debate*. The Independent Institute, pp.110.

The material that I have discussed in this paper has been presented by others on a number occasions with conclusions that range all the way from major warming by the year 2050 C.E[9] to negligible consequences or, even, a generally beneficial result from industrial activities.[10] This wide diversity of conclusions is partly the result of the political, social, or ethical positions of the writer.[11] The "postmodern" aspects of this debate unfortunately obscure the central issue: that the important role for science at this stage of climate research is to reduce uncertainty rather than to support specific policies. Objective and systematic tests of predictions from climate models are possible. No program of tests can lead to certainty about the future, but the room for interpretation can be greatly reduced, if we should wish to make the effort.

Acknowledgments

I am indebted to Robert Stanhope for his work in preparing the figures.

DISCUSSANT

JAMES G. ANDERSON

Harvard University

I WANT TO raise a question that is linked to the issue that Professor Goody has raised and that is the question of the character of scientific exploration. Of course, the American Philosophical Society is uniquely poised to deal with this, with not only Jefferson and Franklin, but Lewis and Clark who defined the character of decisive scientific exploration. But more than that, in this room is contained the expert view of the substance of molecular interactions, the link of radiation dynamics and chemistry, and their link to

---

9. J. Houghton, 1997: *Global Warming: The Complete Briefing*. Cambridge University Press, pp.251.

10. L. Jones, 1997: *Global Warming: the Science and the Politics*. The Fraser Institute, pp.180.

11. D. Bray, and H. von Storch, 1999: "Climate Science: an Empirical Example of Post-normal Science," *Bull. Am. Met. Soc.* 89: 439–455.

public policy and to ethics. And because of this unique capability, we cannot leave this room this morning without dealing directly with these questions. Professor Goody has described a system into which infrared gases are released that create increases in sea-surface temperature, that drive the thermodynamic water engine, that presents a very delicate and non-linear response to changes in the release of gases. He has also described a system in which sulfur, heavy metals, and organics create the formation of aerosols that cool the system. And the question is, how do these balance? The result of these changes, of course, lead to changes in the opacity of the atmosphere, to temperature changes, to the frequency of severe storms, and to changes in the growing season. Some of these things we like and some of these things we do not. We are not going to answer that question this morning, but what we can answer is the question of the national effort related to decisive scientific exploration. And here we have a fundamental problem: we have opted for—for whatever reason—an approach that involves large, complex satellites that cannot diagnose the subtleties of molecular activity, the interplay of angular momentum and entropy in the atmosphere, the interplay of radiation and molecular structures that control delicate and non-linear heating processes. And we cannot accept as a nation a research program in AIDS, for example, that looks at the motion of this problem across the surface of the earth and ignores the immune system. We wouldn't accept it, because it doesn't strike to the heart of an orthogonal issue that's equally important to the spread of the disease. Yet that is what we're accepting in this country with the current program. How we deal with this is really the issue—how we bring decisive, scientific exploration to the table of this debate. The National Research Council, which for many years produced glossy, tepid analyses of how we execute the scientific research, has now come around to the point where it is establishing the detailed scientific questions that link not only the large questions, but through a network of connections, questions of how we test hypotheses related to the truth or lack of truth of individual elements that comprise this climate system. Through the course of establishing this scientific foundations it is now possible to test whether the current "research progress" is consistent or inconsistent with these fundamental scientific principals. So the question before us, in addition to what we have heard today, is how we cast the future. What is the next step we take in order to construct an approach to this problem that's decisive.

The Molecular Biology of Huntington's Disease or in Science Curiosity Pays
—At Least Sometimes

MAX F. PERUTZ

Former Chairman, Medical Research Council Laboratory of Molecular Biology
Cambridge, England

WHILE ATTENDING the Olympic games, Leon prince of Lisle asked Pythagoras how he would describe himself. Pythagoras replied, "I'm a philosopher," and coined this word for the first time. But Leon had not heard the word before and asked him to explain. "Life," Pythagoras began, "may well be compared with these public games, for in the vast crowd assembled here, some will be attracted by the acquisition of gain, others by the hopes and ambitions of fame and glory, but among them there are few that have come to understand all that passes here. It is the same as life. Some are influenced by the love of wealth, while others are blindly led on by the mad fever for power and domination, but the finest type of man gives himself up to discovering the meaning and purpose of life itself. He seeks to uncover the secrets of nature. This is the man I call a philosopher, for although no man is completely wise in all respects, love of wisdom is the key to nature's secrets." That is why I am very honored to be made a member of the American Philosophical Society.

In 1949, Linus Pauling published a sensational paper in Science entitled, "Sickle Cell Anemia, a Molecular Disease."[1] He showed that this inherited disease, which is common among Blacks, was due to a small change in the electric charge of hemoglobin, the protein of the red blood cells. Like all proteins, hemoglobin is made up of chains of amino acids. These are of twenty different kinds, and they are arranged along the chain in a definite,

---

*Read 24 April 1999

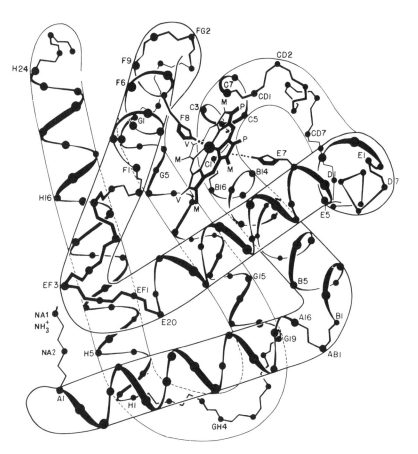

FIGURE 1. Fold of a hemoglobin chain. Each of the black dots marks the position of an amino acid. Much of the chain is coiled into helices which we marked A to M. The numbers mark the sequence of the amino acids along the helices.

genetically-determined order. (fig. 1) Hemoglobin contains two pairs of chains, the α-chains which each contain 141 amino acids and the β-chains which each contain 146.

Pauling and his coworkers found that in sickle-cell anaemia there is a small change in the electric charge of the hemoglobin molecule. In the 1950s my colleague Vernon Ingram took this up in our laboratory in Cambridge; he showed that the change in charge that Pauling, Itano, Singer and Wells had discovered was due to the replacement of a single one of the hundred and forty-six amino acids in the β-chain by another one.[2,3] This minute change produces a severe, fatal, inherited disease. It was a remarkable discovery, because it showed for the first time that a genetic disease is due to a mutation in the DNA which gives rise to the replacement of a single amino acid in a protein. This discovery by Vernon Ingram opened a new field of research; since then over five hundred different hemoglobin mutations have been discovered, most of them harmless, but many of them leading to diseases, and in hundreds of other proteins similar mutations give rise to inherited diseases. They are nearly always recessive.

In the past, you had to isolate the affected protein and find the replaced amino acid. Now, since the advent of recombinant DNA technology, this is no longer needed. All you have to do is to isolate and decipher the gene, and find the base-change produced by the mutation. This new technique has led to the discovery of the molecular causes of many more inherited diseases, but there was one severe one that defied all attempts; that was Huntington's Chorea, a dominantly inherited, late-onset, neuro-degenerative disease that gives rise first to uncontrolled movements and then mood disturbances, dementia and eventually death. Finally, in 1993, a paper in *Cell* reported the isolation of its gene by a team of 61 scientists in 8 different universities in the U.S. & Britain; they called themselves the Huntington's Disease Collaborative Group.[4] By this tremendous international effort they found a gene that codes for a single protein chain nearly six times longer than the hemoglobin chain; the lesion that gives rise to the disease was of a new kind. It did not consist in the replacement of a single amino acid. The normal gene for the Huntington protein codes for a long repeat of the same amino acid, *glutamine,* varying in lengths in different people from six to about 37 glutamines. In patients these repeats were elongated, and that elongation appeared to cause the disease. An extraordinary discovery. The disease usually sets on in middle age, but the longer the repeat, the earlier the onset until, when there are over a hundred glutamines in the repeat, it actually sets on in children. Also, the longer the repeat, the more severe the disease.

I am known as the hemoglobin man, and people wonder how I got into Huntington's disease. Before the gene was known, I worked on an obscure hemoglobin of a parasitic worm and I found that this contained a feature that I had not seen before in any protein: a repeat of amino acids, which produced an alternation of positive and negative charges. I realized that if two such chains came together this would form a "polar zipper," because the positive and negative charges would want to compensate. It occurred to me that this cannot be unique; there must be such sequences in other proteins. One of my colleagues, Roger Staden, searched the data bank and indeed found some in other proteins, but he also showed me that some proteins in the fruit fly, *drosophila*, contained long repeats of glutamines. I was curious what would happen in such a repeat. I built an atomic model of a chain of glutamines and saw that it would form a polar zipper, because of the alternating fractional positive and negative charges along two parallel chains would combine (fig. 2).

I built this model out of idle curiosity, published a little paper on "Polar Zippers," and thought this was the end of the story.[5] But while this paper was in press I read about the discovery of the gene for Huntington's Disease,[1] and it occurred to me that the polar zipper action of long glutamine chains might provide the clue for the molecular cause of that disease.

Was my model right? To find out I asked T. Johnson in our lab to synthesize a short chain of glutamines. Physical tests showed indeed that such chains of glutamines tend to zip together as my model had suggested. After this, I and the colleagues who helped published a paper in the *Proceedings* of the National Academy proposing that the extension of glutamine repeats in Huntington's Disease would make the affected protein molecules aggregate in neurons, and that these aggregates might cause the neurons to degenerate.[6]

However, there was no experimental support for this suggestion because immuno-staining had shown this Huntington's protein as isolated dots spread throughout the neurons, and there was no evidence for aggregates. In August 1997 a paper appeared in *Cell*, which produced a complete turnaround in the research on the disease. It was by Gillian Bates and others at Guy's Hospital and Stephen Davies at University College in London; and they had succeeded in introducing the human, or at least a fragment of the human, Huntington's Disease gene into mice, and reproduced the disease in them. The mice showed neurological symptoms very similar to those of the Huntington's patients. That was a tremendous first step. When they introduced this protein with a normal number of glutamine repeats, it produced no symptoms, but when they introduced the one with long repeats it reproduced the symptoms. Stephen Davies cut thin sections through the brains of the mice and found that the cell nuclei of the neurons contained

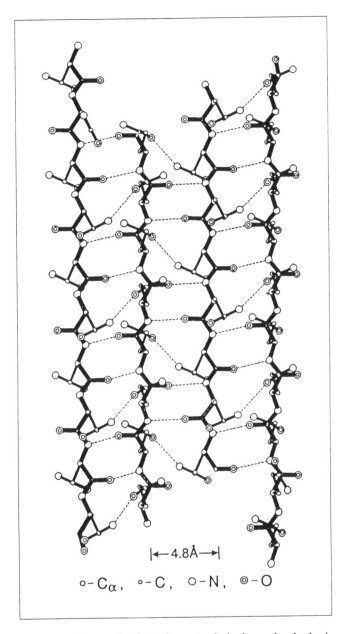

FIGURE 2. Four chains of poly-L-glutamine linked together by hydrogen bonds between their main chain and side chain amides.

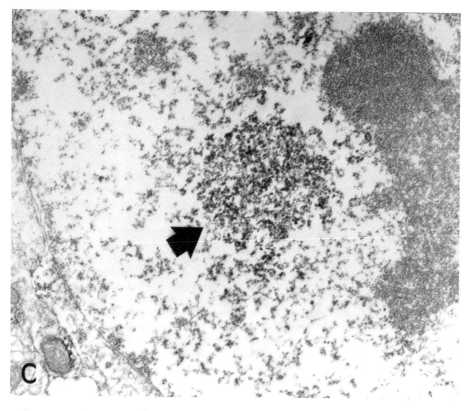

FIGURE 3. Aggregate of Huntington protein in the cell nucleus of a human neuron.
Courtesy Dr. Marion Di Figlia.

fibrous and granular aggregates of the Huntington protein fragment, just as my model had suggested. (fig. 3)

This discovery made Marion Di Figlia and her colleagues at the Harvard Medical School look again at the post-mortem brains of Huntington patients which had been stored in liquid nitrogen; they found such aggregates, but they had been overlooked before.[8] Karl Popper suggested that in science the hypothesis comes first and then you look and see if there is experimental evidence for it. It was the hypothesis that made Steven Davies look at the cell nuclei of the neurons.

Since then, seven other inherited diseases have been discovered which are due to the expansion of the glutamine repeats in various proteins. They affect different parts of the brain and different neurons. For instance, Kennedy disease affects motor neurons and gives rise to difficulties in controlling movement. In several of these diseases similar aggregates have been found. Dr. Nancy Bonini at the University of Pennsylvania had the splendid idea to see if she could introduce a related disease into the fruit fly, *Drosophila*.[9] She found that they developed neurological symptoms similar to man.[5] This isn't just a toy because *Drosophila* would be the ideal organism for testing possible drugs against the disease.

There is one remarkable observation. In all these diseases, glutamine repeats with fewer than 37 glutamins are harmless, and repeats with more than 40 produce disease. This clearly shows that the elongation of these gives rise to a change of structure, and this change of structure gives rise to the aggregates that poison the cell. So the great challenge now is to find out what the change of structure is and how it induces this aggregation. I have suggested that chains with fewer than 37 repeats are disordered, while those with more than 40 fold up to form hairpins.[6] So far there is only theoretical, but no experimental support for this idea.[10]

There is also one encouraging feature in this story: The discovery of the nuclear aggregates in Huntington's protein has brought a new unity to the molecular pathology of neuro-degenerative diseases. Alzheimer's Disease is due to the aggregation of a protein into neuro-fibrillar tangles which aggregate between the neurons. Parkinson's Disease is due to the aggregation of another protein synuclein into Lewy-bodies which are little footballs with spikes on their surface. Prion diseases, like bovine's spongiform encephalitis, or Creutzfeldt-Jakob Disease, are due to the aggregation of prion proteins. I suspect that most, if not all, neurodegenerative diseases are due to the formation of protein aggregates in neurons.

How we can prevent such aggregation is one of the great problems facing us in the next millennium.

References

1. Pauling, L., Itano, H. A., & Singer, S. J., & Wells, I. C. Sickle Cell Anemia, a molecular disease. *Science* 110 (1949): 543–549.
2. Ingram, V. M. (1956) A specific chemical difference between the globins of normal human and sickle cell anaemia haemoglobin. *Nature* 178: 792–794.

3. Ingram, V. M. (1957) Gene mutations in human haemogloblin: the chemical difference between normal and sickle cell haemoglobin. *Nature* 180: 326–328.

4. Huntington's Disease Collaborative Research Group. A novel gene containing a trinucleotide repeat cell is expanded and unstable in Huntington's Disease Chromosomes. *Cell* 72 (1993): 971–983.

5. Perutz, M. F., Staden, R., Moens, L., & De Baere, I. Polar Zippers. *Curr. Biol.* 3 (1993): 249–253.

6. Perutz, M. F., Johnson, T., Suzuki, M., & Finch, J. T. Glutamine repeats as polar zipper: their possible role in neurodegenerative diseases. *Proc. Nat. Acad. Sci. USA* 91 (1994): 5355–5358.

7. Davies, S. W., Turmaine, M., Cozens, B. A., Di Figlia, M., Sharp, A. M., Ross, C. A., Scherzinger, E., Wanker, E. E., Mangiarin, L., & Bates, G. P. Formation of neuronal intranuclear inclusions underlies the neurological dysfunction in mice transgenic for the HD mutation. *Cell* 90 (1997): 537–548.

8. Di Figlia, M., Sapp, E., Chase, K. D., Davies, S. W., Bates, G. R., Vonsattel, T. P., & Aronin, N. Aggregation of Huntingtin in neuronal intranuclear inclusions and dyptrophic neurites in brain. *Science* 277, (1990–1993).

9. Warrick, T. M., Paulson, M. L., Gray-Board, G. L., Bul, Q. T., Fischbeck, K. K., Pittman, R. N., & Bonini, N. M. Expanded glutamine protein forms nuclear inclusions & causes neural degeneration in Drosophila. *Cell* 93 (1998): 939–949.

10. Perutz, M. F. Glutamine repeats and inherited neurodegenerative diseases: molecular aspects. *Current Opinion in Structural Biology* 6 (1996): 848–858.

DISCUSSANT

JEROME KARLE
Naval Research Laboratory

I THINK THAT the audience couldn't have possibly forgotten the marvelous talk that Max Perutz gave earlier today. I had written down a few comments because I knew what he was talking about. His excellent talk has described a large step forward in characterizing, with the aid of structural research, several types of neuro-degenerative diseases. It is a very fine example of a general development of medical insights derived from structural information concerning macro molecules that has begun to accelerate in the past dozen or so years. Examples may be found in many areas such as the structural defects in hemoglobin that Dr. Perutz mentioned already leading to diseases such as thalassemia or sickle-cell anemia, structural characteristics of RNA viruses, the canyon hypothesis for viruses studied by Michael Rossman, and the characteristics of oncogenic and flu viruses. With the help of bioengineering and rational drug design, some of these insights that relate structure to function have begun to yield definitive benefits and others have given suggestive directions for further research.

An outstanding example of a benefit is the current use of protease inhibitors in the treatment of HIV infections. As a valuable peripheral development, a recent issue of *Nature* magazine has indicated that in the presence of "highly active anti-retroviral therapy" the thymus responds rapidly with a sustained increase in output, suggesting an important contribution to immune reconstitution and recovery in HIV patients. Now I might point out that it has been generally thought that the thymus is essentially unresponsive as an immune organ when people reach adulthood. And the article in *Nature* goes on to say that the thymus appears to remain functional, albeit at reduced levels, into adult life in healthy individuals, but its function is repressed in HIV infected patients. And so one finds out that the treatment for HIV stimulates the thymus to again act as a highly-active immune organ.

Another area receiving attention concerns viruses other than the HIV virus, such as oncogenic viruses and the pecora viruses with their vulnerable clefts, which appear to be in the host cell, binding sites, designated as canyons that are referred to earlier by Michael Rossman.

Structural information combined with known function can be a great assistance in correcting disease processes. Sometimes there has been great success; in another cases so far only some suggested paths to follow have been obtained. Unbalanced, however, it is legitimate to say that great advances are taking place over a relatively short period of time. Some of the terms that are used for the processes that facilitate this progress are becoming more and more familiar to us. They are bioengineering, biotechnology, rational drug design, and many other terms that concern the analysis and the manipulation of the myriad of biological entities that enter into the production of final products that are so valuable to human health and the quality of life. When I speak in these terms and think about my own activities, I am profoundly reminded of how indebted we scientists are to the great bounty of facilities and knowledge that are provided to us by our fellow scientists and engineers. It comes from mathematics and from physics as well as from chemistry, biology, and medicine. The best that we as individuals can hope to do is to make worthwhile additions to this fund of knowledge. Our distinguished speaker has for many decades made profound contributions to our fund of knowledge as exemplified by his pleasant presentation.

CLASS II

BIOLOGICAL SCIENCES

Scientists and the Public:
An Ambivalent Partnership*

PAUL L. BERG

Cahill Professor in Cancer Research and Professor of Biochemistry Stanford University

IN A LECTURE delivered at the American Academy of Arts and Sciences meeting at the University of California, Berkeley, J. Michael Bishop framed the issues I want to address this afternoon. He noted that

> We live in an age defined by science, when many of nature's great puzzles have been solved. The fruits of science have vastly improved human welfare and understanding. Despite transcendent achievement, however, science now finds itself in a paradoxical strife with society: admired but also mistrusted; offering hope for the future but also creating ambiguous choice; richly supported yet unable now to fulfill all its promise; boasting remarkable advances but criticized for not serving more directly the goals of society.[1]

How are we to understand this paradoxical "love-hate" relationship? Surveys confirm repeatedly that there is much public interest and support for science although the distinction between science and technology and what each can contribute is poorly understood. This confusion has fostered an unrealistic belief that the fruits of what people believe to be science can cure all problems. But for some, science engenders a deep-seated fear and hostility particularly where it challenges traditional beliefs and values. Thus, science is confronted with apparently conflicting public perceptions—one that bemoans science's shortcomings at having failed to solve society's prob-

---

*Read 22 April 1999.

1. Bishop, J.M. Paradoxical Strife: Science and Society. Presentation at the 1762nd Stated Meeting of the American Academy of Arts and Sciences held at the University of California, Berkeley on 25 March 1994.

lems and the more ominous fear that science is sowing the seeds of dehumanization and the destruction of our society.

In trying to deal with these deeply rooted concerns, we need to understand that scientists believe that they operate in a rational world, one in which interpretations and predictions are based on objective data that are evaluated through a shared systematic process. Whether or not these suppositions reflect the reality of scientific practice, they certainly fall apart when science becomes a public issue. For then political concerns, frequently in the guise of moral and ethical beliefs, intervene in the evaluation process. But experience has shown us that it is far easier to balance differences of scientific opinion than to reconcile differences between conflicting moral values.

The validity and even the value of science's claim to objectivity has not gone unchallenged; these come from two perspectives. The post-modernist criticism dismisses science as being a self-indulgent, wholly fraudulent route to knowing, preferring to dismiss science as "politics by other means"; objectivity is delegitimized as "socially constructed fictions," no more than "useful myths." In Bishop's words, "anyone with a working knowledge of science, anyone who looks at the natural world with an honest eye, should recognize all of this to be errant nonsense."

A somewhat similar but more damning critique of science was unleashed, first in a relatively limited circulation collection of essays and then more widely through the Op-Ed pages of the *New York Times* and the halls of the U.S. Congress. There, the distinguished poet, playwright, philosopher and now President of the Czech Republic, Vaclav Havel, decried the objectivity of science. He charged that science's objectivity denies the binding importance of personal experience including the experience of mystery.[2] Science's insistence on objectivity, Havel believes, replaces the value of the personally experienced measure of the world with a new man-made view, devoid of mystery, free of the whims of subjectivity and as such, impersonal and inhuman. "Modern science," Havel writes, "has killed God and taken His place on the vacant throne so that science becomes the sole legitimate guardian and arbiter of all relevant truth." Havel's prescription for salvation is to take

---

2. Havel, V. The End of the Modern Era. *New York Times* Op-Ed 1 March 1992.

refuge in "the unrepeatable personal, even miraculous, experience," and to rely on intuition and mystery as sources of subjective truth.[3]

However, the essence of scientific understanding rejects the miraculous, for explanations based on miracles resist scientific inquiry. In her President's Commentary for the Carnegie Institution of Washington's *Yearbook*[4] Maxine Singer argues that "we could do away with the words 'truth' and 'faith', as well as 'miracle', in reference to science . . . What science seeks is understanding—not truth." "Scientists," she continues, "do not have 'faith' in scientific understanding and facts. Quite the contrary. They hold only tentative conclusions about any particular scientific understanding—conclusions that become less and less tentative as more and more phenomena are found to be consistent with that understanding." "This tentative, evolving quality of scientific understanding (which Lewis Wolpert called "the unnatural nature of science"[5]) unsettles many people. For them, the impermanence of understanding seems to undermine a common core essential for stability and reliability in human society."

While widely noted and quoted, Havel's metaphysical condemnation of science failed to generate a groundswell of antiscience fervor, with one exception: George E. Brown, Jr., a California Congressman, who had long been a staunch advocate of science. Inspired by Havel's writings, Brown called for a reexamination of the role of science in society.[6] In assessing that role, Brown identified what he referred to as the "knowledge paradox" which he defined as the non-linear relationship between advances in knowledge and advances that benefit society. He cited as examples of what science has failed to solve: overpopulation, traffic congestion, pollution, drug abuse, poorly distributed health care, etc. Brown concluded that there needed to

---

3. V. Havel, Politics and Conscience, one of 22 essays in collection entitled *Living in the Truth,* ed. by Jan Vadislav, Faber & Faber, London, 1987.

4. Singer, M.F. President's Commentary. Carnegie Institution of Washington Yearbook 1993–1994.

5. Wolpert, L. *The Unnatural Nature of Science.* Harvard University Press, Cambridge, MA. 1993.

6. "The Objectivity Crisis: Rethinking the Role of Science in Society." AAAS speech, Feb. 12, 1993.

be a reformulation of the "social contract" with scientists so that their energies would more directly address the problems that confront society.

Brown soon learned, however, that he had picked on the wrong offenders. He was reminded by many that more often than not, failures in the political process undermine or even ignore potential solutions that emerge from scientific research. One need only consider the government's continued support of tobacco growing in the face of irrefutable evidence of its dangers to health; or the government's timidity in promoting greater use of already developed safe and effective vaccines; or society's dalliance in implementing the variety of recommendations for reducing pollution and degradation of the environment. Indeed, political and ideological considerations as well as an unwillingness or inability of our polity to make decisions, may have done more to curtail the societal benefits of research than the unwillingness of scientists to turn their talents and skills to solving our nation's problems. Brown's prescription to target federal research funds to solve society's needs failed also to acknowledge that it was the application of scientific knowledge, the technological fix that had failed society. But it was Brown's perceived threat to basic science that drew the ire of the scientific community.

David Baltimore spoke for many when he pointed out that

> the traditional pact between society and its scientists in which the scientist is given the responsibility for determining the direction of his work is a necessary relationship if science is to be an effective endeavor. This does not mean that society is at the mercy of science but rather that society, while it determines the pace of scientific innovation, should not attempt to prescribe its directions. . . . Major breakthroughs can not be programmed: history tells us that successes are likely to come from . . . people and areas of research that are not predictable. . . . The net effect of constraining biologists to approved lines of investigation would be to degrade the effectiveness of the whole of science . . . the penalty for trying to control lines of investigation seems to be greater than any conceivable benefit.[7]

In short, insisting upon very explicit linkages between national goals and federally-supported research is sowing the seeds for serious damage to our research enterprise. Nevertheless, it is misleading to think that science is not

---

7. Baltimore, D., Limits of Scientific Inquiry. *Daedalus* (Spring 1978):333–344.

directed at all. Brown knew very well that society continually makes crucial decisions about the general directions of science, usually by the appropriation process which allocates available resources.

Proposals to place limits on certain lines of scientific research or to direct it along prescribed lines is not new. During my own career there have been several well publicized attempts to proscribe certain areas of biomedical research, the first of which occurred nearly 25 years ago, involving the recombinant DNA technology, more often referred to as genetic engineering.

Even today, and for nearly 20 years, federally-funded research using human embryos is prohibited by statute in spite of recommendations to permit such research by at least three commissions during three different administrations. These proscriptions are at the heart of the still unresolved debate on whether to permit or prohibit human cloning and the creation of stem cell lines from early stage human embryos. This in spite of the widespread belief that the availability of human embryonic stem cell lines provides new opportunities for exploring the mysteries of differentiation during human embryonic development and offers considerable promise for making cell-based therapies for a variety of human diseases a reality.

For the remainder of my talk I will focus on how the public policy debate concerning the permissibility of recombinant DNA research was framed and resolved. The controversy was triggered by a call for a moratorium on certain experiments using the emerging recombinant DNA methodology. What startled the worldwide scientific community, however, was the source of the call: the scientists who had developed the new technology. It was clear that the new capability created extraordinary and novel avenues for genetic research and could ultimately provide exceptional opportunities for medicine, agriculture and industry. But scientists also considered the possibility that it might engender unforeseen and damaging consequences for human health and the earth's ecosystems. Although there were few data on which to base a defensible judgment regarding the probability of such untoward outcomes, the molecular biological community agreed, not without considerable opposition, that recombinant DNA research should proceed but under strict guidelines; such guidelines were subsequently developed under the auspices of the National Institutes of Health as well as by comparable bodies in other countries.

Some scientists, and public officials as well, were certain that recombinant DNA experimentation was flirting with disaster and that lifting the moratorium was a blunder. Public opinion, after a brief period of reassurance by the scientists' responsible initiatives, turned fearful, in part fanned by the myriad "what ifs" floated by both serious and demogogic commentators and by the allusions to "the Andromeda strain." In the end, however, the guidelines and the mechanism for overseeing them in practice prevailed. Today, after literally tens of millions of experiments throughout the world there have been no documented hazards to public health that have been linked to this line of research.

Frequently heard during the heated debates were criticisms of the scientists for assuming leadership in formulating policies that were matters of public concern. Some scientists felt that the public debate itself was a great threat and that the fall-out of claim and counterclaim would bring debilitating federal and state restrictions or even prohibitions on molecular biological research. Yet the efforts to inform the public also encouraged responsible public discussion, which succeeded in developing a consensus for the measured approach that scientists supported. Legislation was avoided, and in the long run scientists benefitted from their forthrightness and prudent actions in the face of uncertainty. As a result, the recombinant DNA technology now dominates research in biology. It has altered both the way questions are formulated and the way solutions are sought.

An often-voiced criticism of the early recombinant DNA discussions was the failure to consider the ethical and legal implications of genetic engineering of plants, animals and humans. This choice of agenda was deliberate, partly because it was premature to consider applications that were so speculative and certainly not imminent but also because gaining a consensus on how to proceed in the face of differing ethical concerns seemed precarious, if not impossible. At the time, the more urgent concern was the possible effects of recombinant DNA on public health and safety.

Today, however, concern about DNA research is focused on ethical, legal, and environmental issues raised by the rapid pace of genetic advances and the increasing use of genetically modified animals and plants. Discussion of these issues is confounded by the clash of some religious and philosophical beliefs with scientific goals and practical opportunities. For example, a coalition of religious leaders sought a ban on patenting of human genes, cells, organs and genetically modified organisms; their argument is that these are creations of God and not inventions of man. But scientists who synthesize genes by chemical techniques in their laboratories and recognize the near identity of human and other mammalian genes, do not think of human DNA molecules as holy. We are, therefore, continuously confronted with having to resolve the conflict between religious and scientific views about molecules and biological organisms and, as well, the conflict between religious precepts and the moral imperative to do all we can to improve mankind's lot and relieve human suffering.

We are also confronted with other widely expressed concerns stemming from the ability to associate particular mutations or characteristic features in genes with disease manifestations or predispositions. These are the societal stresses, medical challenges, and personal anxieties that are expected to accompany the disclosure of these characteristics. Therefore, protection of individuals against new forms of discrimination (e.g., in employment opportunities and availability of adequate health and life insurance) will be needed to mitigate against these possibilities. Hopefully, in time, new therapies, now woefully lacking, will make the possibilities for early detection more attractive and desirable.

But perhaps the most deeply felt concern is that genetic research in general and the institution of broad based genetic testing will spur a malevolent renewal of interest in eugenics. This view stems from the presumption that current attempts to perform gene therapy by modifying the genetic constitution of somatic cells, i.e., the non-reproductive cells of the body, a goal that most people find acceptable, will ultimately lead to attempts to make alterations in human germ line genes, i.e., those passed on to future generations via sperm and eggs. There are technical reasons for believing that the value of such modifications for humans is questionable and therefore unnecessary. Indeed, many scientists agree that attempts at human germ line modification should not even be considered.

Inferring evil intent and calling for bans on genetic research denies the value of such research in fulfilling human dreams for improved health and the sustenance of a growing human population. Vigorous, informed public debate on all these issues should be fostered if we are not to succumb to ignorance or fear and the tyranny of the minority. As with all changes in human thought and technological developments, we are left with new and unanticipated issues. And, as so often in the past, science, which itself is a uniquely human endeavor, is challenging traditional ideas and values.

But we have to guard against ignorance giving rise to fear. For if we forbid exploration of the unknown territory opened to us by science, we shall not only be condemning ourselves to still existent and yet to be encountered risks but we shall be subverting one of the most admirable expressions of the human spirit.

Let me finish by quoting a passage from Peter Medawar's essay "On the Effecting of All Things Possible" in which he said, "If we imagine the evolution of living organisms compressed into one year of cosmic time, then the evolution of man has occupied but a day. Only during the last 10 to 15 minutes of the human day has our life on earth been anything but precarious. We are still beginners, and for that reason may hope to improve. To deride the hope of progress is the ultimate fatuity, the last word in poverty of spirit and meanness of mind."[8] It is a view we need to keep in mind as we continue to encounter the challenge of dealing with the advancing tide of scientific discovery.

DISCUSSANT

HAROLD T. SHAPIRO

President, Princeton University

IN "SCIENTISTS AND THE PUBLIC" Professor Paul Berg raises a crucial and vexing issue: the ambivalence that society feels about science and its rapid development. His essay focuses on the uneasy relationship that society often has with its scientists and raises the important questions of how and by whom the research agenda should be set, how quickly that agenda should proceed, and who should decide how to apply the fruits of scientific discovery.

---

8. Medawar, P.B. "On the Effecting of All Things Possible," in the collection *Hope of Progress,* Methuen and Co., Ltd., London 1972.

In discussing the ambivalence that many people feel about this process, Professor Berg cites Vaclav Havel's concerns about the limitations of scientific thought. But poets from Sophocles to Yeats to Havel have raised similar objections for what I believe are not very surprising reasons. To begin with, science serves society in two distinctly different ways—functioning as both a servant, making lives better and more comprehensible, and as a critic, responsible for reevaluating existing arrangements and identifying mistaken ideas about how the world works. It's natural to have a certain amount of tension when science is charged with two such conflicting roles.

But perhaps even more important is the fact that every significant development in science, by opening the door to new technologies and applications, raises serious moral questions. As scientists solve problems and increase our understanding of the natural world, they inevitably raise new social and philosophical issues. The inescapable outcome of scientific progress—I'll leave it to others to decide whether "progress" is the right word—is a great deal of complexity and even confusion. And for some groups and individuals within our society, the answer is to try to restrict the flow of discovery or to proclaim that science is nearing the end of what it can constructively accomplish.

Now, scientists ought not to feel too overly persecuted in this regard because calling for a stop to things has virtually become a cottage industry as well as a literary genre. In any bookstore one can find volumes on "the end of God," "the end of history," "the end of empire" or "the end of the nation-state," which gain notoriety, and even sometimes a significant following, by overstating the consequences of certain events or phenomena. Science is a particularly attractive target for such treatment, which is understandable given the dynamics of human nature: our deep curiosity is often at odds with our tremendous desire to create meaning out of the world we experience.

In his essay, Professor Berg suggests a pact between the scientific community and the world at large in which scientists chart the direction of their investigations, while society determines the pace of such activities and the proper use of their results. This leaves the hard moral problem—the use of new scientific information—to the non-scientists. Members of the scientific community should empathize with the rest of us, facing the wonderful but difficult challenge of making moral and meaningful choices about complex and even confounding subjects.

What to do about this dilemma? I think we might all follow the example of Professor Berg, whose efforts encompass both urgent problems of biomedical research and serious issues of public policy debate. He shows us how important it is to have real dialogue between scientists and non-scientists of all views. Scientists will certainly encounter a certain intransigence and mistrust as they move through the world, but that does not absolve them of the responsibility to engage in meaningful exchange with all kinds of people— thoughtful individuals who are trying to make sure that their lives have meaning and that their children have a better future.

The humorist Fran Leibowitz once quipped that science is pursued by those who lack a flair for conversation. She was joking, I am certain, but she touched on an important matter. If human beings are to have confidence in the work of scientists, many broad and continuing conversations must take place.

Cancer: The Revolution and the Challenge*

BERT VOGELSTEIN

Clayton Professor of Oncology Johns Hopkins University School of Medicine

I'D LIKE TO speak to you about cancer, what I work on and what my lab works on, to try to describe the revolution that has occurred in the last twenty years and to indicate some of the challenges that we face in the future.

Now, there has been a revolution in cancer. This revolution was ignited by Al Knudson in the 70s and he will be the discussant of this talk. If I were to summarize that revolution in a single sentence, that sentence would be "cancer is, in essence, a genetic disease." That's the long and the short of it. But it's a very special genetic disease. One can distinguish it from more common genetic diseases—common in the sense that they are widely recognized as genetic. Cystic fibrosis and muscular dystrophy are caused by mutations in single genes. For instance, for muscular dystrophy the gene is dystrophin. A child who has a mutation in the dystrophin gene will be affected by muscular dystrophy in the same way whether that child grows up in Philadelphia, in Los Angeles, or in Sri Lanka. There's a very simple relationship between genotype, the mutation, and the phenotype.

It's not so simple with other hereditary diseases. Atherosclerosis is a reasonable example. Here, individuals can inherit mutations in specific genes, such as LDLR, which controls lipid metabolism, but they won't necessarily get heart disease. A combination of genetics, heredity and environment is what finally determines the type of disease, if any, that these individuals finally end up with.

Cancer is another example of this kind of complex disease, perhaps the most complex one. Certain individuals inherit genetic defects which pre-

---

*Read 22 April 1999

81

dispose them to cancer, but they won't get cancer unless their cells acquire other mutations after birth. These mutations are acquired through mistakes that cells make. Sometimes, perhaps, they are acquired through interactions with the environment, diet, pollution, etc. But more often than not, it's the result of mistakes that cells are programmed to make and it's the combination of mutation that eventually leads to clinical cancer.

Now the revolution is based on the identification of three kinds of genes that together cause cancer. The first are called oncogenes. Oncogenes normally function as the accelerators in the cell. If you permit me to use automobiles as an analogy, oncogenes are the accelerators. A mutation in an oncogene is like having an accelerator stuck to the floor. A car wants to go even if the operator wants to stop it. But just like cars, cells have brakes, and the brakes are called suppressor genes. It's only when at least one accelerator and several breaks within the cell are rendered dysfunctional through mutation that a clinical cancer results. A third and more recently discovered type of gene that can cause cancer predisposition is termed mutator genes. These genes don't directly control cell birth or cell death. They simply control the rate of mutation, a defect in a mutator gene leads to a high rate of mutation and an accelerated rate of tumorgenesis.

Colon cancers illustrate the combination of genetic mutations that cause cancer, but this is true for all kinds of cancers that have been studied. Breast cancer, bladder cancer, lung cancer—they all require mutations in many different genes, either oncogenes or tumor suppressor genes, and the whole process seems to be driven by genetic instability due to mutations of the third class of genes, the mutator genes. And these mutations, as I said, can come about through two ways. In a small fraction of cases, one mutation is present at birth, it's inherited from a parent. Most of the mutations, however, develop after birth. In a nutshell, that's the revolution.

The challenge is to use this information about the genes which cause cancer to help people. There are four ways one can envision doing that: predisposition testing, that is, identifying patients that are at particular risk to develop cancer because they have inherited a mutant gene from a parent; early diagnosis—if one can diagnose tumors early, most patients are cured by a simple surgery, there's no danger of metastasis or death; improved prognosis can obviously be helpful for patients having developed cancer; and of course, new treatments. Now, most of these applications lie in the future. That is the real challenge. It will be just as difficult to get answers to how to use this information to help people as it was to identify the alterations. And most of you are probably aware that it took 25 years from the discovery that the polio virus caused the disease we call polio until the vaccine was created. Polio is a much simpler disease than the group of diseases we call cancer. It would be naïve to believe that it would take less than 25 years to develop any of these applications fully.

But I'd like to focus on one application that is already a real one, the first application, which is genetic diagnosis; that is, identifying patients who have a hereditary predisposition to cancer. In colon cancers about 10 percent of people have such a hereditary predisposition. The other 90 percent develop cancer strictly through mutations which they acquire after birth. But these 10 percent are particularly important because they develop cancers very early. Cancers are always tragic, but these people can develop cancer in their 20s, 30s, 40s, instead of 60s or 70s, which is the median age for colorectal cancer. These families seem almost Jobian in the sense that so many people have become sick with or died of the disease.

A young woman presented to our clinic a few years ago. It was clear that she had hereditary colon cancer from her clinical history—her father had died of colon cancer in his 40s and her paternal grandmother had also succumbed. The real question was whether her siblings, who were teens or pre-teens, were going to come down with the same disease that affected their sister. Through genetic diagnosis, it is now a relatively simple matter to identify the exact mutation that caused predisposition in this young woman, who was 23, and to tell which of her siblings had this mutant gene, and to predict, with 100 percent certainty that they would get this disease. The question is not whether we can do it—that has been answered, we can. The real question, and this is a question that Paul Berg raised, is, should we do it? A headline from the front page of the *New York Times* a few years ago: "Tests to Assess Risks for Cancer are Raising Questions." I'd like to bring to your attention a few very practical questions, which society must answer not a hundred years from now, but next year, because the technology to perform these tests is here.

First question: should results be given to insurance companies or employers? That is, the results of genetic testing. Is that ethical? Audience: how many of you think it is ethical to give results of your genetic testing to your insurance companies or prospective employers? Raise your hands if you think it would be so ethical. Nobody raises their hand. The only people I ever had raise their hand were insurance executives. But I'll ask you another question: how many of you have had physical exams for insurance companies? Raise your hands if you have. Everyone has, right? And you've all had blood pressure tests, right? And that information has been given to your insurance companies. Now what is the conceptual difference between a blood pressure test and a genetic test? They both are simply assaying for genetic disease. A sphygmomanometer is just a poor man's genetic test. If we are willing to give blood pressure information to insurance companies, then we should be willing to give genetic testing information, or we should be willing to give neither to insurance companies.

A second question: Should the results of genetic testing be communicated to prospective spouses? If you or your child, your son, was going to marry a woman, is he morally obligated to tell that woman, or vice versa, that he has a hereditary predisposition to cancer and that he is likely, with 50 percent probability, to transmit that disease to their children? Again, when I asked audiences that question, most people say 50–50, some say yes, some say no. But then if I asked: suppose that gentleman has AIDS. Is he morally obligated to give the information that he has AIDS to his prospective spouse? Does anyone in the room think that he's not morally obligated to do that? No one does.

So let me show you this example. One of our patients from Baltimore who has familial colorectal cancer had six wives and more than a hundred grandchildren, twenty of whom have hereditary colon cancer. He's a one-man epidemic of hereditary colon cancer. Is there any conceptual difference between this and AIDS? Perhaps, perhaps not. But again, not so simple.

And finally, perhaps the most difficult question, should these tests be performed before birth? They *can* be performed before birth, with the idea, of course, that a therapeutic abortion be performed if positive. Now, hereditary cancer predispositions are not lethal diseases during childhood. They usually don't affect people until they're in their 30s or 40s. The patients have normal lives until then and they can often be cured by surgery even if they get cancer. Is it ethical to do therapeutic abortions for diseases which, at worst, allow 30, 40, 50 years of normal life? When I ask most people that question, say "no," it's not ethical to perform genetic testing prenatally for such conditions. But if I ask a support group audience, these are support groups at Johns Hopkins composed solely of members of families who have hereditary cancer, they say just the opposite. They say, who are you to tell us that we can't have this information? We've seen our parents, our sisters, our brothers get very sick, even die with this disease. Who are you to tell us we shouldn't have a therapeutic abortion and spare our families this grief if you have the capacity to do these tests?

One of our mandates in this conference is to project in the future what may happen. And for that purpose, I'd like to extend my discussion of colon cancer to include all genetic diseases. There's a technology that's coming on-line now called micro-array technology, it's often called "CHIPS," because numerous genes are put on chips, literally hundreds of thousands, and assayed within hours to determine whether individuals have specific genetic alterations which predispose them to given diseases. And these tests can be applied at birth, to allow people to know if they're at risk for certain diseases, they can be applied before birth, they can even be applied after fertilization but before implantation. And this is not science fiction. This is real, this will happen, the technology to do this will undoubtedly mature within the next decade, because most of it has already been developed. And you could think of a square for diabetes, one for colon cancer, one for breast cancer, one for prostate cancer and squares for hundreds of other genetic diseases. If people were aware at birth—and again, even before birth—they could do something to minimize their risk of getting the disease or dying from it. And if we're willing to consider this kind of chip, let's go one step further. There are a variety of behavioral and psychiatric diseases which have a significant genetic component: depression, schizophrenia, alcoholism, drug addiction, aggressive behavior, etc. I'm sure all of you can think of many more. And the genes that are associated with, and which in part cause these conditions, will soon be identified or already have been identified. And the technology for assessing whether individuals have those genetic defects or variations will become available soon.

I'd like to leave you with a question. This is not a question, as Paul Berg and Harold Shapiro have said, that should be left to scientists alone and perhaps scientists are not the best people to answer these questions: Should we do this kind of testing? How should we do it? Who should be the recipients? The real question is not how to do them technologically, but how to do them wisely and fairly.

DISCUSSANT

ALFRED G. KNUDSON, JR.

DR. VOGELSTEIN was quite right in calling this a revolution, a revolution that has evolved through the whole century in fact, but with its greatest realization in the last 20 or 25 years. It had been noted at the turn of the century that cancer cells didn't look normal in their cell divisions. Theodore Boveri published a little book in 1914 in which he espoused the idea that cancer cells are different genetically from the rest of the cells in our bodies. That was the beginning of what we call the somatic mutation hypothesis, but it took a long time to give real substance to the idea; in fact, the first specific abnormality in a specific cancer, was reported by Peter Nowell, who is in the audience here, and David Hungerford in 1960. So there was a long interval before there was substantial support for Boveri's notion. If we realize that mutations, whether somatic or germline, can occur spontaneously, one of the questions that arises, and one that I would like Bert to comment on is "If we live long enough, will we all get the somatic mutations that lead to cancer?" At the present time, about 30 percent of people in this country develop cancer. Does this mean that cancer places a limitation on our potential life span? There are also inherited mutations that can strongly predispose to cancer as you've seen from Bert's presentation and these cancers are different from other hereditary diseases in that somatic mutations are also involved and can be selected because they lead to excess growth. So, although a particular somatic mutation may be very rare, a growth advantage for the cell causes it to multiply. This was, for geneticists, a very interesting idea, that a hereditary disease's expression, or penetrance as we call it, may depend upon other mutations (somatic) occurring after birth.

Dr. Vogelstein was the first to clearly demonstrate a specific set of mutations in a common cancer, namely, colon cancer. This leads to the notion that if there are a number of steps in the development of a cancer, there is an increased opportunity to do something. We have some cancers, like the one I originally studied, retinoblastoma in children, in which the number of steps is very small. About 5 percent of the children who have that cancer are born with it, so one cannot imagine that there would be very many events in the pathway, so prevention might be quite difficult. Fortunately, we have a 90 percent cure rate in the United States. But for adults, we have the problem that cancers undergo so many mutations during their evolution that they frequently present great problems in treatment. A cancer may have numerous different clones within it; if a treatment is good for 90 percent of those clones, the other 10 percent will still grow.

Thus, treatment is easier in children and more difficult in adults. On the other hand, prevention is easier in adults and more difficult in children. Now we have a possibility of actually doing something. For example, the von Hippel-Lindau inherited mutation produces little vascular tumors in the retina, which can lead to blindness. If a child has one of these angiomas, we can do something about it. If a child is born to someone who has this disease, we know that there's a 50 percent chance that the child will get it. So we do a gene test in early life. It is interesting to me that we've made some of these decisions in the past and have forgotten them. Arguments against testing in early life disappear when action is possible. We already accept such an idea for some environmental agents. We wouldn't think of abandoning the idea of immunizing young children against diphtheria.

In the matter of insurance, I am very impatient, as I'm sure most of the people in this audience are. An achondroplastic dwarf, who has a bad gene that causes him to have this handicap, wears his genotype on his forehead. Everybody knows that this person has that disease. So what do we do? We say it's illegal to discriminate against this person but if a woman is carrying a breast cancer gene, we don't say that. I don't understand how that happens. Maybe it's just because insurance companies could lose many more people with breast cancer than with achondroplasia. The molecular study of cancer genes suggests new ways to approach intervention, either before any of the steps has occurred, or even after one or more of them have occurred. I think that Bert rightly raises the question, "Should we do testing?" Many of us are coming to the conclusion that for the common diseases heredity and environment are interacting and it might be that most of us will die from a disease to which we have some genetic predisposition. Both environment and heredity are important and for a particular disease there is an age-specific incidence curve. A gene can move the curve 20 years earlier, and it might be quite useful to know who the people are who are predisposed and to try to convince them to make changes in their lifestyles or take new medications.

So, Bert, I have just two questions for you. One is, do you think cancer is inevitable if people live long enough? The other is related to not just cancer, but all diseases: does everybody have a gene that predisposes her or him to a particular disease, and for which testing will become available?

Wiring the Brain: Dynamic Interplay Between Nature and Nurture[*]

CARLA J. SHATZ

Department of Neurobiology
Harvard Medical School, Boston

THE HUMAN brain is the most incredible computational machine imaginable. Our ability to function, to see, to move, and to think depends directly on the precision and detail of brain circuits. How are these circuits assembled during development? One idea is that the brain wires itself up like a computer. That is, chips and components are assembled and connected according to a pre-set circuit diagram, and then with a flip of the switch, the computer turns on and works as it was designed. In the case of brain development, this analogy would imply that the brain only begins to work once it is essentially completely wired according to the adult pattern of connectivity.

The main theme of this essay is that the biology of brain development follows different rules. Neural connections are formed in the brain at very early times in development, and at first they are present in an immature pattern of wiring that only grossly approximates the adult precision. In order for the adult pattern of connections to form, neural function is necessary. This requirement for brain function in order to obtain adult brain wiring is nowhere more essential than in the developing visual system.

The Problem:

First, consider the magnitude of the wiring problem. The adult brain consists of about 1 trillion (10^{12}) nerve cells—neuroscientists argue about the exact number, but within the cerebellum alone it is thought that there are

---

*Read 22 April 1999

10^{11} granule cells. Each neuron makes a very stereotyped set of connections with specific partner neurons. A useful analogy is to think of nerve cells as rather like telephones that employ a mixture of chemical and electrical signals to send and receive phone calls. Each nerve cell sends a long process, an axon—like a phone line—to connect itself to other cells that can be located the equivalent of hundreds of miles away. For example, nerve cells up in the cerebral cortex of the brain connect many feet away with nerve cells down in the spinal cord.

The sites at which one nerve cell connects with another are called "synapses," and each cell can form anywhere from 10 to 10,000 synapses depending on the function and specific circuit. The brain contains well over 1000 trillion connections and none of them are random! A classic example of the precision of connectivity is in the visual system. In the adult visual system, information about the world is transformed from photons to a neural signal within the retina by the rods and cones. These cells send their axons to the retinal interneurons, which in turn, signal to the output neurons of the retina, the retinal ganglion cells. The axons of the retinal ganglion cells travel long distances to reach several visual relay structures within the brain, such as the lateral geniculate nucleus (LGN). LGN neurons then relay visual information to specific neurons located in layer 4 of the primary visual cortex, located in the occipital lobe of the cerebral hemispheres.

The connections between retinal ganglion cells, LGN neurons, and the layer 4 neurons of the primary visual cortex are precise and stereotyped. One important example of this precision is that the connections between eye and brain are organized according to which eye supplies the input. Because only half of the retinal ganglion cell axons from each eye cross over within the optic chiasm to travel to the opposite side of the brain, nerve cells in each half of the brain receive inputs from only one-half of the visual world, but from both eyes. Within the LGN, retinal ganglion cell axons from one eye are strictly segregated from those arising from the other eye to form a series of alternating eye-specific *layers*. The LGN neurons in each layer only receive connections from the retinal ganglion cells of one eye.

The segregation of eye input is then maintained at the next stage, in the wiring between the LGN and the primary visual cortex. LGN axons receiving their input from one eye connect with subsets of visual cortical neurons located in patches or clusters of neurons that alternate with patches of neurons getting their input from the other eye. These patches form the basis for a system of *ocular dominance columns* within the primary visual cortex. The columns, discovered by David Hubel and Torsten Wiesel in the 1960s, represent domains of cortex in which neurons respond best to stimulation of the eye supplying the input. In most higher mammals, including humans, the primary visual cortex is normally subdivided 50 percent–50 percent into an equal number of ocular dominance columns for each eye.

Even more incredible is that during brain development, all these connections have to be formed from scratch—nerve cells are made in different places in the brain by undergoing many successive cell divisions, and then each cell has to spin out its long process—the axon—and grow it towards the appropriate target neurons. For instance, the million or so nerve cells in the eye have to grow their axons long distances to connect up with the "visual" part of the brain; those in the ear with the "auditory" part of the brain; and so on. And then, once the growing axons reach their targets, they must select, from the millions of possible neurons, just the right few with which to form synapses. The process is much like stringing phone lines from one city to another—between New York and Philadelphia, for instance. First, trunk lines between the two cities must be laid down. Then, phones at specific addresses within each city need to be wired so that when a specific phone number is dialed, only that phone rings and not a lot of wrong numbers.

The solution—brain wiring is not like a computer:

How does the brain solve this incredible wiring task during development? As mentioned above, research has shown that the brain's solution is much more elegant and adaptive than simply wiring according to an immutable circuit diagram. In fact, the brain first sets down a basic framework of circuits—rather like trunk lines—according to strict circuit diagrams determined by a genetic blueprint. Then, long before the adult precise circuits are formed, the "switch" is turned on: brain function itself completes the wiring process by running test patterns on the circuits, thereby selecting correct connections and eliminating errors. Using the phone analogy, it is as if, once the trunk lines are strung between two cities, the first set of phone calls to be placed cause *many* phones to ring because many connections, including the correct ones, are formed initially. Then, a process of error-correction occurs, in which phoning itself eliminates the incorrect connections and strengthens the correct ones.

Thus, there are 2 broad phases to brain wiring: an early phase that does not require brain activity, in which basic circuits are established, and a later phase that refines circuits into their adult precision that does. Neuroscientists are beginning to learn a great deal about the molecular rules that govern these 2 major phases. Early on, the growing tips of axons follow road signs and highways of molecules, like netrins, semaphorins, cell adhesion molecules (CAMs), and substrate adhesion molecules (SAMs). These molecules are placed in specific combinations and locations by special early cell types in the brain, and they are sensed molecularly by the growing axon tips of "pioneer" neurons as they spin out the first connections. Once these early connections are formed, neural function begins and neurons signal to each other by sending chemical-electrical signals over their long distance connections. In the phoning process itself, the frequent use of connections strengthens them with rewards of special nerve growth factors and other signaling molecules. The inappropriate use of wrong connections causes their elimination. It is in this second phase of wiring where experience of the world can have a profound influence on the selection and maintenance of connections.

Visual experience places the phone calls after birth:

Here is a specific and famous example. Your grandmother gets a cataract as an adult. She can't see out of her right eye for 5 years. Then, after cataract surgery, she is fine again. In contrast, a child is born with a congenital cataract in the right eye. At 5 years of age, it is operated on and the optics of the eye are restored to normal. Yet tragically, unlike grandmother, the child remains permanently blind in the eye. What is the difference between these 2 cases? To find out, Hubel and Wiesel, Nobel Laureates in 1981, made an animal model of adult versus childhood cataract by simply sewing closed the lids of one eye in adult or in newborn monkeys and then waiting one year before checking on all the connections from eye to brain. What they found was striking. A childhood cataract actually caused that eye to lose so many connections with the visual cortex that it was unable to gain access to

the neural circuits needed for vision; blindness resulted! By tracing the connections between the LGN and primary visual cortex, they discovered that
the ocular dominance columns belonging to the closed eye had withered
away, while those belonging to the open eye had expanded until they occupied over 90 percent of the visual cortex. In other words, the open eye now
controlled over 90 percent of all cortical neurons and circuits. This observation is a graphic demonstration of "use it or lose it"—abnormal visual experience literally caused the weak eye to lose connections in the visual cortex, while the good eye gained far more that its fair share.

But why the difference between the infant and grandmother? The reason has to do with the fact that for an extended period after birth, the visual
system is still wiring itself up. That is, at birth the trunk lines between eye
and brain are all present, but the detailed sets of connections within visual
structures are immature. The phoning process is still going on to correct errors and select appropriate connections. Visual experience is needed to
place the phone calls, and if an eye is blocked by a cataract, calls can't be placed
effectively, so connections wither away: use it or lose it. Grandmother is
fine, though, because once connections are formed in this system, lack of use
does *not* cause them to regress.

The first hint that connections in the developing visual system might not
have the adult pattern and precision came from experiments in which special anatomical or electrical recording techniques were used to trace and
monitor connections from the two eyes in animal models. Such experimental approaches can be used to follow the time course and pattern of formation of the axonal projections from eye to brain. Remarkably, the LGN layers and the ocular dominance columns so characteristic of the adult pattern
of connections are not even present initially in development! Rather, retinal
ganglion cells from each eye *share* connections with many LGN neurons in
common, rather than having exclusive, eye-specific connections with only a
subset of target neurons. Similarly, within visual cortex, LGN neurons rep-
resenting both eyes also share connections with layer 4 target neurons at
early times in development. Thus, the initial circuits that are formed during
brain development are different from those found in the adult. Brain wiring
is a gradual process involving the growth and strengthening of appropriate
connections, coupled with error-correction to eliminate incorrect ones.

With ensuing development, the appropriate connections made by each eye are sculpted and remodeled until the adult pattern is present. The visual pathways develop from outside to inside, with the connections first forming between eye and LGN, and then subsequently between LGN and layer 4 of visual cortex. In all higher mammals (including humans) connections from retina to LGN form (in utero) even before the rods and cones are present, and therefore even before vision is possible! The segregation of LGN axons into ocular dominance columns within layer 4 begins prenatally (primates) but is not complete until neonatal life in all higher mammals. It is during this special postnatal period of development that visual experience can influence the formation of connections between LGN and visual cortex.

Critical periods for use-dependent brain wiring:

This early requirement for visual experience occurs when brain wiring is still happening—and during this period, normal experience is crucial for normal brain wiring. Thus, there is a *critical period,* or window of opportunity, in the visual system when experience is necessary for wiring. Neuroscientists know absolutely in the visual system that during this time, abnormal experience leads to abnormal brain wiring. This observation forms the basis for the classic model of critical periods for brain development. And because different parts of the brain mature at different rates and times, neuroscientists believe there are different critical periods for different functions. A challenge for the future is to learn exactly what those periods are in terms of the specific development of brain circuits, for instance, for language acquisition, or reading.

How early do these windows or critical periods open? In the case of vision, we know from animal models that the phoning process begins even before birth. In utero, of course, vision itself can't place the phone calls. Recall that connections between eye and LGN form before those between LGN and visual cortex. In fact, the eye-specific layers form in the LGN even before the rods and cones are present, Amazingly, nerve cells in the eye are involved in a spontaneous auto-dialing process, and send "test patterns" to the visual centers of the brain to get the process of fine-tuning of connections started extremely early. Groups or local neighborhoods of retinal ganglion cells in each eye all become active in a kind of "wave" of autodialing that is then sent along ganglion cell axons and communicated to target LGN neurons, causing groups of LGN neurons in turn to become active. These retinal waves happen about once every minute for several weeks. and we know that if they are blocked by drugs that block nerve cell chemical-electrical signaling, then the adult pattern of eye-specific layering in the LGN fails to form normally. Thus, as with vision during postnatal life, spontaneously-generated neural activity—the prenatal autodialing—is required for the normal formation of connections at these earlier times in development. Clearly, the brain does not wait until birth to start the activity-dependent phase of wiring. Even in utero, proper brain functioning appears to be essential for proper brain wiring almost as if the brain were in training for experience after birth.

An elegant and adaptive solution to the problem of brain wiring:

In this essay, I have considered the subject of brain wiring in development and the two-step process that occurs—an initial activity-independent step in which the basic framework of connections is constructed strictly according to the genetic blueprint, followed by a step in which brain function selects and refines from a wealth of possible connections. This second step is prolonged in humans, beginning prenatally and lasting to puberty postnatally (and even beyond in special brain regions subserving learning and memory in adulthood, such as the hippocampus). It is during this second prolonged period that experience can profoundly influence the important details of brain circuitry. Although I have restricted considerations here to the developing visual system, there are now examples of similar experience-dependent processes occurring in other regions of the brain, including the auditory and the somatosensory systems. Clearly, the developing brain is not simply a miniature version of the adult. It is a dynamically changing structure that records its experience in its wiring.

Why does the brain use this seemingly risky strategy to wire itself? There are many good reasons. The first relates to the numbers problem I posed in the beginning of this essay. There are just not enough genes in the genome (only about 100,000) to account for the incredible precision of connectivity present in the adult brain (> 1000 trillion connections). An elegant solution is to "hard wire" the trunk lines with specific molecular guidance clues, but then flip the switch to "on" early and let neural function make the final decisions. And this flexibility in final decision-making, after all, is what lets us adapt to our environment. For example, the brain does not know if it is going to have to learn English, Spanish, or Japanese after birth. An elegant solution to the wiring problem is to establish the fundamental framework of language circuitry using strict molecular mechanisms and then sculpt out the details depending on specific experiences after birth. Without this superb flexibility, we could not learn or remember or adapt to our environment—in short, those properties that make us uniquely human.

Useful Background Reading

Hubel, D.H. and T.N. Wiesel 1998 Early exploration of the visual cortex. *Neuron* 20: 401–412.

Shatz, C.J. 1992. The developing brain. *Scientific American* 267: 60–67.

Tessier-Lavigne, M. and C.S. Goodman. 1996 The molecular biology of axon guidance. *Science* 274: 1123–1133.

Katz, L.C. and C.J. Shatz. 1996 Synaptic activity and the construction of cortical circuits. *Science* 274: 1133–1138.

DISCUSSANT

JOHN E. DOWLING

Harvard University

I HAVE JUST one question for you, Carla: Nature clearly provides the initial framework for the brain. And there is now much evidence that the framework can be modified and portions even lost if not exercised early in life. But can one with experience go beyond the framework? The framework must set limits on what a nervous system can do. Put in other words, how much does nature box the brain in? With experience, what you've told us is that synapses can be gained, they can be lost, circuits can be substantially modified; all that I think is now very clear. But how far can nurturing go? That of course has enormous educational implications. Can we improve upon the initial framework?

Shatz Responds:

That's of course a wonderful question and a topic for a whole lifetime of study as many of us realize. Let me just say that I think for me the lesson that I've learned from this kind of knowledge that nature and nurture interact with each other is to look at the other side of the coin and realize that in impoverished environments we can really understand how serious a lack of nurture can be for brain wiring. And that's where I think the lesson has been absolutely clearest. I think we have all taken quite seriously the results of brain research. The more pleasant side of the question whether playing Mozart to your fetus in utero can actually produce a brilliant child is something that's fun to speculate on, but I really don't know the answer.

A Neuroscience of Memory
for the 21st Century*

Christopher Pittenger and Eric R. Kandel

A s the other essays in this volume make clear, in the last few decades biology has undergone a remarkable increase in explanatory power and range. This expansion is likely to have practical implications for all aspects of our lives, including our mental lives.

Biology is beginning to influence our understanding of mind because in the last two decades neurobiology—the science of the brain—has begun to merge with cognitive psychology—the science of the mind. This unification is providing a new analytic framework for a variety of mental functions, including perception, action, planning, language, learning, and memory.

In this brief essay we outline the possibility of advancing this unification further into a *molecular biology of cognition*. We will do so by focusing on memory formation. Using examples of different forms of memory formation from genetically modified snails, flies, and mice, we will illustrate that at least one mental process, the consolidation of short-term memories into long-term memories, can now be studied by combining the tools and conceptual approaches of cognitive psychology with those of modern molecular and cell biology. We also will attempt to illustrate that a molecular approach to cognition might help us understand not only normal cognition but also disorders of cognition, and may soon lead to treatments for memory loss.

There Are Multiple Memory Systems in the Brain

One of the major insights from the merger of neural science and cognitive psychology is the realization that memory is not unitary but can be

---

*Read 22 April 1999

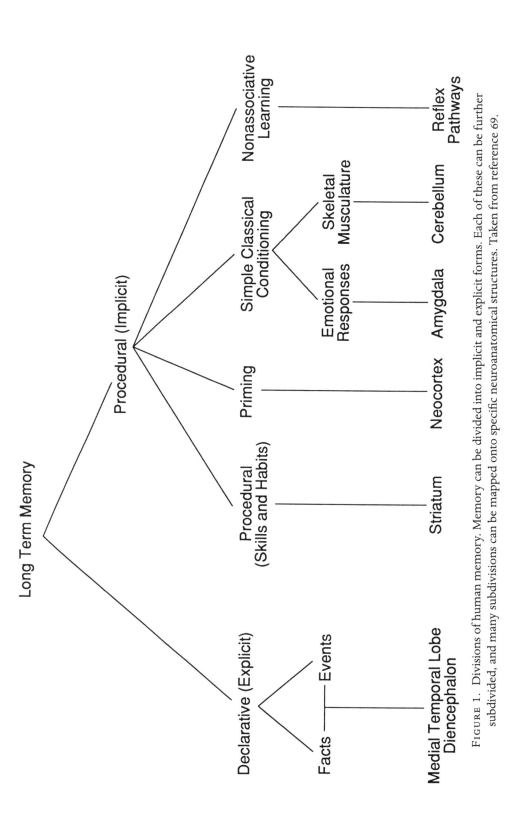

FIGURE 1. Divisions of human memory. Memory can be divided into implicit and explicit forms. Each of these can be further subdivided, and many subdivisions can be mapped onto specific neuroanatomical structures. Taken from reference 69.

divided into (at least) two functionally distinct forms: declarative and non-declarative memory. The hippocampus and surrounding temporal cortex are concerned with memory for facts and events: memories about people, places, and objects that can be brought to conscious recollection and can generally be put into words. This type of memory, referred to as *declarative* or *explicit,* is what one typically means when describing a memory: recalling the name of a friend, last summer's vacation, or this morning's conversation. Declarative memory was demonstrated by Brenda Milner's classic studies of the patient H.M., who suffered complete loss of the ability to store new declarative memories after bilateral removal of the hippocampus and adjacent temporal lobe structures. Studies of memories that were spared in HM revealed the existence of *nondeclarative* or *implicit* memory: changes in perceptual or motor performance that occur as the result of experience but are expressed through performance, without conscious recollection of past episodes. Nondeclarative memory can be further fractionated and is mediated by structures other than the hippocampus; different forms employ the amygdala, the striatum, the cerebellum, and different specific sensory and motor cortices (figure 1).[1]

Are There Common Molecular Mechanisms for Implicit and Explicit Storage?

The finding that there are two different forms of memory with different logic and different anatomical substrates raised a question: Do they share features in common? Can molecular biology reveal molecular similarities in the storage mechanisms?

One clue to mechanisms that may be shared among many types of memory has come from studying the stages of memory storage. Both declarative and nondeclarative memory are commonly divided into at least two stages: short-term memory that is labile and lasts perhaps an hour, and long-term memory that can last for days, weeks, or a lifetime. In each case repetition is required to convert the short-term into the long-term form. In both declarative and nondeclarative memory these stages differ not only in their time course but also in their mechanisms. Long-term differs from short-term memory in requiring the synthesis of new proteins. This conclusion is based on two findings. First, inhibitors of protein synthesis have no effect on learning or on short-term memory, but they specifically block consolidation into long-term memory.[2] Second, this disruption by protein synthesis inhibitors occurs only if they are applied during a certain time window after training—the *consolidation period*. Application of protein synthesis inhibitors at a later time, when the memory has already been consolidated into long-term storage, is without effect.[3,4]

This requirement for protein synthesis during a defined time window is evolutionarily conserved and has been observed not only in vertebrates but also in the invertebrates *Drosophila* and *Aplysia*. It applies to declarative as well as nondeclarative memory. This generality suggests a possible mechanistic conservation, both across evolutionary time and between declarative and nondeclarative memory in vertebrates. The dependence of long-term memory on protein synthesis indicates that new genes must be turned on during the transition from short- to long-term storage. There must be a switch whereby a subset of short-term memories are consolidated into long-term storage; one component of that switch must be the transcriptional apparatus by which new genes are activated.[5] One therefore wonders whether some of the key proteins that make up this switch might be conserved and be used for both declarative and nondeclarative memory. If this is so, identification of the relevant proteins in any one system might provide molecular insights that are important for the study of many other systems. Moreover, information from several different systems, each with its own properties, might be sufficiently complementary as to provide a coherent outline, in molecular detail, of how a transient short-term memory is converted into a stable long-term memory.

Memory Consolidation in the Invertebrates
Aplysia *and* Drosophila *Involves cAMP, PKA, and CREB*

The mollusc *Aplysia* has been a fruitful system for the study of learning and memory for several reasons (figure 2).[6] First, it has a relatively small nervous system of about 20,000 neurons, and has identifiable ganglia and microcircuits dedicated to specific tasks. Second, its neurons are particularly large and robust; this allows one to perform electrophysiological experiments that are much more difficult in vertebrate neurons. Third, its neurons can be readily manipulated in culture, which allows key experiments

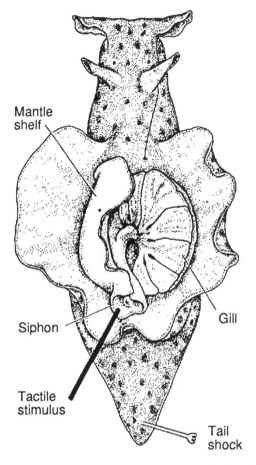

Mantle
shelf

Siphon

Tactile
stimulus

Gill

Tail
shock

FIGURE 2. The mollusc *Aplysia californica*. Structures involved in the gill withdrawal
reflex are illustrated: a light touch to the mantle shelf will stimulate withdrawal of
gill and siphon; a shock to the tail leads to sensitization of this reflex.

to be performed such as the design of specific microcircuits and the injection of proteins into cells—experiments that are not feasible in other systems. Finally, *Aplysia* exhibits a number of well-defined simple forms of
learning that can be readily studied or manipulated both in the intact animal
and in reduced preparations.

To study the cellular representation of memory in *Aplysia* we have used
a simple reflex system, the gill withdrawal response to stimulation on the
siphon. This reflex is subject to a simple form of learning known as *sensitization:* after presentation of a strong aversive stimulus (such as an electric

shock to the tail), the reflex response to a light siphon stimulus is significantly enhanced for a period of time. The duration of this memory is a function of the number of sensitizing stimuli applied to the tail: whereas a single noxious stimulus produces short-term memory lasting perhaps ten or fifteen minutes, four or five tail stimuli produce memory lasting one or two days. Short-term sensitization does not depend on the synthesis of new proteins,[7] whereas long term sensitization does.[8]

We have mapped out the neuronal circuit that mediates this reflex (figure 3).[6] It consists of both monosynaptic and polysynaptic connections between the sensory neuron that innervates the siphon and the motor neuron that innervates the gill. This circuit is modified at multiple points by three classes of modulatory interneurons that are activated by a shock to the tail. In our studies we have focused on the direct connection of the sensory neuron onto the motor neuron, and on its modulation by the neurotransmitter serotonin (also called 5-hydroxytryptamine, or 5-HT). Experimental stimulation of the 5-HT neuron or direct application of 5-HT causes facilitation at this synapse that parallels and underlies behavioral sensitization: after application of 5-HT, a stimulus to the sensory neuron will produce a larger response in the postsynaptic neuron than it did before. This facilitation represents a major component of the changes in the larger circuit that occur during sensitization; in a reduced system changes at this one synapse account for about 50 percent of the total learning that occurs. Changes do occur at other points in the circuit, but we have studied them less. A single pulse of 5-HT, such as might be produced by a single tail shock, produces facilitation lasting 10–15 minutes; multiple pulses of 5-HT produces long-term facilitation (LTF) which can last for days.

The molecular mechanisms of facilitation have been examined at this synapse, first in reduced preparations of the intact animal and more recently in a reconstituted cell culture system (figure 4).[9] The synaptic facilitation that occurs in response to tail stimuli, or more simply to application of 5-HT, occurs by a presynaptic mechanism: There is an increase in the amount of the neurotransmitter glutamate released by the sensory neuron with each action potential.[10] How does this come about? 5-HT activates two kinases, protein kinase c (PKC) and the cyclic AMP-dependent protein kinase (PKA).[11,12] We have more thoroughly investigated the role of PKA. A single pulse of 5-HT produces a transient increase in cAMP, which activates

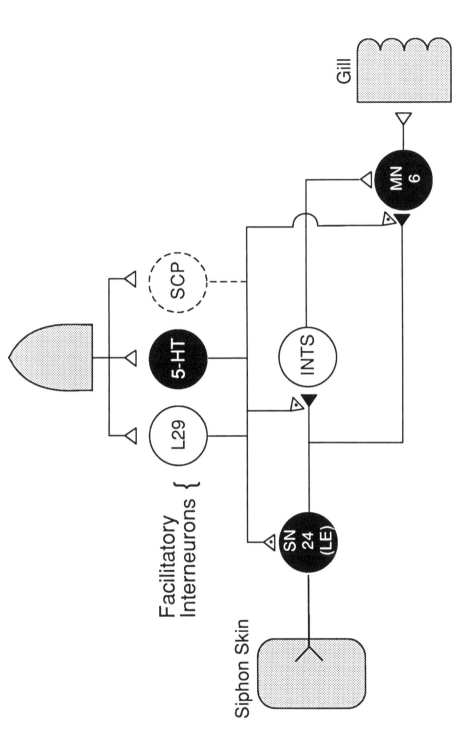

Facilitatory Interneurons {

L29

5-HT

SCP

Siphon Skin

SN 24 (LE)

INTS

MN 6

Gill

FIGURE 3. Schematic of the circuit that mediates the gill withdrawal reflex in *Aplysia*. Tail shock activates three classes of interneuron which release transmitter onto the terminals of the sensory neuron, leading to sensitization; the action of serotonin is particularly important.

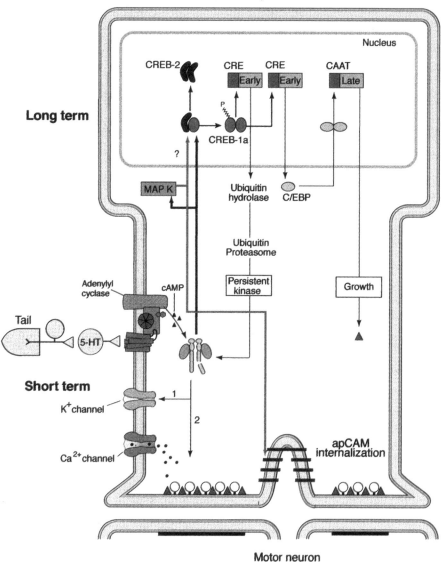

FIGURE 4. Molecular mechanisms of short and long term facilitation in *Aplysia*. Application of 5-HT to the sensory neuron initiates both processes. Modified from reference 69.

PKA. This brief kinase activation has at least two actions. First, it phosphorylates presynaptic K^+ channels, causing a broadening of the action potential in the terminals and a greater calcium influx into the sensory cell each time that cell fires. Second, PKA acts directly on the synaptic release machinery in an as yet ill-defined way.[13,14] Both of these changes cause increased release of transmitter.

After five pulses of 5-HT, PKA is activated in a much more persistent way and its catalytic subunit translocates into the nucleus of the cell.[15] This increased activation of PKA also activates a different set of signal transduction kinases, the MAP kinase cascade;[16] MAP kinase also translocates to the nucleus.[17] These two kinases work together both at the synapse, where they lead to the internalization of the cell adhesion molecule ApCAM,[18] thought to be important for growth, and in the nucleus where they activate transcription of new genes.[19]

Much evidence points to the transcription factor CREB (the cyclic AMP responsive element binding protein) as being critical in the induction of the genes required for LTF. First, a reporter gene driven by tandem CREs, the DNA sequences recognized by CREB, is activated by stimuli that lead to LTF.[20] Second, injection of oligonucleotides encoding the CRE sequence impairs LTF, presumably by binding to CREB and interfering with its normal activating function.[21] Third, injected antibodies against cloned Aplysia CREB (ApCREB) impair LTF, and injection of phosphorylated ApCREB produces LTF in the absence of any application of 5-HT.[22]

Just as there are multiple kinases involved in transducing the signal to induce LTF from the synapse to the nucleus, there are multiple transcription factors involved in the induction of genes. ApCREB2, a protein related to CREB, antagonizes CREB by repressing CRE-driven genes; this repression may be alleviated by phosphorylation by MAP kinase.[23] Yet another transcription factor, ApC/EBP, is induced by CREB, is also required for LTF, and may induce a separate family of necessary genes.[24] A different but related transcription factor, activating factor 1 (AF1), cooperates with ApC/EBP in gene activation.[25]

The end point of this cascade of gene activation is the production of functional changes in synapses, and long-term memories that persist for days, or weeks. Such changes in synaptic strength might best be stabilized by changing the physical structure of the synapse, and if this does occur it should be possible to observe morphological change in synapses that have been potentiated. One of the most exciting developments in the study of *Aplysia* plasticity has been the observation of just such changes.[26] Early studies demonstrated that the entire axonal arbor of the facilitated sensory neuron is increased.[27] Closer examination of potentiated terminals revealed several changes. The number of vesicles ready for release was increased at 24 hours after training but declined by one week, even though the memory persisted. By contrast, the number of synaptic varicosities and active zones increased, and this change decayed with approximately the same time course as the memory.[28] Immunogold electron microscopy allowed examination of the molecular mechanisms of such structural change. Long-term facilitation is accompanied by the internalization of surface antigens by clathrin-mediated endocytosis;[29] among the surface proteins internalized is the cell adhesion molecule ApCAM.[30] These are the sorts of processes one would predict to accompany morphological change: if the shape of the axon is to be permanently altered, distribution of cell surface proteins, including especially cell-cell adhesion molecules, would be required. Strikingly, both potentiation and morphological changes are eliminated by attenuation of CREB-mediated transcription, indicating that the two are coordinately regulated.[24]

Complementary work in the fruit fly *Drosophila* points to many of the same molecular components in neural plasticity and in memory. First, genetic screens have identified a number of genes required for memory storage. Several of these, including the mutants *dunce, rutabaga,* and *amnesiac,* encode components of the cAMP/PKA signal transduction pathway, suggesting that in flies, as in *Aplysia,* this transduction pathway regulates learning-related plasticity. Other genes identified in such screens include cell adhesion molecules[31] and modulators of the MAP kinase cascade,[32] as have been identified in *Aplysia* long-term. Finally, reverse genetic studies, in which candidate genes are disrupted or otherwise manipulated, have shown that disruption of *Drosophila* CREB interferes with learning[33] and that its overexpression enhances learning.[34]

Synaptic plasticity, as opposed to behaviorally measured learning, is difficult to study in *Drosophila,* but a series of studies has examined the relatively accessible neuromuscular junction. Like the vertebrate neuromuscular junction, this synapse is initially weak but is strengthened over development once a successful contact has been made between neuron and muscle. This functional potentiation is accompanied by neuronal growth, as been shown in *Aplysia*. Goodman and colleagues have demonstrated a fascinating dissociation between morphological and functional plasticity. CREB is required for functional potentiation but not for synaptic growth: when CREB-mediated transcription is experimentally attenuated, morphological changes proceed as normal, but the synapse remains weak.[35] The *Drosophila* cell adhesion molecule Fas 1, which is homologous to *Aplysia* ApCAM, is required for morphological changes but not for functional plasticity;[36] this role parallels that demonstrated for ApCAM in *Aplysia* long-term facilitation. Under normal circumstances during development, morphological change and functional potentiation co-occur; presumably the morphological change stabilizes synaptic strengthening, as we have hypothesized in *Aplysia*.

Two aspects of these studies are striking. First, despite the technological advances that have allowed investigation of the molecular mechanisms of learning and memory to proceed in mammals (as we will summarize below), many critical insights in the last decade have continued to come from the simple invertebrate systems *Drosophila* and *Aplysia*. Indeed, even though exciting work in memory is now possible in more complex model organisms, we are experiencing a renaissance of simple systems in recent years as these continue to provide the deepest insights into molecular mechanisms. Perhaps more striking is the conservation of the molecules involved: practically every molecule in *Drosophila* falls in the cascades independently identified in *Aplysia* LTF. This conservation leads us to believe that the mechanisms of synaptic plasticity are conserved across phyla.

The Structural Changes of Implicit Memory Storage May Contribute to the Biological Basis of Individuality

As we have seen, one of the most interesting insights to emerge from studies of long-term memory is the finding of anatomical changes as being the stable self-maintained mechanisms for long-term storage. Does this also apply to the mammalian brain? Does it apply to humans? In mammals, and especially in humans, each functional component of the nervous system consists of hundreds of thousands of nerve cells. In such complex systems a specific instance of learning is likely to lead to alterations at a large number of synapses. The most detailed evidence for this sort of large-scale reorganization has come from studies of sensory systems.

Cortical wiring is heavily influenced during development by activity-dependent rewiring processes[37] reminiscent of the mechanisms of synaptic plasticity we have discussed above. However, rewiring also is possible in the adult cortex. When input is dramatically modified in the adult (such as input to the somatosensory cortex being modified by the removal of a finger), the cortex can adapt such that more of it is responsive to the remaining inputs. This information stored by such means is a form of implicit, or nondeclarative, memory: it does not represent the storage of specific facts or episodes but rather represents a change in the way the cortex processes future input.

The clearest example of cortical rewiring in adults comes from work by Merzenich and Kaas in somatosensory cortex. The primary somatosensory cortex in humans consists of four of Brodmann's cortical areas (1, 2, 3a, and 3b) in the postcentral gyrus of the parietal lobe. Each of these areas contains a separate map of the body surface. Merzenich and Kaas have found that these cortical maps differ systematically among individuals in a manner that reflects their use. If innervation of a portion of the body is disrupted by nerve section[38] or by amputation,[39] the portion of cortex devoted to the absent body surfaces shrinks, and the portion devoted to surrounding, intact structures expands. Similar results have been reported from motor cortex in monkeys[40] and humans,[41] as well as from other primary sensory cortices.[37]

This evidence suggests that the cortical maps of an adult are subject to constant modification on the basis of use or activity of the peripheral sensory pathways. Support for this idea comes from further work from Merzenich. He and his colleagues trained a monkey to use only three of the fingers on one hand to obtain food. After many thousands of such uses, they found that the cortical representation of these three fingers was expanded, whereas the representation of the other two was unchanged. This result confirms that in adults the functional organization of cortex remains subject to use-dependent changes (figure 5).[42] Since all of us are brought up in somewhat different environments, are exposed to different combinations of stimuli, and are likely to exercise our motor skills differently, the architecture of each of our brains will be different. It will be modified in special ways. Even

Cortical representation of fingers

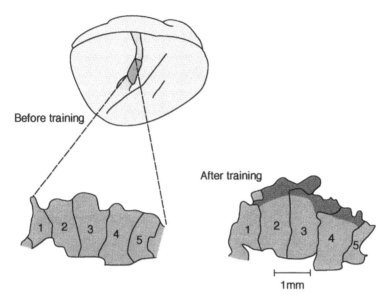

FIGURE 5. Expansion of cortical sensory representation of fingers after differential use. Monkeys trained to preferentially use three fingers show expanded cortical representation of the overused fingers but not of the control two fingers. Modified from reference 70.

identical twins, with identical genomes, will have slightly different experiences and slightly different brains. This distinctive modification of brain architecture presumably constitutes one aspect of the biological basis for the expression of individuality.

Dramatic evidence for cortical reorganization in adult humans has been provided by imaging studies from Taub and colleagues (figure 6). They scanned the brains of string instrument players. During performance, string players are continuously engaged in skillful hand movement. The second to fifth fingers of the left hand, which contact the strings, are manipulated individually, while the fingers of the right hand, which move the bow, do not express as much patterned, differentiated movement. Brain images of these musicians revealed that their brains were different from the brains of non-musicians: the cortical representation of the fingers of the left hand, but not of the right, was larger in the musicians.[43] Such structural changes are more readily achieved in the early years of life. Thus, Johann Strauss Junior

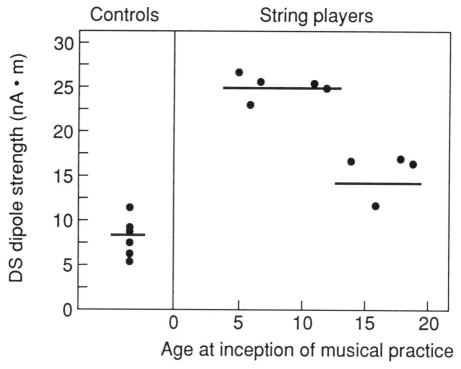

FIGURE 6. Sensory representation of fingers on the left hand in string players. Cortical representation of highly used fingers is expanded relative to controls; furthermore, this expansion is dependent on the age when subjects began their training. From reference 69.

was not simply a great composer and violinist because he had the right genes, but probably also because he began practicing these typically Viennese waltzes, polkas, and marches, some composed by his father, and operettas at a time when his brain was most sensitive to being modified by experience. Indeed, Taub and his colleagues found that musicians who learned to play their instruments by the age of 12 years had a larger representation of the fingers of the left hand, their important playing hand, than did those who started later in life.

Genetic Modified Mice and the Study of Explicit Memory Storage

Declarative, or explicit, memory, as we have described above, encodes all memories that can be consciously evoked and expressed in words: memories for people, places, objects, facts, and events. Formation of this sort of memory seems to require the hippocampus and medial temporal lobe system. This is the memory system that is most affected with age, and a thorough understanding of its workings may allow us someday to treat the dehumanizing ravages of senility; we will return to this possibility at the end of this essay. Aspects of explicit memory formation are well modeled by the formation of spatial memories in mice, which allows us to use the power of mouse reverse genetics to tackle the problem of its mechanisms. Recent advances in transgenic and knockout technology in the mouse allow us to make more and more specific genetic lesions, combining the molecular specificity of genetics with the temporal restriction of pharmacology and a level of spatial restriction that has hitherto been impossible.[44]

The hippocampus is a fruitful place to study the mechanisms of explicit memory for three reasons. First, lesions of the hippocampus, which (as in the case of H.M.) interfere with explicit memories in humans, disrupt memory for spatial tasks in rats and mice.[45] Second, the hippocampus contains a cellular representation of space: specific cells in the hippocampus, called *place cells,* fire only when the animal is in a specific place within an environment, and are stable when the animal returns to that environment;[46] the aggregate of these cells forms a *cognitive map* of space.[47] Finally, the hippocampus contains a robust and much-studied example of neuronal plasticity, termed long-term potentiation (or LTP). In many studies, disruption of hippocampal LTP correlates with disruptions in spatial memory[48] (but see ref.[49] for a counterexample); this suggests that LTP, or more properly more physiological plasticity which it models and resembles, is the cellular mechanism for spatial learning in the rodent.

LTP resembles LTF in *Aplysia* in interesting ways. LTP can be observed at multiple synapses in the hippocampus. To induce LTP at the intensively studied Schaeffer collateral synapse, where cells from the CA3 cell field of the hippocampus synapse on those of the CA1 field, one stimulates the CA3 axons repetitively (typically with one 100Hz train, or tetanus, lasting one second). The strength of the synapse (measured in the entire population of synapses by stimulating the CA3 axons with a single test pulse and recording an aggregate extracellular potential in CA1) is significantly greater after tetanization than before it; this constitutes potentiation (figure 7). As in *Aplysia,* a mild inducing stimulus produces potentiation which is relatively transient (lasting up to two hours) and does not rely on protein synthesis. A

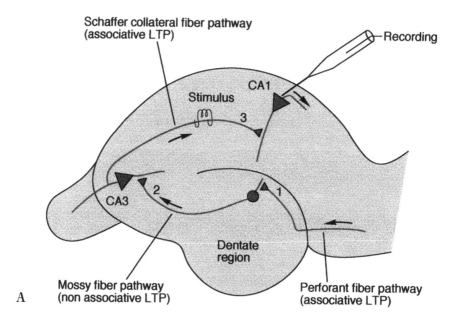

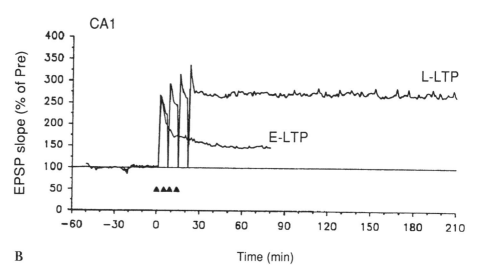

FIGURE 7. Long-term potentiation (LTP) in the mammalian hippocampus.
A. The hippocampal formation consists of three serially connected cell fields; plasticity has been demonstrated at projections between all three. Taken from reference 70.
B. LTP is induced by a train of stimuli, or tetanus; after such induction the postsynaptic response to a constant presynaptic test pulse is enhanced. Short-term LTP is induced by a single tetanus; long-term LTP is induced by four such tetani separated by five minutes.

more robust inducing stimulus (typically four tetani, applied five minutes apart) produces potentiation that can last for as long as the slice remains alive—up to twelve hours or more. Many studies have addressed the mechanisms of the early, protein synthesis-independent phase of LTP. We have turned our attention, as we did in *Aplysia,* to a different question: how induction of LTP at the synapse is coupled to transcriptional events and the induction of the genes required for the late phase.

The mechanisms of the early phase of LTP in the hippocampus are quite different from the induction of short-term facilitation in *Aplysia* (though similar mechanisms may exist in *Aplysia*[50]). Repeated synaptic stimuli trigger calcium influx into the postsynaptic neuron through the NMDA receptor, one subtype of receptor for the neurotransmitter glutamate. (The NMDA receptor does not open during a single synaptic stimulus, which explains why a tetanus is required to induce plasticity.) This calcium influx activates a kinase, CaMKII, which initiates further intracellular events including perhaps the insertion of new glutamate receptors into the post synaptic cell membrane.[51] What happens then remains controversial, but one contributing mechanism is thought to be the production of the retrograde messenger nitric oxide (NO), which travels back across the synaptic cleft to the presynaptic cell and causes increased probability of transmitter release upon future stimulation.[52]

While this early phase of LTP is quite different from what we saw in *Aplysia,* the mechanisms by which the late phase is induced are strikingly similar. First, whereas cAMP and PKA do not seem to be required for the early phase at this synapse (though they are at other synapses[53]), they are critical for the induction of the late phase (and for long-term, but not short-term, spatial learning).[54] Second, as in *Aplysia,* MAP kinase is activated by LTP[55] (and by spatial learning[56]) and is critical for the late phase.[57] Finally, the transcription factor CREB appears to be involved both in late phase LTP[58] and in learning.[59] Many aspects of this mechanism remain to be explored.[60] For example, the evidence for the involvement of CREB is still equivocal; the role of related transcription factors remains unclear (both mammalian CREB variants CREM and ATF1, and other transcription factors like CREB2 and C/EBP that have been implicated in *Aplysia*); the mechanisms of coupling of PKA to MAP kinase remain unresolved; and the role of PKC, if any, is still obscure. However, the striking conservation of mechanism between *Aplysia* and mammals leads us to believe that, whereas the mechanisms of short-term plasticity may vary significantly from synapse to synapse, long term synaptic potentiation is evolutionarily ancient and is likely to proceed by similar mechanisms at different synapses in the mammalian brain.

Disorders of Memory: Benign Senescent Forgetfulness

The fact that people now live longer than they did even 30 years ago has created a major public health problem: how to enhance the quality of life for the ever-increasing fraction of the population that is elderly. One particularly pressing problem is the gradual weakening of memory with age. This difficulty, often referred to as *benign senescent forgetfulness,* is neither completely benign nor necessarily limited to senescence. It first becomes evident in some people in their 40s, and it typically becomes more pronounced and prevalent with time. By age 60, at least 25 percent and perhaps as much as 40 percent of the population is affected to some degree. This memory loss is probably the most bothersome and frequently mentioned complaint of the elderly.[61] This memory loss is not an early phase of Alzheimers disease. It is relatively stable and not associated with cell loss. In the new century, our ever-expanding understanding of the mechanisms of memory storage in experimental animals may allow the development of therapies for this distressing aspect of aging.

As we have seen, lesions of the hippocampus and other structures in the medial temporal lobe interfere specifically with the ability to form long-term memories. People with such lesions can carry on a normal conversation and carry ideas in *working memory,* but they cannot convert this working memory to long-term memory. This defect is very similar to age-related memory loss, an observation which gives us the first clue to the etiology of age-related memory deficits: they may involve the hippocampus. Observations in humans and experimental animals reveal that this is in fact the case.[62]

Age-related memory loss is not limited to humans. We and others have recently developed models in rats and mice to study the effects of normal aging on explicit and implicit forms of memory. Three findings have been consistently supported across several studies. First, aged animals are deficient in explicit forms of memory but not in implicit forms, when compared to young controls.[63] Second, the memory deficit is not restricted to senescence; it begins in mid-life. Finally, not all aged animals are equally impaired: some are very severely impaired, but some perform as well as the youthful controls. The result is that the mean performance of aged animals is reduced, but the variance in performance is dramatically increased in old cohorts.[64] These observations suggest that deterioration in the hippocampal memory system is variable within cohorts of aged animals, which means that aged cohorts represent an ideal place to look for variance in other aspects of the hippocampal system which may correlate with reduced performance.

We have used the Barnes maze, or hole-board maze, to evaluate memory in aged mice. In this task, the animal is placed in the middle of a board which is ringed with 40 holes. One of these holes is connected to a dark escape tunnel, whereas the remainder are useless to the animal. The task is performed in a room with visible cues on the walls, and the escape tunnel is always in the same location, so the animals can learn the position of the escape hole by navigating from the distal cues. (Such navigation is known to be hippocampus dependent.) After the animal is placed in the center of the hole board, an aversive light and sound are turned on, and the animal is motivated to escape. During early trials the animals search randomly from hole to hole until they find the escape tunnel; we call this the *random search strategy*. During later trials, animals pick a random first hole and then search holes sequentially until they find the escape route; this is the *serial search strategy*. Well-trained animals learn to identify the position of the escape tunnel by navigating from distal cues and run more or less directly to it; this is the *spatial strategy*.[65]

This task is particularly useful because of the three strategies used. Only the third strategy, spatial navigation, requires the hippocampus. We confirmed that a subset of the aged animals were deficient in the Barnes maze task and never reached the learning criterion (measured by the number of incorrect holes the animals searched before locating the escape tunnel; figure 8). Interestingly, the aged animals abandoned the random strategy and adopted the serial strategy in parallel with younger controls, but they retained the serial strategy and never adopted the spatial strategy to the extent that younger animals did.[66] This is consistent with earlier findings that the deficit in aged animals is largely specific to hippocampus-dependent forms of learning.

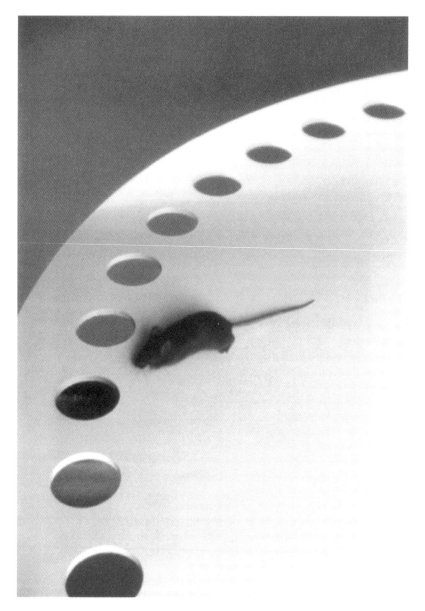

FIGURE 8. Age-related defect in a hippocampus-dependent task.
A. Mouse on the hole-board maze.
B. Layout of the hole-board apparatus, with holes around the circumference, a single escape tunnel, and distal cues for spatial navigation.
C. Aged mice showed a considerable deficit; this deficit proved to be specific to the spatial strategy, which is dependent on the hippocampus. Taken from reference 66.

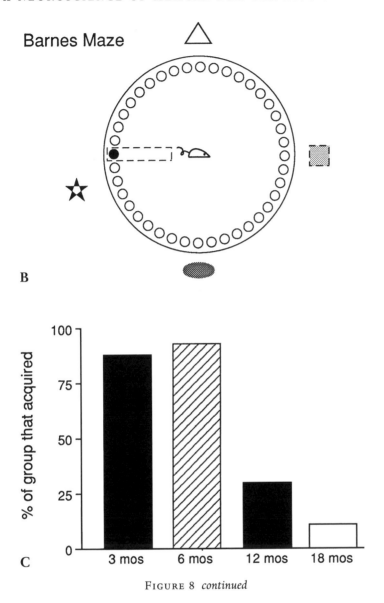

B

C

FIGURE 8 *continued*

As suggested above, we were interested in identifying changes in hippocampal physiology in the aged animals that would correlate with reduced learning. Because of the strong correlations between LTP and hippocampus-dependent learning in pharmacological and genetic studies, we examined late-phase LTP in the aged animals. We found a deficit in late phase LTP that

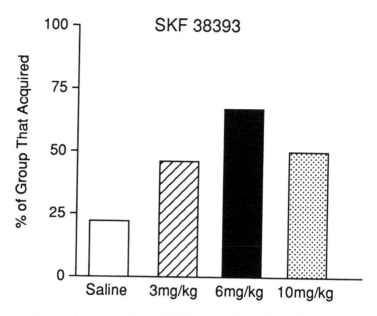

FIGURE 9. Amelioration of spatial defect in aged mice by a dopamine agonist. Intermediate doses of this agonist improved the performance of aged animals; a comparable dose also improved the LTP deficit. Taken from reference 66.

correlated with performance on the Barnes maze in the aged animals, but no corresponding correlation in younger animals.

As we have described above, the late phase of LTP is mediated at least in part by cAMP signaling and PKA. We therefore sought to ameliorate the deficit in LTP and in learning in aged animals by potentiating cAMP-mediated signaling. In hippocampal pyramidal cells, intracellular cAMP can be increased by the binding of the modulatory neurotransmitter dopamine to its receptor. We therefore applied two different drugs that activate the dopamine receptor to hippocampal slices from aged animals and examined their LTP. We had previously shown that high doses of one of these dopamine agonists, SKF 38393, can induce a slowly-developing, long-lasting potentiation in slices that is mediated by intracellular cAMP and shares at least some mechanistic steps with tetanus-induced LTP.[67] These drugs significantly improved late-phase LTP. We then applied SKF 38393 to aged animals in the Barnes maze (the other agonist we used in the LTP studies cannot be dissolved in saline and thus cannot be used in such studies). We found that intermediate doses of the drug ameliorated the learning defect in the aged animals, whereas both saline-injected controls and animals injected with a higher dose of drug remained impaired (figure 9).[66]

Finally, we tried to ameliorate the behavioral deficit in the aged animals by a complimentary manipulation of the cAMP-mediated signaling cascade. We had previously shown that the drug rolipram can improve memory in young animals. Rolipram inhibits the form of cAMP phosphodiesterase that is expressed in the hippocampus. Phosphodiesterease is the enzyme that breaks down cAMP. Rolipram therefore increases cAMP signaling by extending the half life of cAMP that is produced in response to any stimulus; this is in contrast to the dopamine agonists we described previously, which increase production of cAMP but leave breakdown unchanged. A moderate dose, but not a high dose, of rolipram in young animals can increase both LTP and hippocampus-dependent memory, without altering any other measured behaviors or non-hippocampus-dependent memory.[68] In aged animals, a low to moderate dose of rolipram significantly improved hippocampus-dependent learning in the Barnes maze such that the cohort as a whole reached the same learning criterion as younger animals.[66]

Towards a Biology of Memory in the Twenty-First Century: Treatment for Cognitive Disorders?

The results with aged animals summarized above strongly support the notion that an age-related defect in late phase hippocampal LTP at least partially underlies the decline in hippocampus-dependent learning in aged animals. Perhaps more importantly, they suggest that benign senescent forgetfulness might be reversible. In the new century we may see this gradual decline in hippocampus-dependent memory function in the elderly become a treatable inconvenience of old age, not an inevitable disruption. In another decade, we may find that our gradual understanding of the molecular mechanisms that underlie memory formation has led to very significant therapeutic advances, advances that were scarcely thinkable one or two decades ago.

The idea that senescent memory loss might be treatable through a thorough understanding of the molecular mechanisms of memory formation leads one to wonder whether other forms of memory impairment might be amenable to pharmacological treatment if the underlying mechanisms were adequately understood. At the other end of the age spectrum from senescent decline lie a variety of congenital retardation syndromes, such as Down syndrome and fragile X syndrome. The mental retardation aspects of such syndromes are typically assumed to be developmental in nature and thus to be intractable in a child or an adult. However, it is exciting to think that some aspects of the memory impairment associated with such syndromes may be due not to a developmental miswiring of parts of the brain but due to an acute disruption of the normal processes of synaptic plasticity. If this is the case, in any one disorder, it would open exciting new avenues for treatment, postnatally or even in adults, for some aspects of syndromes that have long been intractable.

In the twentieth century the study of memory has largely been one of basic science: scientists have used both humans with lesions and deficits and a variety of experimental systems to attempt to discover how memory works. We have come a long way down this road, though there are an enormous number of questions still unanswered. In the new century, however, we may be able to move beyond basic science, and to begin to treat people with a variety of forms of memory impairment. This may soon be possible at both ends of the age spectrum, with benign senescent forgetfulness in the aged and with certain forms of retardation in the newborn.

It is through a thorough understanding of both the neuroanatomy and the molecular mechanisms of memory storage that these new therapeutic possibilities will emerge. The molecular biology of cognition is maturing and moving onto new ground. An exciting century lies before us.

Notes

1. For further treatment of historical issues and the distinction between implicit and explicit memory, see Schacter, D.L. (1996) *Searching for Memory.* Basic Books, New York; Squire, L.R., and Kandel, E.R., "Memory: From Mind to Molecules," *Scientific American:* New York 1999; Kandel and Pittenger (1999) "The Past, the Future, and the Biology of Memory Storage." *Proc Royal Soc Lond B,* in press.
2. Davis, H.P., and Squire, L.R. (1984) "Protein synthesis and memory: review." *Psychol. Bull.,* 96:518–559.
3. Freeman, F., Rose, S.P., and Scholey, A. (1995) "Two time windows of anisomycin-induced amnesia for passive avoidance training in the day-old chick." *Neurobiol. Learn. Mem.,* 63:291–295.

4. Bourtchouladze, R., Abel, T., Berman, N., Gordon, R., Lapidus, K., and Kandel, E.R. (1998) "Different training procedures recruit either one or two critical periods for contextual memory consolidation, each of which requires protein synthesis and PKA." *Learning and Memory*, 5:365–374.

5. Pittenger, C., and Kandel, E.R. (1998) "A genetic switch for long-term memory." *C R Acad Sci III*, 321:91–96.

6. Kandel (1979). *Behavioral Biology of* Aplysia. W. H. Freeman & Co.

7. Schwartz, J.H., Castellucci, V.F., and Kandel, E.R. (1971). "Functioning of identified neurons and synapses in abdominal ganglion of *Aplysia* in absence of protein synthesis." *J. Neurophysiol,*. 34(6):939–953.

8. Castellucci, V.F., Frost, W.N., Goelet, P., Montarolo, P.G., Schacher, S., Morgan, J.A., Blumenfeld, H., and Kandel, E.R. (1986). "Cell and molecular analysis of long-term sensitization in *Aplysia*." *J. Physiol.*, 81(4):349–357.

9. Rayport, S.G., and Schacher, S. (1986). "Synaptic plasticity *in vitro*: cell culture of identified *Aplysia* neurons mediating short-term habituation and sensitization." *J. Neurosci.*, 6:759–763.

10. Castellucci, V., and Kandel, E. (1976). "Presynaptic facilitation as a mechanism for behavioral sensitization in *Aplysia*." *Science*, 194:1176–1178.

11. Braha, O., Dale, N., Hochner, B., Klein, M., Abrams, T.W., and Kandel, E.R. (1990). "Second messengers involved in the two processes of presynaptic facilitation that contribute to sensitization and dishabituation in *Aplysia* sensory neurons." *Proc. Natl. Acad. Sci. USA*, 87:2040–2044.

12. Brunelli, M., Castellucci, V., and Kandel, E.R. (1976). "Synaptic facilitation and behavioral sensitization in *Aplysia*: possible role of serotonin and cyclinc AMP." *Science*, 194:1178–1181.

13. Klein, M., and Kandel, E.R. (1980). "Mechanism of calcium current modulation underlying presynaptic facilitation and behavioral sensitization in *Aplysia*." *Proc. Natl. Acad. Sci. USA*, 77(11):6912–6916.

14. Shuster, M.J., Camardo, J.S., Siegelbaum, S.A., and Kandel, E.R. (1985). "Cyclic Amp-dependent protein kinase closes the serotonin-sensitive K^+ channels of *Aplysia* sensory neurones in cell-free membrane patches." *Nature*, 313:392–395.

15. Bacskai, B.J., Hochner, B., Mahaut-Smith, M., Adams, S.R., Kaang, B.K., Kandel, E.R., and Tsien, R.Y. (1993). "Spatially resolved dynamics of cAMP and protein kinase A subunits in *Aplysia* sensory neurons." *Science*, 260:222–226.

16. Michael, D., Martin, K.C., Seger, R., Ning, M.M., Baston, R., and Kandel, E.R. (1998) "Repeated pulses of serotonin required for long-term facilitation activate mitogen-activated protein kinase in sensory neurons of Aplysia." *Proc Natl Acad Sci U S A*, 95:1864–1869.

17. Martin, K.C., Michael, D., Rose, J.C., Barad, M., Casadio, A., Zhu, H., and Kandel, E.R. (1997) "MAP kinase translocates into the nucleus of the presynaptic cell and is required for long-term facilitation in Aplysia." *Neuron*, 18:899–912.

18. Bailey, C.H., Kaang, B.K., Chen, M., Martin, K.C., Lim, C.S., Casadio, A., and Kandel, E.R. (1997) "Mutation in the phosphorylation sites of MAP kinase blocks learning-related internalization of apCAM in Aplysia sensory neurons." *Neuron*, 18:913–924.

19. Barzilai, A., Kennedy, T.E., Sweatt, J.D., and Kandel, E.R. (1989) "5-HT modulates protein synthesis and the expression of specific proteins during long-term facilitation in Aplysia sensory neurons." *Neuron*, 2:1577–1586.

20. Kaang, B.K., Kandel, E.R., and Grant, S.G. (1993). "Activation of cAMP-responsive genes by stimuli that produce long-term facilitation in *Aplysia* sensory neurons." *Neuron*, 10:427–435.

21. Dash, P.K., Hochner, B., and Kandel, E.R. (1990). "Injection of the cAMP-responsive element into the nucleus of *Aplysia* sensory neurons blocks long-term facilitation." *Nature*, 345:718–721.

22. Bartsch, D., Casadio, A., Karl, K.Ak, Serodio, P., and Kandel, E.R. (1998) "CREB1 encodes a nuclear activator, a repressor, and a cytoplasmic modulator that form a regulatory unit critical for long-term facilitation." *Cell*, 95:211–223.

23. Bartsch, D., Ghirardi, M., Skehel, P.A., Karl, K.A., Herder, S.P., Chen, M., Bailey, C.H., and Kandel, E.R. (1995). "*Aplysia* CREB2 represses long-term facilitation: relief of repression converts transient facilitation into long-term functional and structural change." *Cell*, 83:979–992.

24. Alberini, C.M., Ghirardi, M., Metz, R., and Kandel, E.R. (1994). "C/EBP is an immediate-early gene required fo rthe consolidation of long-term facilitation in *Aplysia*." *Cell*, 76:1099–1114.

25. Bartsch et al. in preparation.

26. Bailey C.H., and Chen, M. (1988) "Long-term memory in Aplysia modulates the total number of varicosities of single identified sensory neurons." *Proc Natl Acad Sci U S A*, 85:2373–2377.

27. Bailey, C.H., Hawkins, R.D., Chen, M.C., and Kandel, E.R. (1981) "Interneurons involved in mediation and modulation of gill-withdrawal reflex in Aplysia. IV. Morphological basis of presynaptic facilitation." *J Neurophysiol*, 45:340–360.

28. Bailey, C.H., and Chen, M. (1989) "Time course of structural changes at identified sensory neuron synapses during long-term sensitization in Aplysia." *J Neurosci.*, 9:1774–80.

29. Hu, Y., Barzilai, A., Chen, M., Bailey, C.H., and Kandel, E.R. (1993) "5-HT and cAMP induce the formation of coated pits and vesicles and increase the expression of clathrin light chain in sensory neurons of *Aplysia*." *Neuron*, 10:921–929.

30. Bailey, C.H., Chen, M., Keller, F., and Kandel, E.R. (1992) "Serotonin-mediated endocytosis of apCAM: an early step of learning-related synaptic growth in *Aplysia*." *Science*, 256:645–649.

31. Grotewiel, M.S., Beck, C.D., Wu, K.H., Zhu, X.R., and Davis, R.L. (1998) "Integrin-mediated short-term memory in Drosophila." *Nature*, 391:455–456.

32. Skoulakis, E.M. and Davis, R.L. (1996) "Olfactory learning deficits in mutants for leonardo, a Drosophila gene encoding a 14-3-3 protein." *Neuron*, 17:931–944.

33. Yin, J.C., Wallach, J.S., Del Vecchio, M., Wilder, E.L., Zhou, H., Quinn, W.G., and Tully, T. (1994). "Induction of a dominant negative CREB transgene specifically blocks long-term memory in *Drosophila*." *Cell*, 79:49–58.

34. Yin, J.C., Del Vecchio, M., Zhou, H., and Tully, T. (1995). "CREB as a memory modulator: induced expression of a dCREB2 activator isoform enhances long-term memory in *Drosophila*." *Cell*, 81:107–115.

35. Davis, G.W., Schuster, C.M., and Goodman, C.S. (1996). "Genetic dissection of structural and functional components of synaptic plasticity. III. CREB is necessary for presynaptic functional plasticity." *Neuron*, 17:669–679.

36. Schuster, C.M., Davis, G.W., Fetter, R.D., and Goodman, C.S. (1996) "Genetic dissection of structural and functional components of synaptic plasticity. II. Fasciclin II controls presynaptic structural plasticity." *Neuron*, 17:655–667.

37. Katz, L.C., and Shatz, C.J. (1996) "Synaptic activity and the construction of cortical circuits." *Science*, 274:1133–1138.

38. Merzenich, M.M., and Kaas, J.H. (1982) "Organization of mammalian somatosensory cortex following peripheral nerve injury." *Trends Neurosci.*, 5:434–436.

39. Merzenich, M.M., Nelson, R.J., Stryker, M.P., Cynader, M.S., Schoppman, A., and Zook, J.M. (1984) "Somatosensory cortical map changes following digit amputation in adult monkeys." *J. Comp. Neurol.*, 224:591–605.

40. Sanes, J.R., Suner, S., and Donoghue, J.P. (1990) "Dynamic organization of primary motor cortex output to target muscles in adult rats: I. Long-term patterns of reorganization following motor or mixed nerve lesions." *Exp. Brain Res.*, 79:479–491.

41. Cohen, L.G., Bandinell, S., Findley, T.W., and Hallett, M. (1991) "Motor reorganization after upper limb amputation in man. A study with focal magnetic stimulation." *Brain*, 114:615–627.

42. Jenkins, W.M., Merzenich, M.M., Ochs, M.T., Allard, R., and Guic-Robles, E. (1990) "Functional reorganization of primary somatosensory cortex in adult owl monkeys after behaviorally controlled tactile stimulatio." *J. Neurophysiol*, 63:82–104.

43. Elbert, T., Pantev, C., Wienbruch, C., Rockstroh, B., and Taub, E. (1995) "Increased cortical representation of the fingers of the left hand in string players." *Science*, 270:305–307.

44. Mayford, M., Mansuy, I.M., Muller, R.U., and Kandel, E.R. (1997) "Memory and behavior: a second generation of genetically modified mice." *Curr Biol.*, 7:R580–589.

45. Jarrard, L.E. (1993) "On the role of the hippocampus in learning and memory in the rat." *Behav Neural Biol.*, 60:9–26.

46. Muller, R. (1996) "A quarter of a century of place cells." *Neuron*, 17:813–22.

47. Okeefe, J., and Nadel, L., *The Hippocampus as a Cognitive Map*. Oxford: New York 1978.

48. E.g. Bourtchuladze, R., Frenguelli, B., Blendy, J., Cioffi, D., Schutz, G., and Silva, A.J. (1994). "Deficient long-term memory in mice with a targeted mutation of the cAMP-responsive element-binding protein." *Cell*, 79:59–68; Abel, T., Nguyen, P.V., Barad,

M., Deuel, T.A., Kandel, E.R., and Bourtchouladze, R. (1997). "Genetic demonstration of a role for PKA in the late phase of LTP and in hippocampus-based long-term memory." *Cell,* 88:615–626; Tsien, J.Z., Huerta, P.T., and Tonegawa, S. (1996) "The essential role of hippocampal CA1 NMDA receptor-dependent synaptic plasticity in spatial memory." *Cell,* 87:1327–38.

49. Zamanillo, D., Sprengel, R., Hvalby, Ø., Jensen, V., Burnashev, N., Rozov, A., Kaisser, K.M.M., Köster, H.J., Borchardt, T., Worley, P., Lübke, J., Frotscher, M., Kelly, P.H., Sommer, B., Andersen, P., Seeburg, P.H., and Sakmann, B. (1999) "Importance of AMPA receptors for hippocampal synaptic plasticity but not for spatial learning." *Science,* 284:1805–1811.

50. Murphy, G.G., and Glanzman, D.L. (1997) "Mediation of classical conditioning in Aplysia californica by long-term potentiation of sensorimotor synapses." *Science,* 278:467–471.

51. Silva, A.J., Paylor, R., Wehner, J.M., and Tonegawa, S. (1992) "Impaired spatial learning in alpha-calcium-calmodulin kinase II mutant mice." *Science,* 257:206–211.

52. Arancio, O., Kiebler, M., Lee, C.J., Lev-Ram, V., Tsien, R.Y., Kandel, E.R., and Hawkins, R.D. (1996) "Nitric oxide acts directly in the presynaptic neuron to produce long-term potentiation in cultured hippocampal neurons." *Cell,* 87:1025–1035.

53. Huang, Y.Y., Kandel, E.R., Varshavsky, L., Brandon, E.P., Qi, M., Idzerda, R.L., McKnight, G.S., and Bourtchouladze, R. (1995). "A genetic test of the effects of mutations in PKA on mossy fiber LTP and its relation to spatial and contextual learning." *Cell,* 83:1211–1222.

54. Abel et al, ibid.

55. English, J.D., and Sweatt, J.D. (1997) "Activation of p42 mitogen-activated protein kinase in hippocampal long term potentiation." *J Biol Chem.,* 271:24329–24332.

56. Atkins, C.M., Selcher, J.C., Petraitis, J.J., Trzaskos, J.M., and Sweatt, J.D. (1998) "The MAPK cascade is required for mammalian associative learning." *Nat Neurosci.,* 1:602–609.

57. Impey, S., Obrietan, K., Wong, S.T., Poser, S., Yano, S., Wayman, G., Deloulme, J.C., Chan, G., and Storm, D.R. (1998) "Cross talk between ERK and PKA is required for Ca2+ stimulation of CREB-dependent transcription and ERK nuclear translocation." *Neuron,* 21:869–883.

58. Bourtchouladze *et al,* 1994.; Impey, S., Mark, M., Villacres, E.C., Poser, S., Chavkin, C., and Storm, D.R. (1996) "Induction of CRE-mediated gene expression by stimuli that generate long-lasting LTP in area CA1 of the hippocampus." *Neuron,* 16:973–982.

59. Bourtchouladze *et al,* ibid..; Impey, S., Smith, D.M., Obrietan, K., Donahue, R., Wade, C., and Storm, D.R. (1998) "Stimulation of cAMP response element (CRE)-mediated transcription during contextual learning." *Nat Neurosci.,:*595–601.

60. Kandel and Pittenger, 1999.

61. Adams, R.D., Victor, M., and Ropper, A.H. *Principles of Neurology,* McGraw-Hill: New York 1997. Ch. 29.

62. Uttl, B., and Graf. P. (1993) "Episodic spatial memory in adulthood." *Psychol Aging,* 8:257–273.

63. Barnes, C.A. (1979) "Memory deficits associated with senescence: a neurophysiological and behavioral study in the rat." *J. Comp. Physiolog. Psychol.,* 93:74–104.

64. Gallagher, M., and Pelleymounter, M.A. (1988) "An age-related spatial learning deficit: choline uptake distinguishes "impaired" and "unimpaired" rats." *Neurobiol. Aging,* 9:363–369.

65. Bach, M.E., Hawkins, R.D., Osman, M., Kandel, E.R., and Mayford, M. (1995) "Impairment of spatial but not contextual memory in CaMKII mutant mice with a selective loss of hippocampal LTP in the range of the theta frequency." *Cell,* 81:905–915.

66. Bach, M.E., Barad, M., Son, H., Zhuo, M., Lu, Y.-F., Shih, R., Mansuy, I., Hawkins, R.D., and Kandel, E.R. (1999) "Age-related defects in spatial memory are correlated with defects in the late phase of hippocampal long-term potentiation *in vitro* and are attenuated by drugs that enhance the cAMP signalling pathway." *Proc. Natl. Acad. Sci., USA,* 96:5280–5285.

67. Frey, U., Huang, Y.-Y., and Kandel, E.R. (1993) "Effects of cAMP simulate a late stage of LTP in hippocampal CA1 neurons." *Science,* 260:1161–1164.

68. Barad, M., Bourtchouladze, R., Winder, D.G., Golan, H., and Kandel, E. (1999) "Rolipram, a type-IV specific phosphodiesterase inhibitor, facilitates the establishment of long-lasting long-term potentiation and improves memory." *Proc. Natl. Acad. Sci. USA,* 95:15020–15025.

69. Milner, B., Squire, L.R., and Kandel, E.R. (1998) "Cognitive neuroscience and the study of memory." *Neuron,* 20:445–468.

70. Kandel, E.R., Schwartz, J.H., and Jessell, T.M. (1995) *Essentials of Neural Science and Behavior.* Appleton & Lange: Stamford.

DISCUSSANT

VERNON B. MOUNTCASTLE

Johns Hopkins University School of Medicine

ERIC KANDEL has given a luminous overview of many of the molecular and cellular aspects of memory. And both he and Carla Shatz have convinced you, as they have convinced me, that neuroscience is complicated. Along the range of enterprises which Sir Martin Rees mentioned this morning, certainly neuroscience would fall into that group he labeled complexity.

I will not burden you with my own musings on this subject. I had to Dr. Kandel two easy questions—he demurred on one of them but he may answer both of them if he will. The first question is this: how is it that the changes in the molecular and cellular aspects of the hippocampus and the adjacent cortex are transferred into the distributed systems of the neocortex where we know that many long-term memories are embedded? That's the easy one. The second one: Could we induce you to comment on the general phenomenon of recall?

KANDEL RESPONSE

Let me take the second question first. There is no answer to either of those questions. Those are questions for the future, I should say at the beginning, so I will just sort of think out loud about it. Recall is an extremely interesting problem because cognitive psychological studies suggest that it is not simply a question of turning a flash light on a memory process; it's a creative event. One recalls by using a number of different associations. An event is recalled and it's really a reconstruction of a memory. It's never reconstructed in exactly the way it occurs; it's a creative act. And we've been interested in asking the question, if it's a creative act, to what degree does it involve genes involved in laying down memory in the first place? And using genetically modified mice in which you can turn genes on and off we have done the following experiment: we have used the gene that we know interferes with the synaptic facilitation and interferes with memory process, but we've kept the gene off all the time. We've had the animal learn something with the gene off, so it learns it perfectly normally; we test its memory, the memory is perfectly normal. You now turn the gene on a week later and the animal has no memory, cannot recall. So at this particular point you're not sure if you've fouled up the storage process or whether there's a problem with recall. We now turn the gene off again and the animal recalls perfectly well. So that's sort of the first clue that some of the genes involved in laying down the memory need to be recruited for later on. But there's a deep problem, which one is just beginning to be in a position to ask.

The other question that Vernon asks, how does the information move from structures like the hippocampus to the neocortex is really one of the great mysteries. One thought that has been developed by Wilson and McNorton is that there are many connections that lead from the hippocampus back to the neocortex and that when the brain is idling, for example during phases of sleep, it might be replaying this information into the cortex. Simply to put this into perspective for you, when I look at Vernon, his image casts an image on my retina which is projected to an area ultimately in the visual system that specializes in faces. Lesions to that area makes it impossible to recognize Vernon. The initial representation in that area is thought to be weak, and cannot by itself carry the memory. Part of that memory comes to the hippocampus and the hippocampus is thought to work to strengthen that initial representation. And one idea is that in moments of idling, which neither of us is engaging in at the moment, that strengthening is occurring.

SOCIAL SCIENCES

National Sovereignty and Human Rights

Louis Henkin

University Professor Emeritus, Columbia University

I HAD CONCEIVED the following remarks under a title, approximately, "Sovereignty: The Erosion of State Sovereignty by International Human rights." According to standard academic practice, the essential subject of an address is in what follows the colon. But I preface these remarks by brief ruminations on "Sovereignty" generally, and follow them with brief ruminations on what Sovereignty should not be.

1.

"Sovereignty," "national sovereignty," "state sovereignty," is very much in the air of the world s political system. Sometimes it pollutes that air.

The "sovereignty" of states has been a premise of international relations and of international law at least since 1648, from the Peace of Westphalia from which we tend to date the modern international—interstate system. But sovereignty has different meanings, and claims different implications, in different contexts; it is probably the most used term in international law and politics; it is a term also much abused.

That may be due, in part, to its questionable origins: a term deriving from relations between "the Sovereign" and his/her subjects in domestic society; or, identifying the locus of ultimate political authority in domestic society (as in "popular sovereignty"), was transferred to relations between political societies ("states") and became the *urprinciple* of the international political system.

Some of the international uses of "sovereignty" are benign and support important human values. Sovereignty has been the watch-cry of the drive for decolonization and "self-determination." State sovereignty has been the foundation of the most important principle of international law in the Twentieth Century—the provision in the United Nations Charter prohibiting the use or threat of force against the territorial integrity or political independence ("the sovereignty") of another state.

Sometimes,"sovereignty" describes the authority of a state over its for internal affairs. But "sovereignty" is often deemed to imply also that a state, a sovereign state, should not, does not have to, submit to international regulation to agree, say, to a treaty prohibiting land mines or the proliferation of nuclear weapons, or to pay its dues to the United Nations.

(Once I stumbled into a remarkable invocation of "sovereignty." I asked a judge of the International Court of Justice why states appearing in cases before the Court are permitted to present arguments for days, and to pile up "memorials" and briefs, while the Supreme Court of the United States— not an unimportant tribunal—limits each party to a half-hour of argument and a modest number of pages. The reply: "Oh, but one cannot impose limits on a sovereign state.")

These are some of the uses (and abuses) of sovereignty: they cannot all be addressed in brief compass. I turn to my title.

2.

I begin with the invocation by states of their sovereignty to claim autonomy, complete authority, within their territory. And I indicate how that conception of sovereignty has fared under the impact of the international human rights movement.

Until 1945, how a state treated its own citizens in its own territory was its own business. That applied to every state, even Hitler's Germany. Indeed, it required Hitler, and the Holocaust, to bring the international human rights movement to life. Since 1945, how a state treats its own citizens inside its own territory is no longer wholly its own business. It has become a matter of international concern, of international politics, and of international law.

That erosion of sovereignty reflects a striking development. The international system borrowed an idea—"inherent individual rights"—from the seventeenth and eighteenth centuries, and rendered it a universal ideology, applicable to all human beings in every society, within every "sovereign" state.

Human rights are the rights of all human beings. Human rights are implicit in "constitutionalism," in "the rule of law" the ideology of the end of the Twentieth Century from which no one—no "sovereign state"—dissents. In the result, every country in the world, and all of their six billion human inhabitants, have title to all the rights, the human rights, identified and defined by international instruments.

No doubt, we must acknowledge, universal human rights sometimes appears to be only nominal, even hypocritical. But one might do well to recall the insight of the Duc de Ia Rochefoucauld who noted that hypocrisy is the homage that vice pays to virtue: Universal human rights is the virtue to which even the vicious pay homage in the second half of the expiring century.

And so, all sovereign states—the former Soviet Union, and Communist China, and tyrants in parts of the former Yugoslavia, and all others—have recognized, have had to recognize, the idea of human rights as the ideology of our time.

What is more, all have accepted a comprehensive definition of human rights. In 1945, when the world began to speak of human rights, they did not need to define them or to identify their violators. Then, human rights meant freedom from Hitler's ineffable atrocities—genocide and crimes against humanity. Now human rights challenge other states, all states. Now we have defined "human rights" as what is required by human dignity, and spelled out its requirements in the 30 articles of the Universal Declaration of Human Rights which we celebrated last year. And that definition has not been challenged. Now human rights includes freedom of speech and religion as well as freedom from torture and arbitrary detention, and freedom from racial discrimination and from discrimination against women, and the rights of the child. Human rights includes as well, equally, what have been called economic and social rights the right to food, housing, education, and other benefits of "the welfare state" now recognized everywhere (including the United States, though limited here by reluctance to be taxed and by "compassion fatigue").

Needless to say, states—sovereign states—did not rush to embrace this gaping rent in their sovereignty—and some states have been particularly resistant to the ideology I have described. They have felt threatened by the "international human rights movement"—by Amnesty International, and Human Rights Watch, and the Lawyer's Committee for Human Rights, and counterparts in various countries. Some states have seen their sovereignty as increasingly invaded by covenants and conventions, which more and more states have been pressed to ratify, and have ratified. Some states see their sovereignty threatened by professors propagating and teaching the human rights ideology, by litigious lawyers who are after Karadic, and Pinochet, and Milosevic, and others still anonymous, in many parts of the world. Some states feel threatened by the network of organizations and individuals, and the Press and "the Media," engaged in monitoring and shaming governments.

The business of the human rights movement I have concluded, is to shame governments. It has been a matter of some amazement that governments can be shamed and continue to be susceptible to shame.

I sometimes wonder, as I read the newspapers, why China has reportedly been expending huge sums, other resources, and diplomatic goodwill, to keep its name off the agenda of a little-known body called the UN Commission of Human rights. Why does China care? That is part of the process and the influence of shaming. The influence of "shame" as a deterrent in shaping the policy of governments is, I think, grossly underestimated.

Slowly, states have accommodated to this still-young international human rights movement. States—including big, powerful sovereign states—Russia, and China, and the United Kingdom, and France, and Germany—and the United States—all have accepted the principles of the Universal Declaration, all have become parties to human rights treaties, and all are subject to the customary law of human rights. States have accepted the idea of human rights, and have accepted particular human rights standards developed by the international human rights movement, on matters as to which they used to think were for them alone to determine. Have we perhaps now replaced "state sovereignty" with "human dignity"? If so, it is a change that deserves to be celebrated, not least in the halls of the American Philosophical Society.

It requires more time and many pages to explore how much erosion of sovereignty there has been, with what consequences for the lives and the well-being of human beings. I do not wish to paint a rosy picture of the condition of human rights, or a dark picture of the condition of state sovereignty. State sovereignty is alive, if not as well as it once was, international human rights are not as respected as they should be. How much sovereignty, how much international human rights, may not be easy to determine, and may not be agreed. But, I believe, Human Rights are here to stay.[1] They remain prominent on the world agenda for the next millennium.

3.

If there were time, I should consider other forces that weigh on state sovereignty and have implications for human rights. Globalization is now in the

---

1. Since these remarks were delivered, in April 1997, the world has seen "humanitarian intervention" at Kosovo and in East Timor, the drive to oust Milosevic, to extradite Pinochet, to establish an international Criminal Court.

air, as prominently as sovereignty. Like sovereignty, globalization is not carefully defined. What are the consequences of globalization, however defined, for sovereignty in its various senses and uses, and how do they impinge on human rights?

Think about related terms. Who, or what, is "the Market" and where is sovereignty in relation to the market? And "cyberspace"?

Is cyberspace sovereign? Is it subject to the sovereignty of one or more states? And is the international environment sovereign, or is it too subject to the sovereignty of some states, all states?

Globalization, the market, cyberspace, the environment, all have important human rights consequences. And those who care about human rights need to strive to make the state system, as modified by these new forces, more human-rights-friendly. Not least, we have to learn to use the state system, to use state sovereignty, against threats to human rights posed by various forms of globalization.

There are significant implications for sovereignty, and for human rights, in other developments. If the state system of sovereign states is eroding, what of states which may be not exploding but imploding? What can one do about human rights in "failed states"? What of a sovereign state that cannot control what goes on in its territory? A state may assert over and over, that it is sovereign, but it does not act as if it were sovereign, perhaps because it cannot in fact control what goes on inside its territory. In particular, what to do when there is genocide in a country in circumstances where the state cannot prevent or control it?

And what about that famous ingredient of sovereignty, the principle of non-intervention? What do we do with the international commitment that there shall be no intervention inside a country by external forces? If ethnic cleansing and genocide are going on inside a state,[2] and that state is not willing and able to control it, what is the responsibility of the rest of us?

4.

I return to the principal subject. Sovereignty needs serious attention, and it is necessary to resist unworthy accretions to the concept. Sovereignty should not mean international anarchy—that states may refuse to be governed. For a country such as the United States, sovereignty should not

---

2. As at Kosovo and East Timor, later in 1999.

mean isolationism, resistance to cooperation, to assuming obligations; it should not justify failure to comply with obligations we have assumed. Sovereignty is something like individual autonomy and privacy, but it is not an iron curtain. We cannot insist that what we do at home is no one else's business, just as others are not entitled to assume that what they do is not our business. In these Philadelphia halls I remind you that, as a country, we were born with commitment to "a decent respect to the opinions of mankind," but sometimes we, and other "sovereign" states, do not respect the opinions of mankind. Sovereignty does not mean immunity from law, from scrutiny, from the demands of justice. Sovereignty should not mean setting up obstacles to the establishment of international institutions, for example, the currently-developing international criminal court.

In the end, globalization and its variants too may bring home to us the inadequacies of sovereignty, and often the helplessness of human institutions built on state sovereignty.

I have no magic prescription for the ills of sovereignty, and no guarantee of successful cure. But, I am satisfied, we would be better, as a country, as a people, and as an important member of the international community, if we saw, in the tatters of our sovereignty, not obstacles, not pretexts for indifference, but responsibility and opportunity to secure human values, notably human rights and human dignity.

DISCUSSANT

Human Rights: Beyond the National Sovereign
KENT GREENAWALT

IT IS A SPECIAL privilege to open the discussion on the illuminating paper of my friend and colleague, Louis Henkin, because in his academic writing and practical efforts, he has done more than any other individual to develop international protection for human rights. Since I do not find myself in disagreement with anything he has said, I shall offer a few brief comments about problems and possibilities.

1. Globalization of goods and services, dominated by private enterprise, may make it harder for national states to achieve economic justice than has previously been possible. A law raising wages may cause unacceptable competitive disadvantage in relation to producers from other coun-

tries. Of course, countries together can cooperate to see that adequate wages are paid, but some countries, at least, will have incentives not to cooperate in order to acquire a greater share of the market. In the short term, economic globalization may exacerbate inequalities between rich nations and poor ones and between rich and poor citizens within many countries.

2. The intensity of concern of the international community about violations of human rights depends greatly on the human rights involved. Whether wise or foolish, the intervention by NATO countries against Yugoslavia (Serbia) in Kosovo represents a very substantial use of armed force to prevent genocide and ethnic cleansing by countries that have few, if any, narrow interests of their own at stake. Since Croatia broke off from Yugoslavia, the Serbs, and descendants of Serbs, within its borders have been treated as less than equal citizens, and the government has dominated television and radio and harassed opposition press. Saudi Arabia is a long way from permitting the free exercise of religions other than Islam, and Russia has favored traditional religions over groups wishing to attain new converts within its borders. These are examples of a common phenomenon: violations of human rights that hardly rise to the attention of outsiders, much less underlie calls for armed intervention. For a long time to come, the international community is likely to tolerate many infringements of human rights, which will be met by criticisms of human rights organizations but no other practical sanctions.

3. Professor Henkin raised the situation in which entities other than governments are committing terrible acts and the local government is unable to cope. For a long time piracy and slave trading have been regarded as violations of international law, even when engaged in by private enterprise, but we are witnessing an expansion of international regard for non-governmental infringements of human rights. Justifying intervention in response to mass killing is not so difficult when the government at hand has broken down completely; it is more troublesome when that government claims it is in control and doing what it can, but what it does is ineffective.

4. Especially in Europe, regional protection of human rights extends much further than protection given by the general international community. Counties that are subject to the European Court of Human Rights can have their laws and practices challenged before that court. Thus, if Great Britain prevents publication of material that relates to some pending

court case, the European Court can decide whether that violates freedom of the press. A comparison with the United States is instructive. Our original Constitution protected only a few individual rights against state infringement, and the Bill of Rights, which soon followed, initially applied only against the federal government. European nations subject to the European Court of Human Rights are now subject to greater external restraint concerning their treatment of individual rights than American states were subject to national restraints, until the Fourteenth Amendment was adopted and was held in this century to embody the important individual guarantees in the Bill of Rights.

Over time, we can expect both expansion of the countries subject to the European Court, and the growth of similar guarantees in some other regions.

5. Professor Henkin did not talk about "world government." Perhaps that is a loaded term to be avoided; but if transportation continues to become quicker and easier, if the availability of information increasingly brings peoples together, and if commerce grows more and more international, international restraints are bound to increase. If we are lucky enough to avoid the various grave disasters, self-inflicted or fortuitous, that may strike the human race, I am confident that we shall have something reasonably called world government within the next thousand years. Whether we shall manage that in the next two or three hundred years is much more doubtful. Roughly what I mean by world government is an international political order in which major decisions about economic relations, dominant control of physical force, and extensive protection of individual rights lie in international bodies. Again, a comparison with the United States helps. Under the Articles of Confederation, our states were certainly "sovereign," and this arguably continued to be true in the early years of the Constitution. Now, despite rhetoric about sovereign states, everyone supposes that the real sovereign is our national government. Of course differences in religion, culture, and economic institutions, as well as resurgent nationalism, will make any such transition at the world level much more difficult, but over the long reach of history such a development will occur, again barring major disasters that destroy civilization or set back the strong trends toward globalization.

Economics Becomes a Science— Or Does It? [1]

ALAN S. BLINDER

Professor of Economics, Princeton University

I BEGIN BY begging your indulgence. This is, I realize, a scholarly meeting. But my assignment is to review a century of economics, and perhaps to offer some speculations about the discipline's future—all in 20 minutes. Even without the look forward, that works out to 12 seconds per year! Need I ask to be forgiven if my discussion seems superficial in places, or leaves out your favorite topic?

My theme is the union of two phrases. One is the title of this talk: "Economics becomes a science—or does it?" The other appears on the APS letterhead: "Held at Philadelphia for promoting useful knowledge." In particular, I wish to pose and partially answer two deliberately provocative questions:

• Did economics become a science during the twentieth century?
• Has that science, or whatever it is, produced useful knowledge?

Answers to such questions are inevitably subjective, and I want to emphasize that these are my own personal views, not some mythical professional consensus. I will concentrate on three salient changes in the discipline of economics during the twentieth century: *mathematization;* the invention, development, and use of *econometrics;* and the rise of *macroeconomics* as a sub-discipline.

1. This is a longer version of a paper presented at the American Philosophical Society on 23 April 1999. I would like to thank, without in any way implicating, my colleagues Orley Ashenfelter, David Bradford, Gregory Chow, Peter Kenen, Alan Krueger, Jeremiah Ostriker, Uwe Reinhardt, Michael Rothschild, Mark Watson and Michael Woodford for useful suggestions.

Economics as a Science

There is little doubt that economics *circa* 1900 was *not* a science. Peruse copies of the leading economics journals around the turn of the last century, and you will find articles with titles like "The Anthracite Miners' Strike of 1900," "The Commercial Legislation of England and the American Colonies, 1660–1760," and "Our Trade Prosperity and the Outlook."[2] You will find an almost complete absence of equations. And, of course, you will find no regressions or statistical hypothesis testing of any kind—the main techniques having not yet been invented. More generally, you will find little in the way of what I take to be the hallmark of science: formulating theoretical models and confronting them with facts.

That does not mean there were not great economic ideas floating around before 1900. In fact, the opposite is true: Most of the truly great ideas of economics—such as the invisible hand, comparative advantage, and the gains from specialization and division of labor—predate the twentieth century. But ideas alone, even profound ones, do not constitute science. Locke and Madison had some marvelous ideas about government; Beethoven and Monet had sublime ideas about sound and light; Plato and Kant conjured up deep ideas about philosophy. But none of these geniuses were scientists.

We draw a traditional distinction between the sciences and other realms of intellectual discourse partly on *systematization* of the knowledge, partly on *observation,* and partly on the notion that *hypotheses* must be *refutable*— whether through experimentation or otherwise. A century ago, economics lacked all these hallmarks of science. The extant body of knowledge had only recently been systematized (and extended) by the great British economist, Alfred Marshall, who published the first edition of his monumental *Principles of Economics* in 1890.[3] Data were very minimal, and hypothesis testing was essentially nonexistent. Indeed, economists of the day had hardly any theorems or refutable hypotheses; few even talked that language. Adam Smith's brilliant vision was not systematized and turned into theo-

---

2. Respectively, Virtue (1900), Ashley (1899), Giffen (1900).

3. Marshall did not succeed in establishing a separate tripos in Economics and Politics at Cambridge until 1903. Until then, economics was part of Historical and Moral Sciences. See the article on Marshall in *The New Palgrave.*

rems until at least the 1930s and perhaps not until the 1950s.[4] Ricardian comparative advantage was not tested empirically until the 1950s.[5]

By the 1960s or 1970s, economics had been completely transformed into a technical discipline with all the trappings of science. Nowadays, all economics journals are replete with theorems and proofs, statistical estimation of parameters, and hypothesis testing. Indeed, some have claimed that economics is now more mathematical than physics, and nontechnical economics writing has been virtually banished from the academy. It is this scientification that I want to discuss, highlight, and question.

But before doing so, I digress briefly on one other major development that may be of particular interest to the *American* Philosophical Society: During the twentieth century, and especially after World War II, economics became a peculiarly American discipline. The U.S. was home to precious few of the leading economists prior to the 1940s. I think it fair to say that we were a far distant second to our British cousins, and probably even to continental Europe. The leading lights of American economics from the 1890s through the 1940s—people like Irving Fisher, J. B. Clark, Harold Hotelling, and Edward Chamberlin—were outstanding and innovative thinkers. But, other than Fisher, they do not stack up against the great names of English economics: F.Y. Edgeworth, Marshall, John Maynard Keynes, A.C. Pigou, John Hicks, and so on.

By the last third of this century, however, the center of intellectual gravity in the economics profession had shifted dramatically. In fact, it was probably somewhere near Philadelphia! The great names of economics—such as Kenneth Arrow, Milton Friedman, Lawrence Klein, Franco Modigliani, Paul Samuelson, Robert Solow, James Tobin, and many others—were all at American universities (although a number were foreign born), as were virtually all the top Ph.D. programs. The *American Economic Review,* the *Quarterly Journal of Economics,* and the *Journal of Political Economy* had emphati-

---

4. I refer to some seminal papers on mathematical economics by Abraham Wald. While written in the 1930s in German, they were not "discovered" until 15–20 years later. (An English translation of one of them was published in *Econometrica* in 1951.) Economists basically learned these proofs from Arrow (1951) and Arrow and Debreu (1954).

5. My source for the dating comes from Ronald Findlay's article on "comparative advantage" in *The New Palgrave.* Findlay credits G.D.A. MacDougall and Wassily Leontief with the first empirical tests.

cally displaced the *Economic Journal* as the preeminent scholarly journals. And prospective graduate students and young scholars alike knew that the United States was the place to be.

Thus during the last half of the twentieth century, economics became both Americanized and mathematized. But did it also become a science?

Scientification?

Before answering, I should perhaps clarify the terminology. My old unabridged dictionary defines science as "systemized knowledge, derived from observation, study, and experimentation carried on in order to determine the nature or principles of what is being studied."[6] On most of these criteria, contemporary economics qualifies easily. Experimentation is still rare, though it is growing—as is the emphasis on studying so-called natural experiments. But economic knowledge is certainly "systematized" and clearly devoted to understanding "the nature or principles" governing economic life. However, I want to dwell on that first phrase: "systematized knowledge, derived from observation."

A century ago, as I have mentioned, economists had amazingly little data and paltry statistical tools. You will look in vain in Keynes's *General Theory* (1936) for statistical evidence that the marginal propensity to consume is between zero and one. The great man decided this by introspection, and simply asserted it as fact! Marshall had sound logic, but only a slender empirical basis, for claiming that demand curves slope down. Describing the state of economics as late as 1930, the pioneering econometrician Trygve Haavelmo put it this way: "There were lots of deep thoughts, but a lack of quantitative results."[7] This is all quite different today. Introspection is no longer considered a valid method of parameter estimation (though it is sometimes practiced). Deductive logic is not (usually!) considered a substitute for statistical hypothesis testing. There are many more quantitative results than deep thoughts.

---

6. *Webster's New Twentieth Century Dictionary of the English Language, Unabridged, Second Edition* (William Collins, 1979).

7. See his Nobel lecture, which is reprinted, among other places in the *American Economic Review*'s December 1997 membership directory. The quotation appears on page 13.

When I think about what makes contemporary economics a *science,* or when I think about what an economist of the year 1900 would find unrecognizable if he rose from the grave today, I think first and foremost of two interrelated developments: the availability and use of numerous sources of *data,* and the development of *econometric methodology* with which to analyze them. To me, the statement that economics became a science during the twentieth century is almost equivalent to saying that economics became a data-driven, econometrically-oriented discipline—under which heading I include the statistical testing of theories.

I accord such preeminence to econometric theory and practice for a simple reason: Like all the social sciences, economics labors under a severe handicap—its extremely limited ability to conduct controlled experiments. Our (mostly) nonexperimental science uses econometrics as a substitute for the chemist's laboratory. Without these techniques, we would have little hope of deriving systematic knowledge from observation; we might still be a branch of "moral philosophy," as in Adam Smith's time. But with these powerful (though fallible) tools of statistical inference, economists can actually purport to "know" things—though only in a statistical sense. Ours is a probabilistic science, to be sure. To an economist, all numbers are estimates with standard errors.

That was not true a century ago. Economics at the time was more or less limited to purely deductive logic and historical description. Deductive logic is a foundation stone of any science, to be sure. But to advance beyond where we were in 1900, our discipline required, first, the important insight that economic models can be thought of as statements about probability distributions[8] and, second, a set of techniques like multiple regression that purport to control statistically what cannot be controlled experimentally.[9] To sort out cause and effect, we needed practical solutions to what is called "the identification problem" in econometrics[10] Admittedly, these substitutes are inferior to the real thing. A natural scientist who can conduct care-

---

8. My colleague Mark Watson tells me that this idea should be attributed to Haavelmo.

9. Of course, there are many well-known problems with regression.

10. The simplest version of the identification problem is this: Under what circumstances can you use data on price and quantity to infer the shape of the demand curve or the supply curve? The problem was clearly spelled out in Working (1927).

fully controlled experiments in a laboratory has far less need for fancy (and imperfect) statistical methods, many of which intertwine some theory with the statistical inference. But modern econometrics is a vast improvement over what went before it.

Pioneers like Haavelmo, Jan Tinbergen, and Ragnar Frisch paved the way for dozens, then hundreds, then thousands of applied econometricians who sought to estimate the parameters of theoretical models, to test hypotheses, and, more generally, to understand the economic world *inductively* as well as *deductively*. These people built the body of empirical knowledge on which economics' claim to being a science now rests. And virtually all of that work took place after the Second World War.

Naturally, mathematical modeling went hand in hand with the rise of econometrics—or at least it did so until recent decades. Economic models that are expressed in the form of equations have parameters that can be estimated, and often suggest interesting hypotheses that can be tested statistically. Theory generates the maintained hypotheses on which estimation is often based. It is by testing and retesting existing theoretical models and hypotheses, rejecting them when they fail, and formulating new ones, that a science progresses.

Economics embraced mathematics warmly after the Second World War, and nowhere with greater enthusiasm than in the United States. At the turn of the (last) century, relatively few economists had much use for the language of mathematics. Nor were many very skilled at it. There had been, of course, scattered mathematical contributions by Cournot, Walras, Edgeworth, and others prior to 1900. But mainstream economics could hardly be called mathematical.

All this changed dramatically in the twentieth century—especially after World War II, with the war-delayed publication of Samuelson's *Foundations of Economic Analysis* in 1947, the rapid incorporation into economics of advances in optimization by mathematicians, the treatise *Linear Programming and Operations Analysis* (1958) by Robert Dorfman, Samuelson, and Solow, Debreu's *Theory of Value* (1959), and much else. Economics was off to the mathematical races. Intellectual giants like Samuelson and Arrow led the way, sweeping away the old, more literary tradition in economics and attracting a small army of scholars with a more scientific bent.

But somewhere along the way, the warm embrace of mathematics developed first into an infatuation, and then into an obsession. And that, I am afraid, is where economics lost at least some of its scientific moorings — moorings we have yet to regain. By the definition I gave earlier, mathematics would not be considered a science. It is, of course, both a high and exceedingly difficult form of thought and an indispensable tool for every science. I still stand in awe of the great mathematical minds. But mathematics seems entirely too *self-referential,* too *deductive,* one might almost say too *pure* to be considered a science.[11]

Let me dwell on those three words — self-referential, deductive, and pure — for they describe where economics has gone wrong, in my view. Economic science cannot afford the luxury of intellectual purity; our theories are simply not that good. And besides, the economic world is a messy place — with a much lower signal-to-noise ratio than the tidy world of Newtonian physics, on which economics was patterned after Samuelson's *Foundations.* For the same reason, if economics is to be a science rather than an art form, it needs to be at least as inductive as it is deductive. Finally, economics should not be as insular and self-referential as parts of it have unfortunately become — because the source of both ideas and observations is (or should be) the crass real world. The real world may be, as they say, just a special case. But it is an intensely interesting one!

During the last quarter of the twentieth century, it seems to me, the psyche of economics gradually morphed from "physics envy"[12] into "mathematics envy." Patterning our discipline after physics may have been a mistake in the first place. The biological or medical sciences have long seemed to me to offer a better role model for economists. But at least physics has a strong experimental and observational basis. Theorizing is generally motivated by and is ultimately disciplined by facts. Theories must be refutable — at least in principle — to be meaningful. Mathematics is quite different, of course. It is not and should not be experimental. Mathematical theorems

---

11. One might argue, however, as my colleague Michael Rothschild has to me, that important mathematical developments are often responses to real-world problems, frequently in physics.

12. A term apparently coined by Joel Cohen.

are neither proven nor disproven by studying data; they stand or fall on their internal logic and intellectual beauty.

Modern economics has become, in my view, too much like mathematics and not enough like medical research. In the biological sciences, the theory is often thin and perhaps inelegant. The central models often revolve around concepts like evolution, chance mutations, and adaptation, rather than the strong equilibrium theories of physics.[13] Induction trumps deduction. Indeed, large swaths of these disciplines are brazenly empirical—the question is: Does it work? But progress is constantly being made.

Contemporary economics is, in all these respects, quite different. It emphasizes—I might say, it exalts—tightly specified equilibrium models deduced from first principles. (These first principles are normally utility maximization, profit maximization, rational expectations, and competitive equilibrium.) It attaches the highest status to *a priori* theorizing, which it appraises more by cleverness and adherence to the canon than by empirical validity or applicability. It is entirely too deductive. And it welcomes abstract theory undisciplined by facts while often dismissing empirical research undisciplined by theory.

This is not, I hasten to add, a brief against economic theory. Purely deductive theorizing is indispensable in economics, as in other sciences, and it has proven its worth many times. My concern is that modern economics is producing too much *irrefutable* theory and not enough *refutable* theory—which is one reason, I believe, why it has promoted less "useful knowledge" than it should have in the last few decades.

Useful Knowledge

But useful knowledge certainly has been produced—throughout the century. I hope I am not being chauvinistically loyal to my own branch of the

---

13. Not all physical theories are equilibrium theories. Similarly, not all economic theories are equilibrium theories. But the concept of equilibrium, including perturbations therefrom, is absolutely central to economic thinking. And we inherit both from physics.

discipline by nominating macroeconomics for top honors in this regard. I do so for two reasons.

First, since the dawn of the Industrial Revolution, business cycle booms have created wealth and depressions have created misery. And they have done so with some regularity in all the capitalist economies, sometimes with dramatic political and social effects. The Great Depression, for example, paved the way for Hitler in Germany and Roosevelt in the United States. Figuring out what drives the business cycle is therefore more than just a great intellectual puzzle; it is also a practical social problem of the first rank.

Second, macroeconomics is almost entirely a twentieth century invention, whereas the central ideas of price theory are much older. Apart from the notion that inflation is driven by the rate of money growth, which was around for centuries, there was essentially no such thing as macroeconomics before Keynes. The Keynesian revolution slapped the classical tradition in the face (perhaps a bit too brusquely) and opened the door both to the development of national income data by the likes of Simon Kuznets and Richard Stone and to the construction of macroeconometric models by such luminaries as Klein and Tinbergen.

Many economists view macroeconomics as the homely younger sister of microeconomics, which has always been the family's pride and joy. The theoretical basis of macroeconomics is, admittedly, far less elegant than that of microeconomics. But, at least traditionally, macroeconomics has compensated for this deficiency by tying itself more closely to reality and to policy concerns. Above all, macroeconomics has been the source of *useful,* though clearly imperfect, knowledge. And, just as in the story of Cinderella, princes often find macroeconomics more fascinating than her upper-crust sister, microeconomics.

Ungainly they may be. But macroeconomic theory and empirical macro models have, I believe, helped economists and policymakers to understand and quantify the factors that drive business-cycle fluctuations. And this improved understanding has paved the way for policy responses that can mitigate, though certainly not eliminate, business cycles. Modern policymakers do not believe they should stand idly by, waiting for booms and busts to cure themselves naturally. Rather, they think it normal to intervene with monetary and fiscal policy. Many mistakes have surely been made in applying these ideas to real economies, and the ideas themselves are hardly as well-established as the laws of physics. But the practice is improving, and I am not inclined to belittle the achievement.

But, of course, macroeconomics has no monopoly on useful knowledge. Many insights of microeconomics have had profound effects on society in the twentieth century. While economic logic can hardly claim all the credit, or assume all the blame, developments as diverse as antitrust laws, regulation and deregulation, modern tax systems, the welfare state, and much else have their roots in microeconomic analysis. George Stigler (1982, p. 63) once wrote that, "economists exert a minor and scarcely detectable influence on the societies in which they live." I don't believe that is true any longer.

In fact, I think I can detect an element of "life imitates art" in recent history: Real economies have been modified in ways that make them resemble more closely the economist's idealized model. I am thinking of such developments as the conquest of socialism by capitalism, the trends toward privatization and deregulation, the increased global mobility of both goods and capital, the revolution in finance that has proliferated markets, speeded them up, and made them conform ever more closely to economists' arbitrage-based models, a more single-minded concentration by corporations on profit maximization, and a perhaps-regrettable trend toward treating labor like just another commodity that is bought and sold.

You may not applaud all these developments. But you would be hard pressed to deny that economic analysis has played a role in bringing them about. In that sense, economics has surely produced "useful knowledge."

Finally, it is worth pointing out that, unlike the situation a century ago, economists now play significant roles as policymakers and advisers in governments all over the world. This, too, is an objective indicator of usefulness: We have met the market test, although in this case not by providing pure science!

The Greatest Twentieth Century Ideas

I want to close by calling your attention to a few of the greatest economic ideas of the twentieth century. Any such list is subjective, to be sure. My criteria for inclusion were as follows. First, I wanted to keep the list very short;

so please don't be offended if your favorite idea did not make the cut. Second, I include only ideas that were not around 100 years ago. Remember, the greatest ideas of economics predate the twentieth century; I am dealing only with the B-list. Third, I restrict myself to substantive rather than methodological contributions, having already paid homage to econometrics. Fourth, and finally, I concentrate on useful knowledge rather than abstract intellectual achievements. So, for example, I exclude Arrow's (1951) and Arrow and Debreu's (1954) proofs that Adam Smith had it right,[14] Samuelson's wondrous (and numerous) insights into the mathematical structure of many important economic issues, etc.

Here goes. I start my list with Keynesian economics and the associated notion that government actions can mitigate cyclical fluctuations. This accomplishment belongs at the very top, in my view, but I have discussed it already and so will not dwell on it further.

Sticking to macroeconomics for a moment, I would include a dark horse: the so-called "impossible trinity," normally attributed to Robert Mundell. This is the idea that a nation can have no more than two of the following three things: a fixed exchange rate, international capital mobility, and an independent monetary policy targeted at managing aggregate demand. This dilemma, or perhaps trilemma, is one that many of the world's governments are only now just recognizing.

Turning to microeconomics, I begin with a concept that straddles the end of the nineteenth century and the beginning of the twentieth: Pareto efficiency, which is the notion that policy changes are clearly to be recommended if they make some people better off without making anyone else worse off. The Pareto criteria should provide a noncontroversial way to rank alternatives; after all, it amounts to little more than the unanimity principle. To me, the amazing thing about this workhorse of modern microeconomics is that it gets you anywhere at all. But decades of theoretical and applied work in welfare economics have established that Pareto was onto something. It really is useful.

---

14. And I consider Arrow's impossibility theorem one of the great twentieth century ideas of political science, rather than of economics.

Next, I would include the insightful analysis of externalities as market failures, and the use of taxes to correct them, which are generally attributed to A.C. Pigou (1912). For decades, this brilliant idea languished as an intellectual curiosum—beloved in the academy, but ignored outside. But now it is absolutely central to policies to protect the environment, among others.

The elementary notion that "diversification pays," in the sense of bringing the investor less risk for any given expected return, seems to be a twentieth-century idea. Indeed, the basic notions of quantifying risk and using the covariance structure of returns to distinguish "diversifiable" from "undiversifiable" risks date only from the 1950s [15] and option pricing dates only from the 1970s. [16] These developments led directly to the complex hedging and portfolio strategies that—for better or for worse—are at the heart of modern finance.

The basic idea of discounting—that there is a "time value of money"—long predates the twentieth century. Systematic calculations of present value and internal rates of return as ways to make cash flows accruing at different points of time commensurable are commonly attributed to Irving Fisher (1907) and others, but in fact can be found in nineteenth-century writings. Nonetheless, Fisher's (and earlier) analysis was mostly ignored until the 1950s. [17] Without present value calculations, thinking about intertemporal problems was as best imprecise, at worst muddled.

Finally, and most recently, I would nominate the idea that asymmetrically imperfect information—cases in which the seller knows more about the good or service than the buyer does—can destroy markets or make them malfunction. [18] One clear example relevant to public policy is the virtual nonexistence of markets for individual annuities, which is a primary justification for social security programs.

---

15. Harry Markowitz (1952) seems to have been the pioneer, followed soon thereafter by James Tobin (1958) and many others. For an entertaining account, see Bernstein (1996, Chapter 15).

16. The classic reference is Black and Scholes (1973).

17. The history of this idea is nicely told by Faulhaber and Baumol (1988), pp. 583–585.

18. The seminal paper was Akerlof (1970), who used as his example the market for used cars. But Joseph Stiglitz has probably done more than anyone to advance this subject.

Summing Up

The twentieth century, and especially its second half, saw economics cast off its literary and descriptive traditions and become a science — of sorts. I have highlighted three major developments during this century:

- Economics became intensely mathematical.
- Macroeconomics was invented and used to mitigate the ravages of the business cycle.
- Econometric data analysis, estimation, and hypothesis testing became central to the discipline.

Taken together, these three intellectual sea-changes would, I think, make contemporary economics unrecognizable and unfathomable to an economist of the year 1900. That is certainly one sign of scientific progress.

But something may also have been lost along the way. In his justly-celebrated book on the history of economic thought, which first appeared in 1953, Robert Heilbroner called the great economists "worldly philosophers" — a label that would apply to few economists today. Never mind the philosophy, I lament the loss of worldliness. More important, large parts of economics seem to have rushed headlong through the scientific phase and come out the other end as branches of applied, or even pure, mathematics — elegant and difficult, to be sure, but entirely too self-referential, too *a priori,* and too little based on observation to be called a science.

Perhaps this, too, will change as economics matures as a science. But we will have to wait for the 21st century to know.[19]

References

George A, Akerlof, "The Market for 'Lemons': Qualitative Uncertainty and the Market Mechanism" *Quarterly Journal of Economics,* 84 (August 1970): 488–500.

---

19. One optimistic note: A tabulation of papers published in the three leading economics journals (Figlio (1994)) shows a pronounced upward trend from 1975 to 1992 (when the sample ends) in the fraction of articles that included some data analysis as a central part of the research.

Kenneth J. Arrow, "An Extension of the Basic Theorems of Classical Welfare Economics," in J. Neyman (ed.), *Proceedings of the Second Berkeley Symposium on Mathematical Statistics and Probability,* University of California Press, 1951, pp. 507–532.

Kenneth J. Arrow and Gerard Debreu, "Existence of an Equilibrium for a Competitive Economy," *Econometrica,* 22 (1954): 265–290.

W. J. Ashley, "The Commercial Legislation of England and the American Colonies, 1660–1760," *Quarterly Journal of Economics,* 14, No. 1, November 1899.

Peter L. Bernstein, *Against the Gods* (New York: Wiley), 1996.

Fischer Black and Myron Scholes, "The Pricing of Options and Corporate Liabilities," *Journal of Political Economy* (May/June 1973): 637–654.

Gerard Debreu, *Theory of Value* (New Haven, Conn.: Yale University Press), 1959.

Robert Dorfman, Paul Samuelson, and Robert Solow, *Linear Programming and Economic Analysis* (The Rand Corporation), 1958.

John Eatwell, Murray Milgate, and Peter Newman (eds.), *The New Palgrave: A Dictionary of Economics* (London: MacMillan), 1987.

Gerald R. Faulhaber and William J. Baumol, "Economists as Innovators: Practical Products of Theoretical Research," *Journal of Economic Literature,* 26 (June 1988): 577–600.

David Figlio, "Trends in the Publication of Empirical Economics," *Journal of Economic Perspectives,* 8 (Summer 1994): 179–187.

Irving Fisher, *The Rate of Interest* (New York: MacMillan), 1907.

Robert Giffen, "Our Trade Prosperity and the Outlook," *Economic Journal,* 10, No. 3 (September 1900).

Trygve Haavelmo, Nobel Lecture, *American Economic Review,* December 1997.

Robert L. Heilbroner, *The Worldly Philosophers* (New York: Simon & Schuster), 1953.

John Maynard Keynes, *The General Theory of Employment, Interest, and Money* (New York: Harcourt), 1936.

Harry Markowitz, "Portfolio Selection," *Journal of Finance,* 7 (March 1952): 77–91.

Alfred Marshall, *Principles of Economics* (London: MacMillan), 1890.

Arthur C. Pigou, *Wealth and Welfare* (London: MacMillan), 1912.

Paul A. Samuelson, *Foundations of Economic Analysis* (Cambridge, Mass.: Harvard University Press), 1947.

George J. Stigler, *The Economist as Preacher and Other Essays* (Chicago: University of Chicago Press), 1982.

James Tobin, "Liquidity Preference as Behavior Towards Risk," *Review of Economic Studies* 25 (February 1958): 65–86.

George O. Virtue, "The Anthracite Miners' Strike of 1900," *Journal of Political Economy,* 9, No. 1 (December 1900).

Webster's New Twentieth Century Dictionary of the English Language, Unabridged, Second Edition (William Collins, 1979).

E. J. Working, "What Do Statistical 'Demand Curves' Show?," *Quarterly Journal of Economics,* (1927): 212–235.

DISCUSSANT

RECENT CONTRIBUTIONS TO THE DEVELOPMENT OF ECONOMIC SCIENCE[*]

ANDREW F. BRIMMER

President, Brimmer & Company, Inc.
and Wilmer D. Barrett Professor of Economics
University of Massachusetts-Amherst

IN HIS PAPER, Professor Alan Blinder examined the question: "Economics Becomes a Science — or Does It?" He concluded that, during the last 50 years, the answer is YES. Specifically, he states that Economics has become a science because of: (1) "the availability and use of numerous sources of data," and (2) "the development of an extensive toolkit of econometric methods with which to analyze them." ". . . The statement that economics became a science during the 20th century is almost equivalent to saying that economics became a data-driven, econometrically-oriented discipline."

I accept Professor Blinder's conclusions as well as his arguments supporting them. However, the paper sparked my curiosity: I wanted to know *WHO* led the transformation and *WHAT* contributions did they make? *WHEN, WHERE, WHY* and *HOW* were they made?

Evaluation of Contributions

I was able to answer those questions by an examination of the record generated in the process of awarding the annual "Central Bank of Sweden Prize in Economic Science in Memory of Alfred Nobel." Although the Economics Prize was initialed and funded by the Swedish Central Bank in 1968, it is awarded by the Royal Swedish Academy of Sciences, which awards the other Nobel Prizes. In making Nobel selections, the Academy must make awards to persons who have produced the most important discoveries or in-

---

[*]Read 23 April 1999

ventions in Physics, Chemistry, and Physiology or Medicine; or contributed the best in Literature or the most in efforts toward Peace. The same standards are applied to the Economics Prize.

The Economics Committee begins the selection process by sending a form to selected professors at roughly 75 departments of economics around the world asking them to nominate candidates. This canvass usually generates 150 to 200 proposals covering 75 to 125 nominees. A review of the latter typically reduces the list to 20–30 most promising candidates. For them, detailed studies are commissioned by experts in their respective fields. Based on the experts' reports, the Committee ends up evaluating a handful of the very best nominees. Over the course of a number of meetings, a single candidate is selected and sent to the "Social Science Class" of the Academy. To date, the Committee's selection has always been accepted. Thus, the Nobel Prize in Economic Science is awarded in October of each year to the economist who has made the most outstanding contribution to the advancement of the profession.

In awarding the Prize, the Royal Academy issues a statement in which it explains why the winner was selected—along with a substantive summary of his contributions. The winner also provides a biographical sketch in which he describes his research and places it in the context of an advancing profession. I have drawn on all of these materials in making my own evaluation of the Nobel Prize winners' contributions to the emergence of modern economic analysis.[1]

Appraisal of Scientific Advancements

The results of my appraisal are set forth in the attached chart. The awards are grouped under five headings: I. General Equilibrium Theory; II. The-

---

1. The framework I used was an adaptation of that employed by Professor Assar Lindbeck in "The Prize in Economic Science in Memory of Alfred Nobel," *Journal of Economic Literature*, 8, No. 1 (March 1985): 37–56. Professor Lindbeck was a Member of the Economics Prize Committee when it was formed in 1969, and he became chairman in 1980. His assessment covered prizes awarded from 1969 through 1984. My classification and examination covered the years 1985–98.

ory: Special Aspects and Sectors; III. New Methods of Economic Analysis; iv. Empirical Research, and V. Nonformalized Innovative Thinking. Each winner is listed by the year he received the Prize. The field of his definitive contribution and the year in which the latter was published—as cited by the Academy—are also shown.

Several conclusions can be drawn from the data in the chart:

- From 1969 through 1998, 30 Prizes in Economics were awarded to 43 recipients. Ten of the Prizes were joint awards made to 21 persons (9 involved 2 each, and one involved 3).[2]
- In the Nobel Committee's judgment, the most important contributions have been made in *Economic Theory*. The mathematical reformulation of *General Equilibrium Theory* by Paul Samuelson (presented in *Foundations of Economic Analysis,* published in 1947) was the basis for the award of the 1970 Prize to him. Awards to John Hicks and Kenneth Arrow (1972) and Maurice Allais (1988) were in the same field.
- Formulations of specific aspects of *Economic Theory* or its application to particular sectors of the economy were the basis for 12 prizes. Among these, the following stand out sharply: Milton Friedman (1976, Macroeconomics); Theodore Schultz and Arthur Lewis (1979, Development Economics); James Tobin (1981, Capital Asset Pricing); Robert Solow (1987, Economic Growth Theory); Trygve Haavelmo (1989, Econometrics); and Amartya Sen (1998, Welfare Economics).
- The invention, development, and application of *New Methods of Economic Analysis* have been critically essential vehicles in the advancement of economics. At the forefront were Wassily Leontief (1973, Input-Output); Lawrence Klein (1980, Macroeconometrics), and Richard Stone (1984, National Income Accounting).
- Six awards highlight the advances made through the application of Mathematical and Econometric techniques in the analysis of problems in Finance and Financial Markets. The Prizes went to Franco Modigliani

---

2. In passing, it should be noted that fourteen of the Nobel Laureates in Economics are or were members of the American Philosophical Society.

(1985); Harry Markowitz, Merton Miller, and William Sharpe (1990), and Robert Merton and Myron Scholes (1997).

- While pure *Empirical Research* ranked below Theory in the Nobel Committee's evaluations, this activity has become of increasing importance over time. This trend is illustrated by the awards to Simon Kuznets (1971, Development Economics); Gary Becker (1992, Microeconomic Analysis), and Robert Fogel and Douglass North (1993, Economic History).
- *Nonformalized and Innovative Thinking* has received the approval of the Nobel Prize Committee. The prime examples are Friedrich Hayek and Gunnar Myrdal (1974). The Committee praised Hayek's assessment of Comparative Economic Systems. In Myrdal's case, the Academy stated that ". . . when making its decision, it . . . attached great importance to the monumental work, *American Dilemma: The Negro Problem and Modern Democracy* (1944) "The Committee observed further that . . . it is primarily in this massive work of scholarship that Myrdal has documented his ability to combine economic analysis with a broad sociological perspective."

In summary, using the Nobel Prize citations as indicators, I concluded that those working on the frontier of Economic Theory—armed with advanced mathematical and econometric techniques—have done the most to transform economics into a science. This task was greatly facilitated—and supported—by the creation of powerful New Methods and Tools of Economic Analysis. Empirical Research and Innovative Thinking have also contributed to the advancement of the discipline.

Recipients of the Nobel Memorial Prize in Economic Science by Fields
1969–1998 [1]

I.
GENERAL EQUILIBRIUM THEORY

Year	Laureate
1970	Paul Samuelson*
1947	*Gen. Eq. Theory*
1972	John Hicks
1939	*Gen. Eq. Theory*
1972	Kenneth Arrow*
1951	*Gen. Eq. Theory*
1983	Gerard Debreu*
1954	*Gen. Eq. Theory*
1988	Maurice Allais
1943	*Gen. Eq. Theory*

II.
THEORY: SPECIFIC ASPECTS
AND SECTORS

Year	Laureate
1976	Milton Friedman*
1957	*Macroeconomics*
1977	James Meade
1951/55	*Int'l Economics*
1977	Bertil Ohlin
1951/55	*Int'l Economics*
1978	Herbert Simon*
1947	*Adm. Sciences*
1979	Theodore Schultz*
1945	*Dev. Economics*
1979	Arthur Lewis*
1955	*Dev. Economics*
1981	James Tobin*
1958	*Capital Asset Pricing*
1982	George Stigler
1951	*Ind. Organization*
1987	Robert Solow*
1956	*Eco. Growth Theory*

II.
THEORY: SPECIFIC ASPECTS
AND SECTORS (*continued*)

Year	Laureate
1989	Trygve Haavelmo
1941	*Theory and Econometrics*
1994	John Nash
1950	*Game Theory*
1994	Rinhard Selten
1964	*Game Theory*
1994	John Harsanyi
1967	*Game Theory*
1995	Robert Lucas*
1972	*Macro: Rational Exp't*
1996	James Mirrlees
1970's	*Micro/Incentives/Info*
1996	William Vickery
1961	*Macro/Incentives/Info*
1998	Amartya Sen
1970	*Welfare Economics*

III.
NEW METHODS OF ECONOMIC ANALYSIS

Year	Laureate
1969	Ragnar Frisch
1930	*Macroeconometrics*
1969	Jan Tinbergen
1939	*Macroeconometrics*
1973	Wassily Leontief*
1941	*Input-Output*
1975	Tjalling Koopmans
1942	*Norm. Allocation Theory*
1975	Leonid Kantorovich
1939	*Norm. Allocation Theory*

(*continued on next page*)

Recipients of the Nobel Memorial Prize in Economic Science by Fields
1969–1998 [1] (continued)

III. NEW METHODS OF ECONOMIC ANALYSIS (continued)		IV. EMPIRICAL RESEARCH	
Year	Laureate	Year	Laureate
1980	Lawrence Klein*	1971	Simon Kuznets*
1950	*Macroeconometrics*	1951	*Dev. Economics*
1984	Sir Richard Stone	1992	Gary Becker*
1947	*National Income Acc.*	1964	*Microeconomic Analy.*
1985	Franco Modigliani	1993	Robert Fogel
1958	*Macro/Fin. Mkts.*	1964	*Economic History*
1990	Harry Markowitz	1993	Douglass North
1952	*Micro/Fin. Mkts.*	1961	*Economic History*
1990	Merton Miller		
1958	*Macro/Fin. Mkts.*		V. NONFORMALIZED INNOVATIVE THINKING
1990	William Sharpe		
1964	*Micro/Fin. Mkts.*	Year	Laureate
1997	Robert Merton	1974	Friedrich von Hayek
1973	*Micro/Fin. Mkts.*	1935	*Econ. and Instit's*
1997	Myron Scholes	1974	Gunnar Myrdal
1973	*Macro/Fin. Mkts.*	1944	*Econ. and Instit's*

[1] The first date is the year in which the Nobel Prize was awarded. The second date is the year of publication of the principal work cited by the Nobel Committee.

*Note: Member of the American Philosophical Society.

Source: Prepared by Andrew F. Brimmer. Data from Nobel Foundation.

A Millennium of Economics in Twenty Minutes: In Pursuit of Useful Knowledge[*]

WILLIAM J. BAUMOL

Director, C.V. Starr Center for Applied Economics and Professor of Economics,
New York University; and Senior Research Economist and Professor Emeritus,
Princeton University.

The role of merchants in medieval and early renaissance society as instigators of economic, political and scientific innovations is seldom fully appreciated. . . . It is no mere coincidence that Fibonacci, one of the principal conveyors of the Hindu-Arabic numerical system to Europe, was also a merchant.

F.J. Swetz, Capitalism and Arithmetic: The New Math of the 15th Century,
La Salle, Ill.: Open Court, 1987, pp. 291–2.

RECENTLY, IN anticipation of year 2000, I was invited to prepare a paper for a leading journal on major accomplishments in my discipline during the century past. But at the recent meeting of the American Philosophical Society the ante was raised. I was asked to comment on developments in my field during the entire millennium, and at a rate of two minutes per century. The reader will then understand the rather episodic character of my remarks.

I will seek, nevertheless, to incorporate several themes: first, the fact that, with some recent exceptions, economic thought has aimed to provide *useful* knowledge, such as the founders of this Society meant to promote. Second, until the eighteenth century, ideas in the field were contributed predominantly by persons who patently were not economists. Third, two variables that have provided the interstices of economic analysis are the de-

---

[*]Read 23 April 1999.

termination and role of price and the means to achieve economic growth. In this somewhat disorganized survey, with its unavoidable profusion of major gaps, I will also take note of two mysteries, one early in our period and one that emerges toward the end.

King William's Domesday Book and the Medieval Industrial Revolution

To save time, I will simply ignore most of the first century of the millennium, and start with the *end* of the eleventh century and its remarkable statistical compendium, the *Domesday Book* of (approximately) 1085. Arguably, it is the first great data banks available to economic historians, who have not neglected it. Its focus, certainly, is economic growth—not of the economy as a whole, a concept plainly incomprehensible at the time—but that of the only individual who mattered, William the Conqueror.[1] Some 19 years earlier he had multiplied his possessions, adding Britain to his vast holdings in northern France. For, as in ancient Rome and ancient China, pursuit of wealth was considered a respectable activity, provided it was done by respectable means such as aggressive warfare, bribery, and exaction of ransoms. Only productive or commercial transactions were considered reprehensible avenues to wealth.

Thus, the new wealth that William surveyed in the Domesday Book was not tainted by contribution to economic growth for the society. Yet Domesday reveals that somehow a major contribution to growth had managed to emerge—a profoundly revolutionary innovation. It was not like that other revolutionary innovation, the stirrup, whose primary contribution was military (indeed, it has been suggested that William's possession of the stirrup may have made the difference at Hastings). Rather the crucial innovation was the water mill, which, for the first time in history, freed producers from reliance on human or animal power. True, the Romans and others had pos-

---

1. It will understandably be objected that William of Normandy can hardly be deemed to have been a professional practitioner of the dismal science. But then, as will be noted later, neither were such noted contributors as Adam Smith, James Mill, or David Ricardo.

sessed the water mill, but the evidence suggests that it was used little, and used only for the most obvious tasks.

In contrast, in what historians have called the "medieval industrial revolution" (eleventh to thirteenth centuries), the water mill was put to a striking variety of uses: pitting olives, fulling wool, sawing lumber, grinding mash for beer, crushing cloth for paper making, milling coins, hammering metal, and operating the bellows of blast furnaces, all of these using a variety of sophisticated gear arrangements. These mills were widespread in southern France, were sufficiently numerous to impede shipping on the Seine at Paris and, the Domesday book tells us, they dotted the landscape in the south of England. Nearly 6,000 mills in this circumscribed area are recorded in the survey, which, it has been estimated, provided on average one mill for every 50 families.

Here, indeed, is a contribution to economic growth, and it facilitated the prosperity of the twelfth and thirteenth centuries when so many of the great cathedrals were built. But this is where my first mystery enters.

Unlike other growth episodes, this unprecedented industrial revolution, with its widespread and effective utilization of a great invention for productive purposes, was *not* introduced and operated primarily by private enterprise. Certainly the guilds in the growing towns did not take the lead— indeed, they were prone to resist change with determination. Rather, its entrepreneurs were predominantly monastic, and those predominantly from one order—the Cistercians. Why? I have some hypotheses, but so far I have found no medieval historian able to provide an answer.

A Word on Just Price and Practical Pricing

Modern economists, with their predisposition to focus on the analysis of pricing, generally turn to the theological discussions of just price as the central topic of medieval economic thinking. It is true that writers such as Saint Thomas in the thirteenth century did devote attention to the subject. Here I will merely note that while the modern reader may well doubt whether any useful knowledge emerged from these discussions, that is far from what the theologian of the time would have concluded. Surely to them there was no knowledge more useful than knowledge that could contribute to salvation of the soul.[2] Indeed, it was only in the late Middle Ages that avid opposition to the search for knowledge (on the ground that it constituted prying into God's secrets) began to recede. In the thirteenth century this view was still powerful, as that genius Roger Bacon found to his misfortune. Thus, knowledge of the paths to salvation was the most permissible form of useful knowledge, and discussions of just price were designed to contribute such knowledge.

Yet pressures of the growing commerce were forcing thinkers to turn to the search for ideas and information we would more readily consider practical today. An example is the application of mathematics to economic decisions. Here we must not forget that as late as the fifteenth century Europeans were still having trouble using the Arabic number system and decimal notation. A fourteenth-century example indicates how limitations of the available mathematical tools affected business. By this time merchants had devised various evasive procedures to overcome the prohibition of usury. We have records of a transaction in Siena, an example of repayment of a debt before its due date. The parties to the transaction recognize that the amount the borrower should consequently pay the lender was smaller than if payment had been delayed to the due date. But they could not figure out how the reduction should be calculated, and in fact, they got it wrong. This should not be surprising for an era in which multiplication and division were considered advanced and difficult calculations.

The type of calculation required for the Sienese lender's problem, now common in the economics literature, was not actually understood until the seventeenth or eighteenth centuries, and the mathematical relationships were worked out fully in a publication on forestry (!) in 1849.[3] By the beginning of our century, the concepts were well understood and written about by a number of economists. It is remarkable, then, that this type of analysis did not become commonplace in the business school curriculum or in business practice until after the Second World War.

---

2. It is noteworthy that religious considerations did not disappear from economic writings until the nineteenth century. For example, specialists recognize that the 1776 invisible hand of Adam Smith was no less than the hand of providence.

3. See Martin Faustmann, "Calculation of the Value Which Forest Land and Immature Stands Possess for Forestry," *Allgemaine forst-und jagt-zeitung,* (15 Dec. 1849), pp. 441–55.

Useful Economic Knowledge and Employment of Mathematics

The noted writers who populate writings on the history of economic ideas first make their appearance in the seventeenth century. They did indeed write on economics, but they were not trained economists, nor would they have considered this their profession. William Petty was a seaman, physician, surveyor, professor of anatomy and of music, land speculator and jack of other trades; Cantillon was a merchant; Adam Smith a professor of logic and, then, of moral philosophy; and David Ricardo a stockbroker. Arguably, T.R. Malthus was the first professional economist. And all of them wrote on economics not in order to provide knowledge for its own sake, but because they believed it to be useful. Adam Smith, for example, emphasized the importance of economic growth, and a central purpose of the *Wealth of Nations* was to indicate what governments should *not* do, in order to avoid handicapping of the process. Ricardo was concerned with freedom of trade as a means to facilitate growth and as a way to benefit the members of the labor force and the nascent class of capitalists. Going all the way to Alfred Marshall, who can be considered the bridge between the nineteenth and twentieth centuries, I doubt whether one can find a major contributor to my discipline who would have admitted to being driven by what Veblen characterized as "idle curiosity," the motive, in his view, of most academic research.

It was only in our century that many economists began to devote themselves to what they considered pure research. Arguably, this work has provided deep and illuminating insights, though it has also encountered skeptics, notably Marshall, Keynes and Viner (who described some of the literature as illegitimate intercourse with beautiful models). It is ironic that, as will be described later, some of this "pure research" has constituted the basis of a new flowering of applied economics in which economists are not merely offering unsolicited advice, but rather, find their services heavily demanded.

The redirection of research and writing away from application was accompanied by another phenomenon: the emergence of formal mathematics as one of the economist's primary tools. When French mathematician A.A. Cournot published his great contribution to our discipline in 1838, there had already been a number of writings in the field that made use of algebra and a little more. But Cournot was the first to show what mathematics really could do for economic analysis. It took half a century and more for the lesson to take hold, and only in the 1950s was mathematical economics able to sweep all before it in the graduate schools and in the specialists' literature. Today, it is the nonmathematical article that is a curiosity, as a glance at any of the leading journals readily confirms. But mathematics has also emerged as a prime tool of applied economics, in widely disparate applications including work designed to help combat inflation and unemployment, in the analysis of government finance, in study of effective measures for regulation of industry and rules for antitrust activity.

On Useful Knowledge Related to Pricing

So we have leaped forward to the eighteenth century and beyond—to the era in which economics finally emerged as a distinct discipline with investigation and practice carried out by specialists. Economists have, of course, dealt with a vast range of topics, and time forces me to confine myself to two: pricing and growth, which pervade the literature and serve as interstices for the rest of the workings of the economy to a degree that nonspecialists are unlikely to recognize.

Price theory, in particular, has been a focus of writings in economics for at least three centuries. The theory seeks to explain both how the magnitudes of prices are determined by economic forces, and what effects they have upon economic behavior. Consumers obviously care about the magnitude of the prices they pay, and pricing decisions can seriously affect the financial condition of firms. But the importance of price goes well beyond this.

To see why else prices matter, it is suggestive to recall the propensity some decades ago for Marxists (basing themselves on nothing Marx had ever written) to say that chaos was a prime attribute of the capitalist economy. Millions of producers daily and *independently* make decisions about what and how much to produce and how to produce it. At the same time, millions of consumers *individually* decide how much of each good to demand, doing so without consultation or systematic guidance. Why are markets not flooded with unwanted goods and chronically short of things consumers urgently desire? As it turns out, for reasons now well understood, it is the planned economies that fell into the chaos that their central direction was intended to avoid, while the individualistic, uncoordinated free-market economies, though not immune from other serious problems, conducted their day-to-day activities in a manner whose orderliness must be astonishing when the matter is considered.

The secret of the synchronized behavior of the market economies is price. Its operation can be described in simple terms. If producers happen to err and produce fewer buttons than the market demands, their price will rise. That will induce button makers to expand their output and consumers to cut back on demand. If the price rise proves still insufficient to equate demand and supply, that price will rise even further. It will continue to do so until the button shortage is eliminated. Thus, without anyone having planned it, with no conscious intervention by anyone, with no deliberate coordination, the market *automatically* manages day after day, in every geographic area to bring supplies and demands together.

That is even more of a miracle than it may seem at first, because the demands and output needs of different commodities are mutually interdependent, characterized by implicit simultaneous solution of millions of equations with millions of variables. The production of energy for example, requires steel, copper, labor and a vast variety of other inputs. But none of those inputs can be supplied without obtaining adequate quantities of energy whose required amount depends on the size of the outputs of the user industries. The manufacture of transport vehicles to bring those inputs to the energy production facilities in turn requires energy and all the other inputs as well, in interdependent quantities. Thus the economy's production mechanism is a complex tangle of interdependencies and mutually determined requirements. It is the set of prices of all of these items that conveys the requisite information to all of the decision makers involved and automatically induces them to coordinate their decisions so that the entire mechanism works reasonably smoothly and rarely collapses into chaos.

If one accepts this standard piece of economic analysis, it must surely be recognized to be informative. But is it also *useful* knowledge? The answer is, emphatically, yes. It is proving vital in a variety of areas, in business decision making, in government policy and elsewhere. And it is the modern mathematical analysis of the workings of price that has played a crucial role here.

Let me give just one illustration, which happens to involve an issue that affects many industries in nations throughout the world. In particular, in telecommunications, after decades of operation as legal private monopolies or as nationalized monopoly firms, the world has begun to recognize that full competition offers great advantages in the form of improved service, new products, and lower prices. Accordingly, in 1997 some 70 nations signed an agreement permitting foreign suppliers of telephone service to invade their borders as competitors to each nation's former monopoly supplier.

The problem is that modern telecommunications networks have vast capacity and are extremely costly to construct. With the native supplier often already having much of the capacity that is likely to be needed, and with the cost of replication of the facilities by a new competitor prohibitive, entry with new facilities is unlikely to occur. To salvage competition in such circumstances, governments have turned to an alternative course of action. The entrant firms are encouraged to rent access to the facilities already in existence, and the incumbent firms are *required* by their government to rent the access to their prospective competitors.

However, unless a rental price is specified along with the rental requirement, the latter becomes an empty gesture. If the incumbent telecommunications monopolist is left free to charge prohibitive access prices to prospective entrants, that is patently tantamount to complete withdrawal of any rental offer. But the rental price can also be too low. If a government forces the incumbent firm to rent access to its facilities at a price that is not compensatory, that amounts to requiring that firm to subsidize its competitors. The result can well be destruction of the native telecommunications firm while handing over the business to foreign rivals, who then conquer the market not by superior performance but by virtue of the subsidy with which they have been provided.

Thus, either too low or too high a rental price can have disastrous consequences, and a method for determining the "right" price is clearly useful knowledge. And economics has indeed provided such a formula, one which, as the cliché goes, yields the only price that provides a "level playing field" for the incumbent and entrant firms. This pricing principle has already been adopted in a number of arenas and countries and is under (heated) discussion today before government regulators in virtually every industrialized nation of the world.

Finally—On the Mystery of Capitalist Growth

Despite the importance of price, in many firms it is being replaced by *innovation* as the prime weapon of competition. Enterprises focus on improved products and increased productive efficiency as the most effective means to deal with their rivals.

This brings us to the issue of innovation and its role in the incredible growth record of capitalism. As Marx and Engels put the matter:

> The Bourgeoisie [i.e., capitalism] cannot exist without constantly revolutionizing the instruments of production. . . . Conservation of the old modes of production in unaltered form was, on the contrary, the first condition of existence for all earlier industrial classes. . . . The bourgeoisie, during its rule of scarce one hundred years has created more massive and more colossal productive forces than have all preceding generations together. . . . It has accomplished wonders far surpassing Egyptian pyramids, Roman aqueducts and Gothic cathedrals. . . . (Marx and Engels, *The Communist Manifesto,* 1847).

The growth of per-capita income and productivity in the free-market economies is so enormous that it is virtually impossible to comprehend. Since the beginnings of what we think of as *the* Industrial Revolution (which occurred around the time of George Washington), per-capita income and productivity have probably grown more than 2,000 percent in the U.S. In contrast, average growth rates of per-capita incomes were probably approximately *zero* for about one and a half thousand years before the Industrial Revolution. In 1776, even the wealthiest consumers in England, then the world's richest country, had only a half-dozen consumers' goods that had not been available in ancient Rome. These new products included (highly inaccurate) hunting guns, (highly inaccurate) clocks and watches, paper, window glass and very little else. Besides, Roman citizens enjoyed a number of amenities, such as hot baths and paved roads, that had long disappeared at the time of the American Revolution. In contrast, in the past century and a half, per-capita incomes in the typical capitalist economy have risen by amounts ranging from several hundred to several thousand percent. Recent decades have yielded an unmatched outpouring of new products and services, and the flood of new products continues. When a few years ago many of the world's communist regimes collapsed and when even the masters of China turned toward capitalist enterprise, surely part of the reason was their public's desire to participate in the growth miracle of the capitalist economies that Marx and Engels—those high priests of anticapitalist movements—were among the first economists to discern.

This leaves us with my parting mystery. Just what is it that is so different about the free-market system—the capitalist economy—that permits it to attain levels of prosperity and rates of growth unmatched at any time in human history under any other economic arrangements? The inventiveness of medieval China, the vast military construction of ancient Rome and the central planning of the recently defunct Soviet economies produced no such record. In the West, as recently as the seventeenth century, famines and mass starvation were common occurrences. But in today's industrialized countries, that is all incomprehensible ancient history.

Economists are increasingly devoting study to the explanation. And that, too, promises to provide useful knowledge, particularly to the more than two-thirds of the world's nations that are impoverished, and that continue to fall further behind the prosperous societies of which our nation continues to be a leader.

DISCUSSANT

JOSEPH E. STIGLITZ

WILLIAM BAUMOL in his remarks has described very forcefully the attempt of academics to make useless knowledge and the futility of turning that into useful knowledge. He also discussed the possibility of a third category—dangerous knowledge that is counter-productive. I want to focus on that, particularly in the context of some of the remarks that Alan [Blinder] made about what might be called "pre-scientific" knowledge—ideology that is clothed in the guise of knowledge.

During the last hundred years there have been two very important social experiments. The first is the now defunct socialist experiment that everybody agrees was a failure. But there's been another very interesting experiment in the last ten years. Economies that were formerly socialist have attempted to move into a market economy. This has been a massive experiment in which an enormous number of people have been involved. Economists had a lot to say; textbook economics had very strong views about that process of conversion from socialist economy to market economy. Old wisdom speculated that a country like Russia was inefficient because it had central planning, distorted prices, no profit motive, and needed incentives. To get these, you have to have property rights and a key part of the strategy is privatization. So you had this terribly inefficient socialist-communist economy and you had a clear prescription from all the textbooks, or at least most of the textbooks, about what ought to be done in order to liberate an economy and make it grow. As Will pointed out, there is an enormous demand for economists. There is an old economic law, Say's Law, that people don't believe any more that states supply creates its own demand. And that's true about economists. We tend, particularly when we get into positions of power, to try to increase the demand for our colleagues and it's a self-generating business. So economists have played a significant role in economies in transition. They were called on to provide advice. What should countries do? They took textbook models and advised privatization and relinquishing central planning. It was very clear what the implied prediction of that model was, and to go back to what Alan said, if economics is a science, it has to be based on predictive powers and it was clear that "here was a theory and we're gonna test it out in as close to a natural experiment—nothing is ever perfect." And there was a prediction—going from an inefficient system to a market-based economy, even if imperfect, (given how bad things were before,) should have increased output and standards of living. What has happened basically a decade later? At the beginning of the transition, there were about 14 million people in the Eastern Bloc living in poverty defined as income under four dollars a day. Today there are almost 150 million people in that region living on less than four dollars a day. Almost every country in that region has seen their incomes plummet. They have fallen by between 30 and 40 percent. Here we had a huge experiment and it's clear that something went wrong. Now there's a big debate, something like medieval medicine—there are some people who say they should have let more blood; with more bloodletting the patient would have recovered. There is a another school that says: because they didn't suffer enough, they didn't recover. I find that a very implausible theory.

What is interesting and what makes the experiment a very telling one is that, on the other side of the world there was another country, China, with 1.2 billion people, which was going through a process of transition from a communist system to what they called a market socialist economy with a Chinese character. In many ways, however, it was a transition to a market economy. They had the good fortune of not reading the textbooks and not having Western advisers and they took a very different course. They had a lot of interesting discussions. They consulted with people in the United States and elsewhere but they chose their own course and came up with a lot of unique solutions like "township and village enterprises" BTVEs— which in economic theory, as it is presented in the economic textbooks, should have been a disaster because it provided no clear property rights. And what is the consequence? Over the last 20 years, overall income in China has increased by about 10 percent per year. Although at the beginning of the decade, China's income was about 40 percent less than Russia's, today China's income is 40 percent greater than Russia's. It's an amazing experiment— one of the most interesting in terms of what lessons we can learn. I talked about increase in income. In terms of reduction of poverty, the reduction of poverty in China has been greater than virtually anywhere else in the world.

Actually, it isn't quite as much of a mystery as I've suggested because one of the things we've learned in the last few decades is what was wrong with the textbook model, in particular—economics of information has really cast a different light on these issues and a particular application here is the issue that we call "governance"—how resources are managed. The system of governance that we envisioned, which is a simple private property system, doesn't work well unless you have the appropriate legal structures.

The important information innovation in the Middle Ages, was the clock. It's one of the things economic historians emphasize because the clock allowed coordination of production. Nobody's talked about the next millennium. My conjecture is that, just as the Industrial Revolution was the major economic event of the last thousand years, the information revolution, with all its implications, is going to be the major catalyst for change in the next millennium.

Population in the Twentieth and Twenty-first Centuries *

Joel E. Cohen

Professor of Populations, Rockefeller University and Columbia University

T HE TWENTIETH century will differ dramatically from the twenty-first century in demography, economics, culture and environment. Demographic changes can be expected in the growth rate, size, urbanization, and aging of the global human population.

In the twentieth century, world population increased 3.8-fold. The United Nations estimated that the world population in 1900 was 1.65 billion, and in the year 2000 will be 6.1 billion. World population is very unlikely to increase 3.8-fold in the twenty-first century. Some demographers think there is a better-than-even chance that the world's population will never double to 12 billion people. At the end of the twentieth century, after 35 years of slowing population growth, a continued slowing of population growth in the twenty-first century seems very likely. If the rate of increase of population continues to fall, then the twentieth century was and will be the only century in the history of humanity to see a doubling of Earth's population within a single lifetime. Human numbers will probably never again nearly quadruple within a century.

Despite a slowing rate of increase, the twenty-first century is unlikely to see a reversal of world population growth for several decades at least. The 1998 long-term *low*-fertility projection of the UN estimated that global population will peak near 7.7 billion in the middle of the twenty-first century, and will fall to 5.6 billion by 2100. The world previously had 5.6 billion people around 1993. Unless future population growth is much lower than antici-

---

pated in the UN's low projection, the twenty-first century will have billions more people than the twentieth century.

The twentieth century saw the fraction of world population living in cities rise from 13 percent in 1900 to 47 percent by the year 2000. That is a 3.6-fold increase. The absolute number of city dwellers increased even more dramatically, by nearly 14-fold, from 0.2 billion people to 2.9 billion. At the beginning of the twentieth century, no cities had 10 million people or more. One city did in 1950 — New York. By the century's end, there will be 20 cities of 10 million people or more. These figures on urbanization disguise ambiguities and variations in definitions of "urban." While the numbers should not be taken too literally, the trend toward urbanization is clear. In Europe, the rush of people from the countryside to cities dates back to the eleventh century. Urbanization has occurred worldwide for at least two centuries.

The twenty-first century is unlikely to see a reversal in the relative growth of urban population. The UN estimated in 1996 that almost all population growth in the next half century will be located in cities, while the rural population of the world will remain nearly constant around 3 billion people. If urbanization occurs as anticipated, then the twentieth century was and will be the last century in human history in which most people live in rural areas. In the next century, humanity will be predominantly urban.

The twentieth century saw the world fraction of children aged 0 – 4 years gradually decline, and the world fraction of older people aged 60 years or more gradually increase. Both percentages will meet at 10 percent in the year 2000. This trend results from improved survival and reduced fertility. Improved survival raised the world's expectation of life from perhaps 30 years at the beginning of the twentieth century to more than 66 years at the beginning of the twenty-first century. Reduced fertility rates added smaller cohorts to the younger age groups.

The twenty-first century is unlikely to see a reversal in the aging of world population. In its 1998 medium-variant projection, the UN estimated that by the middle of the twenty-first century, the fraction of the population aged 0 – 4 years will fall from 10 percent to less than 7 percent while the fraction of the population aged 60 years or more will rise from 10 percent to more than 22 percent. In this projection, the ratio of older people to young children is expected to rise from 1-to-1 now to 3.3-to-1 in half a century. In all the variant projections developed by the UN, the ratio of elderly to young children is expected to grow. The lower future fertility, the higher the ratio of elderly people to young children. If the future resembles any of the UN projections, then the twentieth century was and will be the last century in human history to see younger people outnumber older people. The next century will be a world of predominantly older people.

PLAUSIBLE FORECASTS of a more slowly growing, larger, more urban and older world population presuppose that the next century will not be afflicted by lethal global pandemics of novel infectious diseases, by massively destructive warfare, nor by a meteoric impact that darkens the skies for years. These forecasts assume no abrupt shift in oceanic circulation, global climate, and sea level and no collapse of conventional agriculture. All of these catastrophes are conceivable. None is exceptionally unlikely. For example, it has been suggested that every past 10-fold increase in human population density has been associated with new human infectious diseases. Unless the sanitary infrastructure of the next century's megacities improves dramatically, large cities could become incubators for new infectious diseases. The difference between the future and the historical record for infectious diseases is that people know far more now than in the past about how to prevent and contain the spread of infection. I exclude catastrophic possibilities because I have nothing useful to say about what would follow.

The world experienced a drastic decline in the human population growth rate once before in the present millennium. In the fourteenth and fifteenth centuries, waves of the Black Death, brigands, war lords, and famines killed somewhere between one-third and two-thirds of the people between India and Iceland. Economic and medieval historians have argued that the Black Death shook Europe loose from a stable equilibrium of high population density, intensive grain production, and widespread poverty. Before the Black Death, admission to guilds had been hereditary or strictly limited. A scarcity of workers following the drop in population forced guilds to recruit more widely from among the poor. Parents shifted much of their bequests from pietistic charity to their children. Increased lands per person shifted diets toward more meat, previously the food of the rich. The scarcity of people raised the wages of both agricultural and urban laborers and stimulated the development and spread of labor-saving technology. From an over-simplified economic perspective, when the supply of people dropped, the price of people rose. A dramatic fall in the abundance of people was followed by an increase in their value.

Other key factors in the development of Europe were urbanization and technological innovation. The rise of urban society in Europe in the eleventh to thirteenth centuries gave professionals a prominent place. Technological innovations in both agriculture and manufacturing occurred as people moved to cities. The Black Death saved these gains from being eaten up, as they were in Asia, by the rise of population. These trends seem relevant to the twenty-first century if population growth slows and cities grow rapidly as expected.

However, the effects on well-being of major demographic changes depend as much on the relations of power in a society as on numbers. Many localities in Europe passed anti-labor laws in the fourteenth and fifteenth century in unsuccessful attempts to control the demands of workers. If the decimation of the Amerindians following the European conquests raised the price of people in the New World, it led the European colonists to tighten their control of the subjugated populations.

In the twentieth century, the supply of people surged to unprecedented levels. To judge by the preventable ills of the human population today, people are collectively valued cheaply. Perhaps three-quarters of a billion people are chronically undernourished. At least another billion are malnourished. A billion adults are illiterate. Roughly 2 billion people — one in three people on the planet — are infected with the bacillus of tuberculosis, though isoniazid, an inexpensive drug that can cure tuberculosis when taken properly, was discovered in 1952. Hundreds of millions of people are under threat from other infectious diseases.

WILL THE relations between the rich world and the poor world follow the European experience, with growing equity and wealth for all, or will it follow the Amerindian experience, with prolonged subjugation and deprivation for the poor? The twentieth century shows the seeds of both possibilities. The growth of economic inequality is an ominous trend. The spread of primary education is a promising trend.

Economic growth during the twentieth century more than quadrupled the average gross domestic product (GDP) per person, from less than $1,300 to $5,200. Measured by aggregate GDP, the size of the world economy grew sixteen-fold. Of course, the GDP has important limitations as a measure of economic well-being. To an important extent, the process of economic development substitutes market production for domestic production: eating in a restaurant replaces cooking at home; paying for childcare replaces parental rearing of children. Hence the GDP rises faster than real (including domestic) production. The GDP also includes commercial gains from market activities but neglects their drawing-down of environmental and social capital. Though the numbers that economists use to measure economic growth have uncertain interpretations as indicators of welfare, it seems clear that economic well-being has improved for many people during the twentieth century.

People shared the improvement in average incomes very unequally. Between 1870 and 1985, the ratio of average incomes per person in the richest countries to average incomes per person in the poorest countries increased sixfold. When the 1997 gross national product per person was adjusted for purchasing power parity, the poorest 2 billion people on the planet had incomes of $1,400 per year, less than one-sixteenth of the average incomes of the richest billion. These comparisons of income between groups at different levels of economic development suffer from the same limitations as long-term comparisons of average GDP.

A more promising trend in the twentieth century is that primary education spread across the world. A standard indicator of educational activity is the primary gross enrollment ratio (PGER). A gross enrollment ratio is calculated by dividing the number of children enrolled in school by the school-age population. Because children who are over age or under age may also enroll in school, the PGER over-represents the proportions of children of school-going age who are actually enrolled in school. The PGER may exceed 100 percent.

In the wealthy regions of northwestern Europe, North America and the Anglo Pacific, the PGER rose this century from 72 percent to 103 percent. Latin America, the Caribbean, East Asia and Southeast Asia saw much more dramatic increases, from as low as 4 percent in Southeast Asia to more than

100 percent in all these regions. Sub-Saharan Africa lagged other regions. Its PGER progressed from 16 percent to 85 percent. Late in the twentieth century, about three-quarters of the children eligible to attend primary schools in developing countries did so. The 130 million children who were out of school were disproportionately girls, and were mainly illiterate.

The improved status of women and the spread of primary education, human rights and effective democratic governments are major cultural trends of the twentieth century that bode well for the twenty-first. A continuation of these trends in the next century could bring an unprecedented growth of equity and spread of prosperity. A wealthier, better-educated populace could demand environmental quality and the knowledge needed to achieve it. Changes in the composition and function of families—associated with falling fertility, rising longevity, and economic and cultural changes in the relations between men and women—will have unknown but probably very important effects.

On the other hand, the gulf between rich nations and poor, the ever-present seeds of violence and corruption, and growing material through-puts of the human economy could undermine the benign environmental assumptions of these speculations.

HUMANS HAVE been a geological force on the face of the Earth since they mastered fire hundreds of thousands of years ago. Energy consumption is one index of capacity to transform the Earth. Between 1860 and 1990, the use per person of inanimate energy from all sources grew nearly 20-fold while global population quadrupled, giving a nearly eighty-fold rise in aggregate inanimate energy consumption. Partly as a consequence of the increased production and consumption of energy, human interventions in biotic and geological processes grew tremendously in the twentieth century. I will illustrate with the global cycles of carbon, water and nitrogen.

Although individual human well-being is appropriately measured per person, human impact on global biogeochemical systems is appropriately measured on an aggregate basis. The reason is that the mass of the atmosphere, the area of the continents, the volume of the ocean, the number of species, and many other planetary systems are independent of the size of the human population.

In the twentieth century, human-induced atmospheric carbon emissions grew from 0.5 billion to 7.3 billion tons of carbon per year. The carbon dioxide concentration in the atmosphere rose in this century by about 20 percent. Atmospheric carbon dioxide concentrations are now higher than they have been in the last 150,000 years, a period that includes the emergence of modern humans and the multiple inventions of agriculture. The human and biological implications of this rise are hotly debated. Current models are the subject of controversy, some scientifically motivated and some politically motivated.

World water withdrawals grew eight-fold from 500 cubic kilometers per year around 1900 to roughly 4,000 cubic kilometers per year currently. Humans now withdraw annually roughly a quarter to half of all available renewable freshwater. The two-fold uncertainty in this estimate reflects current ignorance of humans' place in the world's water cycle. While aggregate supplies of freshwater remain ample, local water shortages currently affect billions of people.

Human emissions of nitrogen in NO_x from the combustion of fossil fuels grew from 1.5 million to 25 million tons per year between 1900 and 2000. The mass fraction of nitrates in ice grew from 45 parts per billion at the beginning of the century to 120 parts per billion at the end. Current human activities emit 40 percent of the nitrous oxide (N_2O), 70 percent of the ammonia (NH_3) and at least 80 percent of the nitric oxide (NO) emitted to the atmosphere from all sources.

People converted forests to agricultural land throughout the twentieth century. The application of chemicals to agricultural lands intensified greatly in the last third of the century. Through the uses of land for agriculture, cities, industry and infrastructure, humans have altered the habitats and populations of many non-human species.

WHETHER AND for whom the twenty-first century goes well or ill is not determined by the situation today. Nothing is inevitable about any of the human changes anticipated here. Human changes result from individual and collective choices. One choice often constrains another. People collectively choose the growth rate, size, age composition, and concentration in cities of the human population. Through investments in education, capital and environmental protection, people choose who shall acquire the capacity to generate wealth and to share in global prosperity. People choose whether to let their interventions in the biogeochemical mechanics of the globe run ahead of their ability to foresee the impacts of those interventions.

Unfortunately, humans do not yet understand well how the interacting system of the human-natural world works. People cannot yet choose how the natural world will treat them. In the twentieth century, the physical, chemical and biological world has surprised people repeatedly. Lead in gasoline poisoned children and adults. Asbestos products injured many workers. Above-ground atomic tests put strontium in milk. Chlorofluorocarbons created ozone holes. Human immunodeficiency viruses and antibiotic resistance emerged. The Aral Sea shrank from the fourth to the eighth largest lake in the world. The Colorado River ended in a trickle.

As long as people remain stunningly ignorant of how the natural world works, surprises from the natural world will continue. Not all of the surprises may be pleasant. In the recent geological past, very abrupt, major transitions in oceanic circulation have taken place over intervals as short as a decade or a few decades. These transitions were accompanied by equally abrupt changes in climate over large parts or all of the globe. Such abrupt changes could be highly unfavorable to the well-being of humans and many other living species on which humans depend. Improved scientific knowledge of the interactions between humans and the rest of the Earth is needed to estimate the risks of such abrupt changes more realistically, and to offer guidance on how humans can avoid undesirable transitions.

Will we follow the example of Noah, who anticipated environmental change, prepared for it, and left a human and biological legacy that has enriched all following generations? Or will we follow the example of Samson, whose foolish passions led him to blind enslavement, and whose power finally brought the temple down on his own head?

ACKNOWLEDGMENTS. I am grateful to Nathan Keyfitz, Samuel Preston, George Whitesides, Valerie Herr, and Jonathan Messerli for helpful comments. I acknowledge with thanks the support of U.S. National Science Foundation grant BSR92–07293 and the hospitality of Mr. and Mrs. William T. Golden during this work.

DISCUSSANT

SAMUEL H. PRESTON

University of Pennsylvania

I AM GOING to make several remarks that are stimulated by points that Joel raised. First, this has been a wonderful century. It wins the most valuable century award hands down, in this or any other millennium. Choose any indicator of human well-being, life expectancy at birth, infant mortality rate, proportion literate, per capita income, political participation, and the gains of the twentieth century exceed the gains of all previous centuries put together. This is a remarkable achievement. The gains are so persistent that I sometimes think they have acquired an air of inevitability, but of course they are not inevitable. We have just heard from Joe Stiglitz several and backsliding many others could be added. So understanding how these gains occurred I think is vitally important. I think, and this is certainly not highly original, the evidence is completely in favor of the proposition that it has been in a primitive sense the march of ideas that has made the difference—the greater understandings that we have of the natural world and of the social world. I am convinced that this is true in the improvements that I know best, those in longevity. During the twentieth century the germ theory of disease and its implementation in innovative social organizations has for the first time given us secure protection against one another's microbes. This is unquestionably one of the great advances in human welfare.

One idea did not fare so well during the twentieth century. Last year marked the 200th anniversary of Thomas Malthus' *Principle of Population*. The twentieth century was not especially kind to Reverend Malthus. That these massive twentieth century gains in human well-being occurred during a period of unprecedentedly rapid population growth is, I think, a good indication of the basic paucity of the model that Malthus proposed. Nevertheless it is possible that our liberation from Malthusian constraints is only temporary. The most worrisome constraint is no longer the availability of land, but rather as Joel has stressed, the absorptive and regenerative capacity of the biosphere. The problem here is not the mass of human beings. If all humans in the world gathered themselves together in the circle and stood side-by-side, the radius of that circle would be nine miles. The problem, of course, is the ecological damage that this little group is capable of doing. But it's also capable of turning the Earth into English gardens and amber waves of grain. Controlling population numbers is surely one of the crudest means available for affecting outcomes. But if all else fails, if we cannot develop the incentives, the institutional structures, the international agreements that are required to direct human activity in salutary ways, it is conceivable that we would have to invoke a population solution to the problems, as has been advocated by many in the past.

Finally, I'd like to add one uncertainty to Joel's list about the twenty-first century. This relates to the future of families—the basic unit responsible for reproduction and child-raising in all societies. Malthus peered across the sea and saw a population that was liberated from land-constraints and the restrictions on marriage that those constraints implied. He saw a population in which women completed childbearing with an average of eight children. Benjamin Franklin referred to children swarming across the land like locusts. It's obvious that families have changed dramatically, not only in the United States but around the world. Relations between the sexes have become more tentative, rates of cohabitation and divorce have risen, rates of marriage and fertility have fallen. One-third of American births last year occurred to unmarried women. Fertility is below the replacement level in one out of every three countries in the world, a list that grows every year. And once you are on that list it appears that there is no escape. Fertility has fallen as low as 1.2 children per woman in Italy, of all places. I think we have some clues about why this has happened, why these dramatic changes have occurred. I am personally persuaded by Gary Becker's emphasis on the declining gains from trade in exchanges between the sexes, but I'm surprised at how little research is being done on this very fundamental social change. Until we understand it better, it's hard to predict where we are headed. I think it's entirely possible that the American Philosophical Society meeting a century hence is going to be faced with a very different set of questions about the human species than it is faced with today.

CLASS IV

HUMANITIES

Reconstructing the Past*

Sir John Elliott

Regius Professor Emeritus of Modern History, Oxford University

FUTURE HISTORIANS looking back on the world as it stands today are likely to be struck by two apparently contradictory, although connected, phenomena. On the one hand they will record and investigate a process of fragmentation. They will note how, in the aftermath of the collapse of the Soviet empire and the ideology which it promoted, old power-blocs were dissolved, long-standing structures weakened and crumbled, and communities or sectional groups asserted with growing vigour their rights to autonomous status on grounds of colour, creed, gender, ethnicity, language or tradition. But they will also note how, amidst this scene of fragmentation and disintegration, powerful forces were simultaneously working in a contrary direction. Accelerating technological advance, the information revolution, the rise of international organizations and multi-national corporations, will be seen as bearing witness to an irreversible process of globalization, running counter to the process of fragmentation.

I believe that, over the past few decades, historical writing, which tends to mirror the general movements of society, has been reflecting these two divergent tendencies. In the short time at my disposal I want to sketch out very briefly what I think has been happening in the world of historiography, and to comment on some of the challenges and the opportunities which, as I see it, currently confront those who attempt to record, understand, and reconstruct the past for the benefit of present and future generations.

Since the emergence of historical writing in the western world on a professional basis there has never, of course, been a total unanimity of approach, but there have always been dominant tendencies. The dominant influence on historical writing in the years after the Second World War was the

*Read 23 April 1999

Annales School, based in Paris, which had risen in reaction to what was perceived as the narrowness of the political and diplomatic narrative history cultivated by the followers of Ranke. Many elements, not all of them mutually coherent, flowed together to form what in due course was to become the *Annales* approach, but it borrowed heavily from the social sciences, turned its back on narrative history, and, in its greatest age, gave primacy to economic or social forces in human development, in line with contemporary Marxist and neo-Marxist thinking.[1]

The *Annales* School, under the leadership of Fernand Braudel, aspired to produce "total" history, providing an all-embracing synthesis which would make history the queen of the social sciences. But the claims of the *Annalistes* were weakened by the inevitable gap that emerged between theory and practice. They were criticized for their neglect of the political dimension of the past, and also for what was increasingly perceived as a failure to give sufficient place to its cultural context, at a time when Anglo-American anthropologists, reacting against Marxist or structuralist determinism, were developing a cultural anthropology directed towards the decoding of meaning. Heavily influenced by the cultural anthropologists, the post-Braudel generation of *Annalistes* increasingly turned their attention to the history of collective representation or, in what became the fashionable terminology, the history of *mentalités*.

The history of *mentalités* had its own inherent tendency to fragment, as cultural historians pursued their interest in particular aspects of the theme—for instance, the history of the book—or explored the *mentalité* of particular and localized groups, or even of single individuals, like Menocchio, the miller of Friuli, who, after four centuries of total obscurity, suddenly became an international celebrity in the 1970s as a result of Carlo Ginzburg's skill in reconstructing his unique vision of a cosmos emerging like worms from cheese.[2] Ginzburg's book, written from outside the *Annales* School,

---

1. For a useful short account of the *Annales* School, see Peter Burke, *The French Historical Revolution. The Annales School, 1929–89* (Polity Press, Cambridge, 1990).
2. Carlo Ginzburg, *The Cheese and the Worms. The Cosmos of a Sixteenth-Century Miller,* trans. John and Anne Tedeschi (The Johns Hopkins University Press, Baltimore and London, 1980). The original Italian version, *Il formaggio e i vermi,* was published in 1976 (Einaudi, Turin).

heralded the arrival of new and powerful trends in historical writing—cultural history and micro-history—in reaction against the socioeconomic approach of the *Annalistes*.

The very term "micro-history" implies the dissolution of the past into fragments, sometimes very small fragments, indeed. A close study of an obscure sixteenth-century Italian miller, or of an equally obscure one-legged soldier in the period of the French wars of religion,[3] would seem to represent a polar opposite to "total history," the proclaimed objective of the *Annales* School. But the process of fragmentation in the world of historical scholarship extended much further than this, and reflected institutional as well as ideological changes. The proliferation of universities and history departments, the multiplication of national and international conferences, and the vast outpouring of technical and monographic studies resulting from all this activity, led to an escalation of historical writing so vast in its scope and so bewildering in its diversity as to overwhelm the most conscientious of scholars, even when they confined themselves to their chosen field of expertise.

In this increasingly pluralist climate of the western world, it was inevitable that a thousand flowers should bloom. Different sectional groups had understandably come to demand their own place in the sun. Women's history, Black history, minority studies of every shape and hue abounded. Self-proclaimed revisionists, reacting against the disappearance of the contingent and the individual in Marxist and *Annaliste* historiography, sought to restore political actors and high politics to center stage. Lawrence Stone announced in 1979 the return of narrative history, although there were some of us, even then, who were unaware that we had ever abandoned it.[4]

Even as the process of fragmentation gathered pace, the whole conception of history as traditionally practiced was to come under sustained assault, initially from departments of literature, where the "canon" of great books was systematically being dismantled. The new relativism inherent in

---

3. See Natalie Zemon Davis, *The Return of Martin Guerre* (Harvard University Press, Cambridge, Mass., 1983).

4. 'The Revival of Narrative: Reflections on a New Old History' in Lawrence Stone, *The Past and the Present Revisited* (Routledge and Kegan Paul, London and New York, 1987), pp.74–96. Originally published in *Past and Present*, 85 (1979).

the post-modernist movement, the attack on the assumptions about the relationship between language and extra-linguistic "reality" on which the whole historical enterprise had rested, threatened history itself with dissolution, as it was absorbed into textuality. If language itself is a closed system, and text and context merge, the historian is left without an object of study, and all certainty—or even the possibility of certainty—is gone.

Running counter to this process of fragmentation, both within and beyond the boundaries of the historical enterprise, have been a succession of macro-historical undertakings, ambitious syntheses spanning the history of nations and even continents, and challenging the parochialism that has beset so much specialist historical writing. Many of these great synthesizing efforts—ranging from S.N. Eisenstadt's *The Political Systems of Empires: the Rise and Fall of Historical Bureaucratic Societies* (1963) to Perry Anderson's *Lineages of the Absolutist State* (1974), and Immanuel Wallerstein's *The Modern World System* (1974–80)—have either come out of, or are heavily indebted to, the world of the social sciences, and have been received with a certain scepticism by the guild of historians, who have tended to treat them as alien intruders.

Yet at the same time, advances from within the discipline have also been tending in recent years to push at least some guild members in a macro-historical direction, although in ways that may be helping to widen the gulf between professional historians and the reading public, which is one of the most preoccupying features of the current historical scene. While lay readers still expect history to be written as the narrative of the nation, there has been a growing awareness among many professional historians that a narrowly national approach is inadequate for dealing with many of the complex questions thrown up by the results of new research, and that such topics as the causes, consequences, and character of slavery, or the encounter between Europe and the non-European peoples of the world, pose problems that require a global treatment, very often on a comparative basis. What was once the history of the colonization of North America, for instance, is now being transformed into "Atlantic history," with Europe, Africa, and America itself as the participants in a vast movement of peoples spanning four centuries.[5]

---

5. See Bernard Bailyn, "The Idea of Atlantic History," *Itinerario,* 20 (1996):1–27.

The tensions between the fragmentation of the past which has been such a dominant feature of historical writing over the last two decades, and the contrary process of globalization, which is now gathering pace, would seem to me to reflect the tug of contradictory forces in the world around us, and to spring from comparably interconnected causes. In the world of scholarship, the breakdown of the traditional compartments into which the humanities have been organized has led on the one hand to a process of splintering, in which, to paraphrase Carl Becker, every man or woman becomes his or her own historian,[6] and on the other to invasions across disintegrating disciplinary frontiers in a bid to conquer new territory and impose a new hegemony. The world of politics has seen a similar tug of competing forces as a new world order struggles to emerge from the wreckage of the old, and as smaller political units and ethnic communities react to the imposition of supra-national organisms and overarching political or economic structures by redefining and reasserting their own sense of collective identity.

This search for a lost or suppressed identity is in turn having a major impact on current historical writing over a whole range of fields, running from the history of gender to the history of the traditional nation states. It is instructive, for instance, to observe the shifting attitudes of historians to the past of two countries with which I happen to be reasonably familiar, Spain and my own. In the Spain of General Franco, the dominant historiography, as might be expected, was centralist and centralizing. The history of Spain tended to be equated with that of its dominant region, Castile, and was presented as the story of the success of the state in controlling the inherent tendencies of the Iberian peninsula to fragmentation, thus enabling it to uphold a series of transcendental values with which the official idea of Spain was closely identified. With the end of the Franco regime and the emergence of a democratic and pluralist Spain, the dominant historiography began to collapse, to be replaced by a set of increasingly specialized histories of seventeen autonomous regions, each seeking to establish or reestablish its unique historical identity.

A comparable process of fragmentation is now overtaking what used to

---

6. Carl Becker, "Everyman his own Historian," *American Historical Review*, 37 (1932): 221–36.

be known as "English history"—currently, if sometimes only for cosmetic purposes, undergoing a metamorphosis into "British history." As the constitutional reordering of the United Kingdom gathers pace, and Scotland and Wales reassert their separate historical identities, so the master story which tended to identify the history of Britain with that of England is subjected to the challenge of alternative stories, just as happened with the master story which identified the history of Castile with that of Spain.

The increasingly agonized debate over the writing and teaching of British history raises questions which seem to me to go to the heart of the dilemmas that currently confront the world of historical scholarship. The history of Great Britain, as traditionally written, is dissolving into a set of national histories—English, Irish, Scottish, Welsh—which in turn, and partly in response to the sheer multiplication of historical research, show signs of further breaking down into regional or local histories, as investigation focuses with growing intensity on smaller and smaller units. Such fissiparous tendencies are, of course, neither new nor unique: the study of colonial America has long been subjected to comparable processes, as historians of Virginia or Pennsylvania go their own ways, and reject a master narrative written from the standpoint of Puritan New England.

But the conjunction of political change with intense historical inquiry has posed the dilemma for historians of Britain and Spain in a particularly acute form, since it is tied up with a question of great current moment—the problem of national identity. Is there any such thing as British history—as distinct from English, Scottish, or Welsh history—and, if so, how should it be written? It is, I think, a straw in the wind that Norman Davies, the author of a recent very successful history of Europe,[7] is now engaged on a comparable volume about my corner of the world, which he plans to call a history not even of the British Isles, but simply the Isles.

The challenge to what had once looked like a coherent account of the British past is a particularly vivid example—not least because of its current political relevance—of the wider process in historical scholarship that I have been describing. In assessing that process, it would seem helpful to begin with one or two observations of a general nature. In the first place, it is

---

7. Norman Davies, *A History of Europe* (Oxford University Press, Oxford and New York, 1996).

worth remembering that the challenge to coherence is itself an integral part of the historical enterprise. Insofar as we can speak about "progress" in history, much of it comes from confronting and overthrowing accepted paradigms that are no longer able to accommodate conclusions arising from new approaches, or from the results of new documentary research. The dissolution of outmoded paradigms is therefore a necessary and salutary constituent part of historical scholarship. In the second place, there has always been division and competition between macro-historians and micro-historians—between the "lumpers" and the "splitters," as the late Jack Hexter called them,[8] or between what Emmanuel Le Roy Ladurie described as the "parachutists" and the "truffle-hunters."[9] Both kinds have an important contribution to make. This in turn emphasizes the desirability of avoiding the dichotomy of an either/or approach. There are horses for courses, and some of the best historians are equally adept at the flat race and the steeplechase.

But in assessing the course and picking the horse, it is important to be aware both of the opportunities and the risks. The sheer diversity of historical scholarship over the past few decades has itself been a source of enrichment. Intense scrutiny of documentary sources that had been neglected or under-used by earlier generations of historians—notarial or inquisitorial records, for instance—has given us insights into private worlds that were previously closed to us. One important result has been to restore the individual to a position from which he or she had tended to be displaced by the intense emphasis placed by the dominant historical schools of the immediate post-war era on the great impersonal forces, demographic or economic, in the shaping of society. In historical writing at least, human agency is back, and, with it, intention and intentionality.

The effect of the recovery of the individual has been to give a new respectability, both to biography, and to historical narration, as life-stories

---

8. J. H. Hexter, *On Historians* (Harvard University Press, Cambridge, Mass., 1979), pp. 241–3.

9. After searching through Professor Le Roy Ladurie's writings for this reference, and failing to find the hoped-for truffle, I eventually appealed to the author for help. He, too, does not know where he published it, but assures me that I can safely attribute it to him. The contrast is between parachutists who range over large areas of territory, like French soldiers in Algeria around 1960, and truffle-hunters who unearth a treasure.

have been pieced together from the archives. As someone who firmly believes in the importance of individual agency in shaping events, I naturally find this a positive development. Much of the fascination of the past, for me at least, lies in the interplay between individuals and the environment — geographical, cultural, social — in which they conduct their lives. To what extent, for instance, was a Philip II of Spain the prisoner of circumstance, and to what extent did his own beliefs, attitudes and temperament mould the world around him? I also believe that the resurgence of the narrative mode has restored something that was at least temporarily in danger of being neglected as historians came excessively under the sway of the social sciences — the importance of change (or sometimes the lack of it) over time. Without a sense of the dimension of time, history has lost its bearings.

But there have been losses as well as gains in the renewed concern with the reconstruction of individual experience, just as there have also been losses and gains in the resurgence of the narrative mode for relating it. To restore a lost life, or to give new utterance to voices silenced by time or oppression, is a heady experience for any historian. But a piece-by-piece recovery of the intimacies of the past can easily lapse into little more than historical voyeurism. The accident of the survival of documentation is not in itself an adequate reason to reconstruct a life unless the reconstruction can give us a sharper insight into the social and cultural world in which that life was lived. The life that is being reconstructed may be a more or less representative one — and it is hard to know whether there were others beside the heretical miller of Friuli who believed that the world had its origin in putrefaction — but it only becomes of historical, as distinct from antiquarian, interest when it is in some way related, as Carlo Ginzburg succeeds in relating it, to its contemporary context.

There is, too, a danger that, in concentrating on the minutiae of individual lives, we lose a sense of proportion. If I may be allowed to quote a remark that I made on another occasion, "There is surely something amiss when the name of Martin Guerre becomes as well or better known than that of Martin Luther," [10] though I hasten to add that in this instance it is also

---

10. John. H. Elliott, *National and Comparative History* (Inaugural Lecture, Clarendon Press, Oxford, 1991), p. 11.

a tribute to the skills of the narrator. But the very act of sympathetically re-covering the voices of the unknown and the underdog can create its own distortions. One of the great collective historical achievements of our times has been the slow and painstaking reconstruction of what has been called "the vision of the vanquished"[11]—of the peoples of the world conquered and colonized by an expansionist Europe. But the achievement has come at a price. Historians of empire have become so attuned to picking up distant signals from the vanquished that they are in danger of ignoring the variety of voices among the victors, who in some respects have today become more alien than their victims. It is relatively easy to paint an understanding por-trait of those to whom one is sympathetically drawn. The challenge to the historian is to enter the mind-sets of those whose attitudes and behaviour elicit no sympathy, often for very good reason.[12]

It is, however, in the blurring of fact and fiction in the narration of the past that the greatest danger lies. The current mode for relativism, the as-sumption that one story is no more or less trustworthy than another, is a negation of all scholarship that is founded on the careful accumulation and testing of evidence. This is not to say that a "reality" out there can, with time and patience, be fully recovered. But it is to say that there are degrees of plausibility in the reading and interpretation of the past, and that the in-terpretation which is most plausible is the one that shows the most respect for the available evidence, of whatever kind, and the most regard for the context of place and time.

To make a story plausible is, of course, to give it coherence—both an in-ternal coherence, and a coherence with the world to which it relates. To some extent the coherence is bound to be spurious—stories are tidy; life, as we all know, is not. It is for this reason that the best history allows room for

---

11. The phrase seems to have originated with the Mexican historian of Nahuatl cul-ture, Miguel León-Portilla, who entitled his anthology of indigenous accounts of the Span-ish conquest of Mexico *Visión de los vencidos* (Universidad Nacional Autónoma de México, 1959). It was later used by Nathan Wachtel as the title of his study of Peruvian Indian reac-tions to the conquest of Peru, *La Vision des Vaincus* (Gallimard, Paris, 1971).

12. For a brave attempt to grapple with this challenge, see Inga Clendinnen, *Reading the Holocaust* (Text Publishing, Melbourne, Australia, 1998), especially pp. 104–8 ("Under-standing Unpleasant Others").

the operation of the irrational and the contingent, for the sudden upsurge of emotion, or the apparently fortuitous conjunction of circumstances. The past is, no doubt, more or less chaotic, but as historians we abdicate our responsibility to the present and the future if we renounce the attempt to make some sense of it.

How we do this, or should do it, depends very much on contemporary perceptions and needs. Each age will want to recover and validate a particular aspect of the past, at the inevitable expense of others. Our age, as I have suggested, has been particularly diligent in the pursuit of lost or submerged identities, and has displayed remarkable technical virtuosity in the process. But if one function of the historian is to respond to the demands of the moment, the other is to point to the alternative options presented by the past, so that the store of historical memory is not unnecessarily diminished.

If, as I believe, the search for submerged identities has led to an unprecedented fragmentation of prevailing interpretations of the past, there is now a particularly strong case for attempting to put the fragments together again. Pluralist societies will want, and get, their pluralist histories, but a global society requires a larger coherence than that of a multiplicity of compartmentalized units categorized by ethnicity, class, gender or creed.

Therefore the challenge for the next generation of historians, as I see it, is to connect, in terms both of method and content. We need new syntheses, which will transcend traditional disciplinary boundaries, and incorporate into plausible constructs some of the vast quantity of new information and new ideas produced by a generation of research. We need, too, to think in terms of new and larger categories. The process, as I have suggested, is already under way. It is under way in the move, to which I have already referred, to construct an Atlantic history, transcending but not suppressing that of the different societies that border the Atlantic ocean. It is under way in the growing trend among cultural historians to break away from the earlier rigid dichotomy between so-called 'high' and 'low' culture, and to identify instead a world of shared behaviour and beliefs.[13] It is under way, too, in

---

13. See James S. Amelang, *The Flight of Icarus. Artisan Autobiography in Early Modern Europe* (Stanford University Press, Stanford, 1998), p. 243. I am grateful to Dr. Amelang for his comments on an early draft of this paper.

the history of European overseas colonization, as historians become more aware of the part played by cultural *métissage* in the formation of colonial societies.[14]

One way to make connections is through the discovery of hidden, or not so hidden, links. Another is through the comparison of distinctive entities. Comparative history, although technically one of the most difficult kinds of history to write, has an important part to play in challenging on the one hand the atomization of the past, and on the other its endowment with a factitious coherence achieved by glossing over the individual and the distinctive.[15] By identifying at once the similarities and the differences, it can suggest what is truly exceptional and what is experienced in common. In so doing it can introduce fresh questions to the historical agenda about the infinitely varied process of development over time, which is central to historical understanding. The answers to these questions, as to all historical questions, can only be partial, reflecting both the standpoint of the historian and the necessarily partial nature of the evidence. But this is no reason to turn one's back on a challenge that confronts not only historians but all those engaged in the humanist enterprise—a challenge once succinctly summarized by E. M. Forster in his famous injunction: "Only connect."

DISCUSSANT

Anthony Grafton

Princeton University

John's observations seem to me absolutely correct. It's not surprising because they reflect his own extraordinary career as a historian. John is himself the horse who can run all courses. He began as a young historian in Franquista Spain, rebelling with the Catalans, writing one of the first great regional studies of Early Modern Europe. He then came, in his later career, to study both the creation of the Spanish monarchy, to compare it

---

14. See, for example, Serge Gruzinski, *La pensée métisse* (Fayard, Paris, 1999).

15. See my discussion, "Comparative History," in Carlos Barros, ed., *Historia a Debate* (3 vols. Santiago de Compostela, 1995), vol.3, pp. 9–19, and the footnote references.

with the creation of the French monarchy in early modern times, and to write a small book on global history, *The Old World and the New,* composed and published more than twenty years before the Columbian bicentenary. If you took all of the literature written on the Columbian bicentenary and put it on one end of the beam and *The Old World and the New* on the other, we know which end would go down. I can say that having written one of the others myself.

I'd like just to add three or four points of comment and expansion. First of all, John suggests that the features of historical writing, which he's emphasized, are especially characteristic of professional history and reflect a growing separation between professional history and the rest. From my own vantage point in the mudflats of New Jersey, things look a little different. In fact, I'd say that some of the most creative history that's been produced in the last two decades has cut across traditional boundaries, traditional periodizations, traditional unities of place, but has been written by non-professionals. Just to give you one example, Neal Ascherson's extraordinary *Black Sea,* a very fine piece of historical writing but written outside the university and one which anyone who teaches what we laughingly call the West should try to contend with in organizing his teaching and thinking.

Secondly, I'd like to suggest that in other fields besides the history of early modern Europe, some of these tendencies have been in operation for a long time. Here I think especially of the history of science, the history of the exact sciences, which probably was one of the first fields in the study of the ancient world to challenge the belief that there was a classical and non-classical world. It has been carried on by a great member of this Society, Otto Neugebauer, and by others who are in this room, who did a great deal to turn Classics into the Ancient World or the Ancient Mediterranean, a transformation which has been taking place for more than two decades now and which is really extraordinarily interesting to watch. So it seems this process is even older than John suggested. There are also other factors which will keep this process in motion and perhaps make it more radical, more difficult to terminate with a concluding synthesis, than he suggested. Again, from an American vantage point, just two. One is demographic: our student bodies are increasingly diverse. At elite universities in North America, between 12 and 30 percent of the undergraduates are of Asian origin. Nobody can predict, of course, what anyone will want to study. One winner of our prize for the best undergraduate in Princeton last year was a Korean who wrote her senior thesis on *Middlemarch*. And happily, these crossings will always take place. Nonetheless, more and more, from Princeton to Berkeley, we see student bodies that demand something different from the European history, the English history, the American history of the past. And I think that those demands are actually going to become more and more urgent as those parts of the student body become more and more prominent. This is altogether a good thing, but not easy to deal with pedagogically.

Secondly, we're seeing among young scholars, those going to graduate school to study European history, efforts to create something new, somewhat along the lines John described. Every young student I know who has gone to graduate school from Princeton to study European history in the last two or three years, and everyone who has come to us, has been possessed by the desire to study both Europe and its empires. They do in a very serious way, learning both the European and the non-European languages involved, steeping themselves in both historical and ethnographic traditions of scholarship, working both sides of the line. That sounds wonderful in theory. What jobs do we have for them? There is no post in most history departments for someone like this, though we desperately need them. And a task for those of my generation who are wise by our beards is to think about how to create such jobs. A new kind of scholarship and teaching is forming, one whose nature we are not in a position to predict and for which we simply must make room. In a world increasingly dominated by market and metaphors, even in the university, we need non-market ways of explaining why these new fields must be opened.

Finally, one more point which John didn't mention but which also contributes to the fragmentation rather than the reunification of history. Historians are increasingly obsessed by their own subjectivity. One feature of much of the most exciting historical writing done both inside and outside the university, one that links Natalie Zemon-Davis to Neal Ascherson, is the historian's sense of the way his or her own approach stems from a time, a place, a particular set of prejudices, a particular training, the sense of the fragility and the provisional character of all historical argument is prevalent more and more. Historians acknowledge it explicitly. Some of the most fascinating historical work now written takes a double form, when the study of the past accompanies a biographical or autobiographical study of the historian's way of reaching it. The literary results of this, as in Ascherson's case, can be stunning, compellingly readable, fascinating. But if every historian is to be his or her own autobiographer in every book, we confront a level of intellectual atomization the results of which are dizzying to imagine: the historian as Humpty Dumpty.

Art and Architectural History in the Twentieth Century*

HENRY A. MILLON

Dean, Center for Advanced Study in the Visual Arts,
National Gallery of Art

THIS PAPER consists of three sections: first, brief descriptions of the origins of several current directions in the field; second, an examination of Modernism as it came to be defined in non-representational painting at mid-century in the United States and; third, a discussion of museum exhibition practices, one of the major sites of encounter between the public and art historians.

What we describe today as the history of art resulted from a merging of object study, artists' biographies, and philosophical thought in the late nineteenth and early twentieth centuries. The discipline of the history, theory, and criticism of art and architecture as practiced in the first third of this century in universities, museums, and art journals was constructed on the intersection of empirical and antiquarian studies with those in the philosophy of art history by scholars in Germany, Switzerland, and Austria that were partially dependent on the aesthetics of Kant and Hegel.

Philosophers and scholars pondered how it was possible, given the diversity of the arts of the past, fashioned at different times, in different societies with belief systems unknown or not shared by contemporary society, that the art of the past could be rationally examined and of consuming interest to them in the present. They were not willing to accept a premise of mere fascination with artistic technique or composition for, in that case, the objects would have artistic value only, thereby ignoring a larger context of

---

*Read 23 April 1999.

original purpose and function. The art object would be only of antiquarian interest.[1]

The work of Charles Peirce in the United States and Ferdinand de Saussure in Switzerland established the basis of semiotics with works on sign theory and on structural linguistics.[2] Their approaches began to be applied systematically to material culture, including the visual arts, first through structuralism and then, in the 1960s, via poststructuralism. These studies were primarily produced by scholars in Germany, France, Austria, Czechoslovakia and later in the United States.[3] Saussure's structural linguistics were then applied to philosophy in France in the work of Maurice Merleau-Ponty who became more interested in the texts and images produced than in the individual who may have conceived them, leading eventually to what Roland Barthes called the "death of the author."[4]

---

1. See Michael Podro, *The Critical Historians of Art,* New Haven and London: Yale University Press, 1982; David Watkin, *The Rise of Architectural History,* London: Architectural Press, 1980; and Michael Ann Holly, *Panofsky and the Foundations of Art History,* Ithaca and London: Cornell University Press, 1984.

2. Charles S. Peirce, *The Peirce Papers. Collected Papers,* ed. by Charles Hartshorne, Paul Weiss, and Arthur W. Burks, 8 vols. (1931–1958). Peirce's major work on semiotics (*A System of Logic, Considered as Semiotic*) remained unfinished at his death in 1914.

Ferdinand de Saussure, *Cours de linguistique général,* Lausanne: Payot, 1916 (*Course in General Linguistics,* trans. Wade Baskin, New York: Philosophical Library, 1959). For Saussure, see also Jonathan D. Culler, *Ferdinand de Saussure,* Hassocks, England: Harvester Press, 1976. For a discussion of Peirce and Saussure, see Margaret Iversen, "Saussure versus Peirce: Models for a Semiotics of Visual Art," in A.L. Rees and Frances Borzello, eds., *The New Art History,* London: Camden Press, 1986, pp. 82–94. For a recent examination of semiotics and the history of art, see Mieke Bal and Norman Bryson, "Semiotics and Art History," *Art Bulletin* 73 (1991): 174–208.

3. For structuralism in anthropology, see among others Claude Levi-Strauss, *Anthropologie Structurale,* Paris: Plon, 1958 and *La penseé Sauvage,* Paris: Plon, 1962. For semiotics and language, see Roman Jakobson and Morris Halle, *Fundamentals of Language,* 's-Gravenhage: Mouton, 1956; R. Jakobson, *Main Trends in the Science of Language,* New York: Harper and Row, 1974; R. Jakobson, *Coup d'oeil sur le développment de la sémiotique,* Bloomington: Indiana University Press, Atlantic Hylands, NJ: Humanities Press, 1975; R. Jakobson, *Six Lectures on Sound and Meaning,* (translated by John Mepham), Cambridge, Mass: MIT Press, 1978.

4. Maurice Merleau-Ponty, *Phenomenology of Perception,* (trans. from the French edition of 1945 by Colin Smith), London: Routledge and Kegan, Paul: Atlantic Highlands, NJ: Humanities Press, 1962; M. Merleau-Ponty, *The Primacy of Perception and Other Essays on Phenomenological Psychology, the Philosophy of Art, History and Politics* (edited, with an introduc-

Poststructuralism, arising after World War II principally in France from the work of Roland Barthes (1915–1980), Michel Foucault (1926–1984), and Jacques Derrida (1930–), questioned the humanist consensus that individuals—like each of us—have the ability to analyze and comprehend the world, and to determine meaning through the acquisition of objective knowledge. Poststructuralists argued that meaning is not likely to be based on objective standards, and that value systems are more likely to be the product of interest groups that intend to maintain or advocate positions of power. Further, poststructuralists, in negating the relevance of authorship, argued that an author's intentions cannot be known and, therefore, the meaning of a text is contingent upon what the reader brings to the text. The result will differ for each reader and every reading will be a recreation. Poststructuralism is seen to question the notion of genius, the notion of art, the ineffable nature of a work of art, and even the concept of a museum of art—an issue to be addressed in the third section.[5]

In the 1920s and 1930s, scholars in the Soviet Union, Germany, and the United States sought to apply Karl Marx's observations about art, found in his *Introduction to the Critique of Political Economy,* in which he advocated directing attention to the production of art, the relationship of art to the

---

tion by James M. Edie), Evanston, Illinois: Northwestern University Press, 1964; M. Merleau-Ponty, *Signs* (trans. from the French edition of 1960 and with an introduction by Richard C. McCleary), Evanston, Illinois: Northwestern University Press, 1964; M. Merleau-Ponty, *The Visible and the Invisible,* followed by working notes (edited by Claude Lefort, trans. by Alfonso Lingis), Evanston, Illinois: Northwestern University Press, 1968.

Roland Barthes, *Elements of Semiology,* (trans. from the French by Annette Lavers and Colin Smith), New York: Noonday Press, 1968; R. Barthes, *Critical Essays,* (trans. from the French by Richard Howard), Evanston, Illinois: Northwestern University Press, 1972; R. Barthes, *Image, Music, Text* (trans. from the French by Stephen Heath), New York: Noonday Press, 1977 (contains the essay "Death of the Author" on 142–148).

5. Michel Foucault, Roland Barthes, Jacques Derrida, Jean-Louis Baudry, et. al. *Théorie d'ensemble,* Paris: Éditions du Seuil, 1968; J. Derrida, *Dissemination* (trans., with an introduction and additional notes by Barbara Johnson), Chicago: University Press, 1981; J. Derrida, *Positions* (trans. and annotated by Alan Bass), Chicago: University of Chicago Press, 1981; M. Foucault, *This is not a pipe* (with ill. and letters by René Magritte; trans. and edited by James Harkness), Berkeley: University of California Press, 1983; J. Derrida, *Signéponge = Signsponge* (trans. by Richard Rand), New York: Columbia University Press, 1984; J. Derrida, *The Truth in Painting* (trans. from the French edition of 1978 by Geoff Bennington and Ian McLeod), Chicago: University of Chicago Press, 1987.

working class, and the exploitation of art by the ruling class. The rise of Stalin, the replacement of modern art by socialist realism in the Soviet Union, the exile of Trotsky and, in 1939 the Soviet-German pact and the invasion of Finland frustrated scholars intent on developing a Marxian analysis. Nonetheless, an interest in a social history of art was maintained by scholars in Europe and the United States who rejected Stalinist communism.[6] Subsequent to the political unrest of the late 1960s, a renewed interest in a Marxist social history of art gained adherents and advocates in the universities of western Europe and North America, and became one of the animators of the "new art history".[7]

---

6. Serge Guilbaut ("The New Adventures of the Avant-Garde in America: Greenberg, Pollock, or from Trotskyism to the New Liberalism of the 'Vital Center'," in *October 15*, Winter 1980, 61–78; reprinted in Francis Frascina, ed., *Pollock and After. The Critical Debate*, New York: Harper and Row, 1985, 153–166) has described the political and artistic problems faced by Marxist literary and art critics in New York in the 1930s and 1940s in reconciling the internal policies of the Soviet Union with the theoretical positions advocated by André Breton and Leon Trotsky.

In the mid-1930s Meyer Schapiro seems to have assumed a leading role in maintaining a commitment to a social theory of art while disassociating himself and others of the like mind from Soviet politics and foreign policy, as well as from rigid Soviet art theory. See Schapiro's "Social Basis of Art," *First American Artists' Congress*, New York, 1936, 31–37. For Clement Greenberg's account of the period, though written twenty years later, see "The Late Thirties in New York," *Art and Culture*, Boston: Beacon Press, 1961, 230–235.

7. The renewed interest in a Marxist or social history of art manifested itself in the 1970s. See Kurt Forster, "Critical History of Art. On Transfiguration of Values?," *New Literary History*, vol. 3 (1972): 462–463; Beryl Lang and Forrest Williams, *Marxism and Art: writings in aesthetics and criticism*, New York: Longman, c. 1972; Maynard Solomon, compiler, *Marxism and Art: essays classic and contemporary, selected and with a historical and critical commentary by Maynard Solomon*, New York: Knopf, 1973; Timothy J. Clark, "The Conditions of Artistic Creation," *Times Literary Supplement*, 24 May 1974, pp. 561–562; Francis D. Klingender, *Marxism and Modern Art: an approach to social realism*, London: Lawrence and Wishart, 1975; Max Raphael, *Proudhon, Marx, Picasso: three studies in the sociology of art*, translated from the first published edition of 1933 in French by Inge Marcuse; edited, introduced, and with a bibliography by John Tagg, Atlantic Highlands, New Jersey: Humanities Press, 1980; Oscar K. Werckmeister, "Radical Art History," *Art Journal* 42 (1982): 4, 284–291; O. K. Werckmeister, "A Working Perspective for Marxist Art History Today," *Oxford Art Journal* 14 (1991): 83–87; Wolfgang Kirsten and Joan Weinstein, eds. *Radical Art History: Internationale Anthologie: Subject, O.K. Werckmeister*, Zurich: ZIP, c. 1997.

For a view that rejects Marxist determinism, while advocating a social history of art, see James S. Ackerman, "Toward a New Social History of Art," *New Literary History*, 4

Many anthologies of modern art include an article by Timothy J. Clark from the *Times Literary Supplement*, 24 May 1974, in which he argued for a renewal of the history of art. Clark thought the intellectual ferment among its practitioners in Germany and Austria in the late nineteenth century and early twentieth century was evidence of a need for rigorous debate and commitment absent in contemporary art history. Clark calls for a new social history of art, as well as renewed historiographical studies, a history of art that would give greater attention to history, economics, politics and social life: a history of art that examined the relation between art and ideology and the "conditions and relations of artistic production."[8]

Clark's exhortation added to influences besetting art history from semiotics, linguistics, structuralism, phenomenology, and post-structuralism.

In addition, studies in psychology, psychology of perception, and psychoanalysis played an increasing role in the formation of the philosophy and theory of art history. Freud's psychobiographical study of Leonardo (1910) and psychological analysis of the statue of Moses by Michelangelo (1914) initiated a series of psychoanalytic studies of symbolism, sublimation, creativity, biography and autobiography.[9] Among these were Ernst Kris and Otto Kurz's *Legend, Myth and Magic in the Image of the Artist* of 1934, Kris's *Psychoanalytic Explorations in Art* in 1952, Meyer Schapiro's psychoanalytic discussion of still-life paintings and drawings of Cezanne in 1968 and of the Merode Altarpiece at the Metropolitan Museum in 1945, as well as his corrective analysis of Freud's study of Leonardo.[10] More recently Norman

---

(1973): 315–330 and "The Demise of the Avant-Garde: Notes on the Sociology of Recent American Art," *Comparative Studies in Society and History*, 11 (1969): 371–384.

8. The *TLS* article was preceded by Clark's *The Absolute Bourgeois: Artists and Politics in France, 1848–1851*, London: Thames and Hudson, 1973, and *Image of the People: Gustave Courbet and the 1848 Revolution*, London: Thames and Hudson, 1973.

9. Sigmund Freud, *Leonardo da Vinci: a psychosexual study of an infantile reminiscence* (trans. by A.A. Brill), New York: Moffat, Yard and Co., 1916 and "The Moses of Michelangelo," *S.E.* 13 (1914): 211–236.

10. Ernst Kris and Otto Kurz, *Legend, Myth and Magic in the Image of the Artist*, (trans. from the German edition of 1934 by Alastair Lang and Lottie M. Newman), New Haven: Yale University Press, 1979; Ernst Kris, *Psychoanalytic Explorations in Art*, New York: International Universities Press, 1952; Meyer Schapiro, "The Apples of Cezanne. An Essay in the Meaning of Still-Life," *Art News Annual*, 34 (1968): 34–53 (also reprinted in Meyer Schapiro, *Modern Art 19th and 20th Centuries*, New York: George Braziller, 1978, pp. 1–38; Meyer

Bryson and others have applied psychoanalytic approaches to the analysis of art historians and their work.[11]

Feminist art historians seek to do more than insure that women artists receive appropriate recognition, a largely futile attempt if the ideological social and intellectual structure is, as feminists argue, a patriarchal one. For this reason feminist art historians such as Griselda Pollock, one of the more vocal spokespersons, argue that art historians "should be studying the totality of social relations which form the conditions of the production and consumption of objects designated in that process as art." Such study, Pollock observes, should lead to "wholly new ways of conceptualizing what it is we study and how we do it." From its beginnings in the early 1970s, feminist art history has grown to become a significant voice in the field.[12]

Schapiro, "Freud and Leonardo: An Art Historical Study," in P.O. Kristeller and P.P. Ivener, eds., *Renaissance Essays from the Journal of the History of Ideas,* New York: Harper and Row, 1968, pp. 303–337, reprinted in Meyer Schapiro, *Theory and Philosophy of Art: Style, Artists and Society,* (vol. IV of selected papers), New York: Braziller, 1994, pp. 153–192.

11. One example might be Norman Bryson, "Philostratus and the Imaginary Museum," in Simon Goldhill and Robin Osborne, eds., *Art and Text in Ancient Greek Culture,* Cambridge: Cambridge University Press, 1994, quoted in Stephen Bann, "Art History and Humanism," in Mark A. Cheetham, Michael Ann Holly, and Keith Moxey, eds., *The Subject of Art History. Historical Objects in Contemporary Perspective,* Cambridge: Cambridge University Press, 1998, p. 234.

12. Lucy R. Lippard, *From the Center: Feminist Essays on Women's Art,* New York: Dutton, 1976; Norma Broude and Mary D. Garrard, eds., *Feminism and Art History: Questioning the Litany,* New York: Harper and Row, 1982; Griselda Pollock, *Framing Feminism: Art and the Women's Movement, 1970–1985,* edited and introduced by Rozsika Parker and G. Pollock, London: Pandora Press; New York: Routledge and Kegan Paul, 1987; Linda Nochlin, *Women, Art and Power and Other Essays,* New York: Harper and Row, 1988; G. Pollock, *Vision and Difference: Femininity, Feminism and Histories of Art,* London and New York: Routledge, 1988; Arlene Raven, Cassandra Langer and Joanna Ellen Frueh, eds., *Feminist Art Criticism: An Anthology,* Studies in the Fine Arts 27, Ann Arbor, MI: UMI Research Press, 1988; Whitney Chadwick, *Women, Art, and Society,* New York: Thames and Hudson, 1990; N. Broude and M. D. Garrard, eds., *The Expanding Discourse: Feminism and Art History,* New York: IconEditions, 1992; Richard Kendall and G. Pollock, eds., *Dealing with Degas: Representations of Women and the Politics of Vision,* New York: Universe, 1992; Carol Duncan, *The Aesthetics of Power: Essays in Critical Art History,* Cambridge and New York: Cambridge University Press, 1993; C. L. Langer, *Feminist Art Criticism: An Annotated Bibliography,* New York: G.K. Hall, 1993; G. Pollock, *Avant-Garde Gambits, 1888–1893: Gender and the Color of*

It is within this milieu of competing authoritative voices that the Modernist program, as manifested in painting in New York in the late 1940s and 1950s, received increasing attention from critics and art historians.

2

Writing the history of Modernism, particularly that of Cubism and Abstract Art, has transformed the history of art since World War II. Curators, connoisseurs, critics, and academic art historians still seek to address the historical and interpretive necessities of abstract and non-representational art within a larger history of twentieth-century art or image making, while also accommodating the demands of emergent epistemological theories.

In the spring of 1936 the Museum of Modern Art in New York presented an enormously influential survey of Modernist art in an exhibition called *Cubism and Abstract Art,* curated by Alfred Barr. In the exhibition, Barr delineated the variety of art movements that contributed to the art of the 1930s, both non-geometrical and geometrical abstract art. The text eschewed discussion of any relationship between the development of modern art and the cultural history of the period, seeing the sequence of art forms during the previous fifty years as independent and self-reflexive.[13]

Meyer Schapiro, the next year, in an article on the "Nature of Abstract Art," addressed the exhibition at the Museum of Modern Art. He acknowledged the richness and range of the material assembled by Barr, but argued, using a series of examples, that abstract art, as well as its precursors, was

---

Art History, New York: Thames and Hudson, 1993; Yves Michaud, *Feminisme, art, et histoire de l'art,* Collection Espaces de l'art. Paris : Ecole nationale superieure des beaux-arts, 1994; A. Raven, C. L. Langer, and J. E. Frueh, eds., *New Feminist Criticism: Art, Identity, Action,* New York: IconEditions, 1994; Katy Deepwell, ed., *New Feminist Art Criticism: Critical Strategies,* Manchester: Manchester University Press; Manchester; New York : Distributed exclusively in the USA by St. Martin's Press, 1995; Rozsika Parker, *Old Mistresses: Women, Art and Ideology,* London: Pandora Press, 1995; Fred Orton, *Avant-Gardes and Partisans Reviewed,* Manchester: Manchester University Press; Manchester; New York: Distributed exclusively in the USA by St. Martin's Press, 1996; G. Pollock, *Mary Cassat: Painter of Modern Woman,* New York: Thames and Hudson, 1998; G. Pollock, *Differencing the Canon: Feminist Desire and the Writing of Art's Histories,* London and New York: Routledge, 1999.

13. Alfred H. Barr, *Cubism and Abstract Art,* New York: Museum of Modern Art, 1936.

necessarily engaged with the society that produced it and not the result of some inexorable artistic force.[14]

By contending that abstract art was not conceived within an independent artistic world, Schapiro indicated that abstract art must have a significance that extends beyond art itself, as artists sought to come to terms with a modern world in all its complexities. The article also refuted the communist argument that abstract art was isolated from society. It provided, thereby, a theoretical avenue for artists, with a socialist inclination as well as critics, including notably Clement Greenberg, and art historians, to engage in the modernist program.[15]

In 1961 Clement Greenberg read a paper entitled "Modernist Painting" on *The Voice of America Forum Lectures: The Visual Arts.* It was the fourteenth in a series of eighteen lectures and is generally acknowledged to describe the aims of Modernism as they were realized in the work of Jackson Pollock (Fig. 1), Mark Rothko (Fig. 2), Barnett Newman, Clyfford Still, Kenneth Nolan and others in the preceding decade and a half.[16] Greenberg's interpretive scheme saw the essence of modernism "in the use of the characteristic methods of the discipline to criticize the discipline itself . . . to entrench it more firmly in its area of competence." In Greenberg's philosophical and historical justification or explanation for abstract expressionist painting, it was the task of self-criticism of the art of painting to purge any effects that might have been borrowed from any other art. Once extraneous effects were eliminated it was the "ineluctable flatness of the surface that remained . . . for flatness alone was unique and exclusive to pictorial art." Greenberg continues, "to achieve autonomy, painting has had above all . . . to exclude the representational or literary . . . painting has made itself abstract. The flatness . . . can never be an absolute flatness. The heightened sensitivity of the

14. Meyer Schapiro, "The Nature of Abstract Art," *Marxist Quarterly,* 1, no. 1 (January 1937): 47–98 (reprinted in Meyer Schapiro, *Modern Art: Nineteenth and Twentieth Centuries,* New York: George Braziller, 1978, pp. 185–211).

15. For an account of the relation of Marxist art criticism to abstract art in New York in the 1930s seen within a wider international context, see the article by Serge Guilbaut, cited above in note 6.

16. The lecture was first published in *Arts Yearbook,* no. 4, (1961): 101–108. The lecture series, *The Voice of America Forum Lectures: The Visual Arts,* United States Information Agency, Washington, D.C., appeared four years later in 1965.

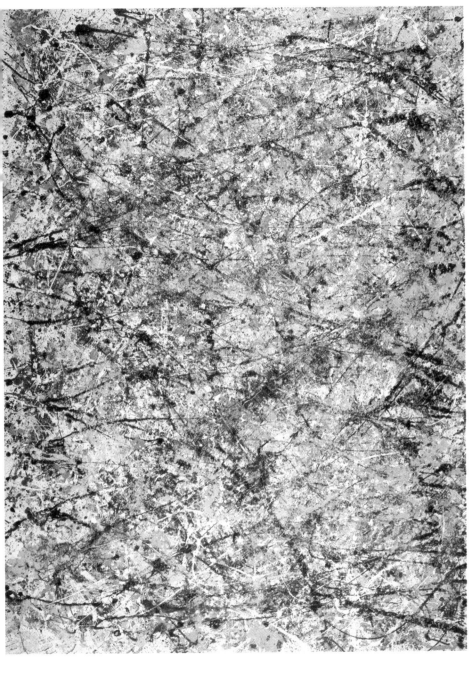

FIGURE 1. Pollack, Jackson, American, 1912–1956. Number 1, 1950, *Lavender Mist*. Oil, enamel, and aluminum on canvas. National Gallery of Art, Washington

FIGURE 2. Rothko, Mark, American, 1903–1970. Untitled (Rothko number 5068.49), 1949. Oil on canvas. 81 × 66 inches. National Gallery of Art, Washington

picture plane . . . must permit optical illusion . . . a strictly pictorial, strictly optical third dimension [not an illusion of space to imagine walking into] but the analogous illusion . . . can only be seen into . . . traveled through . . . only with the eye." With respect to earlier painting, Greenberg cites precedents from the Old Masters as well as from the nineteenth century and notes, "modernism has never meant . . . a break with the past. It may mean a devolution, an unraveling of tradition, but it also means its further evolution."

Greenberg had, much earlier, begun to formulate his interpretive scheme. In 1939, in an article on the avant-garde and kitsch, Greenberg described the relation between the avant-garde and "an elite among the ruling class," arguing that "no culture can develop without a social basis, without a source of stable income." [17] A second new, cultural phenomenon, kitsch, comprised of "popular, commercial art and literature . . . ersatz culture, destined for those who, insensible to the values of a genuine culture, are hungry nevertheless for the diversion that only culture of some sort can provide," Greenberg locates the advent of kitsch as "a product of the industrial revolution which urbanized the masses of Western Europe and America and established what is called universal literacy." He observes further that kitsch "has become the official tendency of culture in Germany, Italy and Russia . . . because kitsch is the culture of the masses in those countries as it is everywhere else." With this article Greenberg invigorated the notion of an avant-garde and provided it with an elevated artistic mission—that of countering kitsch which had become a cultural force in the United States and, in the totalitarian states, a virtual government cultural policy. Greenberg proposed that artists have produced an "avant-garde culture. A superior consciousness of history."

The next year, 1940, in a narrative account of the development of Modernism, Greenberg further defined the task of the new avant-garde as "to perform in opposition to bourgeois society the function of finding new and adequate cultural forms for the expression of that same society, without . . .

---

17. Clement Greenberg, "Avant-Garde and Kitsch," *Partisan Review* 6, no.5 (1939): 34–39. Reprinted in Clement Greenberg, *Art and Culture. Critical Essays,* Boston: Beacon Press, 1961, pp. 3–21, and also reprinted in Francis Frascina, ed., *Pollock and After: the Critical Debate,* New York: Harper and Row, 1985, pp. 21–23. The quotation is found in *Art and Culture* on page 6.

succumbing to its ideological divisions and its refusal to permit the arts to be their own justification." [18]

By 1948 Greenberg was able to state "the conclusion forces itself, much to our own surprise, that the main premises of Western art have at last migrated to the United States, along with the center of gravity of industrial production and political power." [19]

Almost twenty years later, in 1967, his continued eminence as an art critic led him to declare, in a piece about the complaints of a critic, that aesthetic judgments are "immediate, intuitive, indeliberate, and involuntary [with] no room for the conscious application of standards, rules, and precepts." For Greenberg criticism can be classed as objective only when it produces a consensus: a consensus based on a qualitative principle or norm in subliminal operation and which appears in the several verdicts of "those who care most about art and pay it the most close attention." [20] With the publication of his collected essays and reviews in 1961, *Art and Culture,* Greenberg's status as the pre-eminent critic of Abstract Expressionism and Modernism was unquestioned.

Barbara M. Reise in 1968 argued that Greenberg had written an article in 1962 entitled "After Abstract Expressionism," in which he revealed an acceptance of the historical evolution of forms that followed a predetermined course. [21] Greenberg in 1962 could no longer agree with Greenberg in 1940

---

18. Clement Greenberg, "Towards a Newer Laocoön," *Partisan Review* 7, no. 4 (1940): 296–310. (Reprinted in Francis Frascina, ed., *Pollock and After: the Critical Debate,* New York: Harper and Row, 1985, pp 35–46).

19. Clement Greenberg, "The Decline of Cubism," *Partisan Review,* March 1948. (Reprinted in Charles Harrison and Fred Orton, *Modernism, Criticism, Realism,* London and New York: Harper and Row, 1984).

20. Clement Greenberg, "Problems in Criticism II: Complaints of a Critic," *Art Forum,* (October 1967): 38–39. (Reprinted in Charles Harrison and Fred Orton, *Modernism, Criticism, Realism,* London and New York: Harper and Row, 1984, pp. 3–8).

21. Barbara M. Reise, "Greenberg and the Group: A Retrospective View," *Studio International,* 175, no. 901 (May 1968): 254–257 (part 1), 175, no. 902 (June 1968): 314–316 (part 2). Reprinted in Francis Frascina and Jonathan Harris, eds., *Art in Modern Culture: an anthology of critical texts,* London: Phaidon Press Ltd., 1992. Clement Greenberg, "After Abstract Expressionism," *Art International* 25 (October 1962): 24–32. (Reprinted in Henry Geldzahler, ed., *New York Painting and Sculpture: 1940–1970,* New York: E.P. Dutton and Co., 1969, pp. 360–371).

that "it is quite easy to show that abstract art like every other cultural phenomenon reflects the social and other circumstances of the age in which its creators live, and that there is nothing inside art itself, disconnected from history, which compels it to go in one direction or another,"—a commitment to a social history of art.[22]

Though Greenberg had developed a group of followers who supported his conceptions of Modernism, he had also, by the mid-to-late 1960s generated an array of critics of his aesthetic developmental dogma. It was at this juncture that the advocates of the new art history entered the scene. The museum has provided a vibrant theater for the subsequent engagement.

3

Two of the modes of presentation of works of art in a museum (chronological arrangements and the agglomeration of period artifacts) have been thought to have their origins in Paris after the French Revolution, as the existence of a lost historical past came to be appreciated.[23] Works of sculpture and fragments of architecture were deployed chronologically by Richard Lenoir as he sought in 1795 to salvage objects for public instruction in the Musée des Monuments Français. The second mode, the display of associated artifactual remains of all types and media, paintings, tapestries, tableware, kitchen utensils and toiletries, all from coherent periods or moments, was realized when Alexandre du Sommerard opened the Musée de Cluny in 1834 with its wide variety of Medieval and Romanesque objects.

These modes of display in museums have given rise to, on the one hand, curatorial departments and chronological displays by media—painting, sculpture, decorative arts—and by geographical and national schools. On

---

22. Texts are found in Greenberg, op. cit, note 21 and Greenberg, op. cit, note 18.

23. For an account of the formation of the Musée des Monuments Français by Lenoir and the Musée de Cluny by Sommerard (1834), see Stephen Bann, *The Clothing of Clio: A Study of the Representation of History in Nineteenth Century Britain and France,* Cambridge: Cambridge University Press, 1984, pp. 77–92; Francis Haskell, *History and its Images: Art and the Interpretation of the Past,* New Haven: Yale University Press, 1993, pp. 237–252; and Stephen Bann, "Art History and Museums," in Mark A. Cheetham, Michael Ann Holly and Keith Moxey, *The Subjects of Art History,* Cambridge/New York/Melbourne: Cambridge University Press, 1998, pp. 230–249.

the other hand, the same museums may well have specific period rooms with a plethora of objects (usually of high quality) of mixed media, as for example the program of period rooms for the Philadelphia Museum of Art planned by the director Fiske Kimball in the late 1920s.[24] We all have come to know the attraction of house museums.

Interest by the public in temporary exhibitions in the last half of the century has played an increasing role in the public programs of museums. In these years a significant number of exhibitions in major museums have been devoted to works that earlier in the century would have remained the responsibility of museums of ethnography, anthropology, or history.[25] This

---

24. See Lauren Weiss Bricker, "The Writings of Fiske Kimball: A Synthesis of Architectural History and Practice," in Elizabeth B. MacDougall, ed., *The Architectural Historian in America,* Studies in the History of Art 35, Washington, D.C.: National Gallery of Art, 1990, pp. 215–235, esp. 225–227.

25. A few of the more recent exhibitions of other than Western art include the following: Douglas Newton, *Art Styles of the Papuan Gulf,* New York, Museum of Primitive Art; distributed by University Publishers, 1961; *Treasures of Peruvian Gold. An exhibition sponsored by the Government of Peru. National Gallery of Art, Washington; Dallas Museum of Fine Arts, Dallas; Cleveland Museum of Art, Cleveland; Gallery of Modern Art, New York; Seattle Art Museum, Seattle; William Rockhill Nelson Gallery of Art, Kansas City, 1965–1966,* Washington, D.C,: H.K. Press, 1966; Peter Gathercole, Adrienne L. Kaeppler, and D. Newton, *The Art of the Pacific Islands,* Washington, D.C.: National Gallery of Art, 1979; Suzanne Abel-Vidor, *Between Continents/Between Seas: Precolumbian Art of Costa Rica,* New York: H.N. Abrams; Detroit: Detroit Institute of Arts, 1981; Robert Farris Thompson and Joseph Cornet, *The Four Moments of the Sun: Kongo Art in Two Worlds,* Washington, D.C.: National Gallery of Art, 1981; Henry B. Nicholson and Eloise Quiñones Keber, *Art of Aztec Mexico: treasures of Tenochtitlan,* Washington, D.C.: National Gallery of Art, 1983; William Rubin, *"Primitivism" in Twentieth Century Art: Affinity of the Tribal and the Modern,* New York: Museum of Modern Art, 1984; Roy Sieber and Roslyn Adele Walker, *African Art in the Cycle of Life,* Washington D.C.: Published for the National Museum of African Art by the Smithsonian Press, 1987; D. Newton, *The Pacific Islands, Africa, and the Americas,* New York: Metropolitan Museum of Art, 1989; Richard B. Woodward, *African Art: Virginia Museum of Fine Arts,* Richmond, VA: The Museum, 1994; Elizabeth P. Benson and Beatriz de la Fuente, *Olmec Art of Ancient Mexico,* Washington, D.C.: National Gallery of Art; New York: Distributed by H. N. Adams, 1996; J. Weldon Smith, *Forms and Forces: Dynamics of African Figurative Sculpture,* San Francisco: Fine Arts Museums of San Francisco, 1998; Tim Barringer and Tom Flynn, *Colonialism and the Object: empire, material culture, and the museum,* London and New York: Routledge, 1998; Richard F. Townsend, *Ancient West Mexico: Art and Archaeology of the Unknown Past,* Chicago: The Art Institute of Chicago, 1998.

phenomenon has been accompanied by the appointment in departments of history of art and architecture of specialists in other than Western art including prehistory, pre-Columbian, African, and Oceanic art as well as Islamic, West, South and East Asian art. Some smaller museums with global aspirations now have only two curatorial departments—eastern and western hemispheres. Photography, film, and the history of landscape have since mid-century also come under the purview of both the museum and university.

Public education programs, after early starts in North America and the United Kingdom, have received increased attention in European and other museums. As the research interests of the curator on objects and the academic art historian in theory have diverged, new programs have been devised to challenge the separateness of the two.

The desire to meet the requirements of a diverse public has led, for example, in one British museum to the planning of each exhibition by a three-person team—curator, education specialist, and academic art historian.[26] Many visitors to these exhibitions have been stimulated by unexpected and revealing juxtapositions of works that disclose unanticipated relationships. Other visitors, however, have deplored a consequent dilution of the captivating force of great works of art.

Some museums have recently chosen to exhibit portions of their collections by period without regard to nations or schools. Works from late medieval and early renaissance from both northern and southern Europe may be shown together as, for example, in the new Sainsbury wing at the National Gallery in London.

The hanging of works that customary curatorial concern would deem inappropriate, though not a new phenomena, is by its increasing frequency invigorating the museum environment. Almost a century-and-a-half ago when the English painter Turner made his bequest of paintings to the National Gallery, London, he specified that two of his paintings, *Sun Rising through Vapour* . . . (Fig. 3) and *Dido Building Carthage* (Fig. 4), should be hung adjacent to two paintings executed two centuries earlier by the French

---

26. The observation was made by Stephen Deuchar (Tate Gallery of British Art, London) about the policy of the Tate Gallery, Liverpool, during a presentation at a conference at the Clark Art Institute on 9 April 1999 (see below, note 29).

FIGURE 3. Turner, Joseph Mallord William, 1775–1851. *Sun rising through Vapour, Fishermen cleaning and selling Fish.* Oil on canvas. National Gallery, London.

FIGURE 4. Turner, Joseph Mallord William, 1775–1851. *Dido building Carthage, or The Rise of the Carthaginian Empire.* Oil on canvas. 155.6 × 231.8 cm. National Gallery, London.

seventeenth-century painter Claude Le Lorrain, *Landscape with the Marriage of Isaac and Rebecca* (Fig. 5) and *Seaport with the Embarkation of the Queen of Sheba* (Fig. 6).[27]

Needless to say, this juxtaposition invites us to ponder what Turner saw when he studied the two Claudes after they came into the collections of the Gallery in 1824, and to speculate on the extent of his assimilation of the issues Claude addressed in these paintings. But the juxtaposition also suggests there are many beguiling ways to assemble the works in a collection. Museums in Paris, Rotterdam, Madrid, New York and London, among others, have done so in the past decade by inviting notables from outside the museum environment to propose a theme for an exhibition utilizing works from the museum's own collections.

The Louvre, for example, has sponsored four exhibitions in this decade, the first by Jacques Derrida in 1990 entitled *Memories of a Blind Man;* the second by the British filmmaker Peter Greenaway, in 1992, called *The Noise of Clouds=Flying out of this world;* a third by Jean Starobinski, in 1994, titled *Largesse;* and a fourth by Hubert Damisch in 1995 devoted to the *Treatise of the Trace.*[28] These imaginative and idiosyncratic assembling of objects with suggestive and sometimes fanciful texts, labels, and catalogues attracted and stimulated visitors while offering provocative and illuminating observations

---

27. J.M.W. Turner (1775–1851), *Sun Rising Through Vapour: Fishermen Cleaning and Selling Fish* (most likely exhibited at Royal Academy, 1807), oil on canvas, NG 479, Turner Bequest 1856; J.M.W. Turner (1775–1851), *Dido Building Carthage, or the Rise of the Carthaginian Empire,* 1815, NG 498, Turner Bequest 1856; Claude Gellée (Le Lorrain), *Seaport with the Embarkation of the Queen of Sheba,* signed and dated 1648, oil on canvas, NG 14, Bought 1824; Claude Gellée (Le Lorrain), *Landscape with the Marriage of Isaac and Rebekah,* signed and dated 1648, oil on canvas, Insc: MARI[AGE] / DISAC / AVEC / REBECA, NG 12, Bought 1824.

Stephen Bann, 1998, note 23, cites the Turner bequest as an example of innovative presentation of paintings by the National Gallery in the middle of the nineteenth century.

28. Jacques Derrida, *Mémoires d'aveugle: l'autoportrait et autres ruines,* Paris: Éditions de la Réunion des musées nationaux, 1990; Peter Greenaway, *Le bruit des nuages = flying out of this world,* Paris: Réunion des musées nationaux, 1992; Jean Starobinski, *Largesse,* Paris: Réunion des musées nationaux, 1994; Hubert Damisch, *Traité du trait: Tractatus tractus,* Paris: Réunion des musées nationaux: Diffusion, Seuil, 1995; Peter Greenaway, *Flying over water = volar damunt l'aigua,* London: M. Holberton; Barcelona: Fundació Joan Miró, 1997; Jonathan Miller, *On Reflection,* London: National Gallery Publications; New Haven, Conn: Distributed by Yale University Press, 1998.

FIGURE 5. Claude, 1604/5?–1682. *Landscape with the Marriage of Isaac and Rebekah* ('The Mill').
Oil (identified) on canvas. 149.2 × 196.9 cm. National Gallery, London.

Figure 6. Claude, 1604/5?–1682. *Seaport with the Embarkation of the Queen of Sheba.*
Oil (identified) on canvas. 148.6 × 193.7 cm. National Gallery, London.

about relationships seen by these individuals between works of art that normally remain in separate worlds.

In April, a conference at the Clark Art Institute in Williamstown addressed the Two Art Histories, intending thereby art history as practiced in museums and universities.[29] While uncovering large areas of mutual concern, the gathering also revealed divergences that centered on exhibition practices. Many curators, though not all, in planning exhibitions, resisted the introduction of objects that might inhibit an "unmediated encounter" between a painting—a work of art—and a viewer.

Most academic art historians, on the other hand, felt that both a greater understanding of issues addressed by the work and an appreciation and enjoyment of a painting would follow from a planned accompanying presentation of the cultural and historical milieu within which the work was produced. The professors argued that seeing a work of art is more an acquired or learned practice than an aesthetic experience.

From among the academics occasionally involved in exhibition planning, came John House from the faculty of the Courtauld Institute in London. He prepared an exhibition in 1995 entitled *Landscapes of France: Impressionism and its Rivals* for the Hayward Gallery in London that paired modernist and academic paintings executed at the same times.[30] In contrast to the curators who wished to insure the possibility of a transcendental aesthetic experience by a viewer, House felt compelled at the gathering to declare categorically "no work of art can speak for itself." In preparing the exhibition House believed it essential in understanding the revolutionary importance of modernist painting to see it together with the academic painting of the same moment.[31]

---

29. "The Two Art Histories: The Museum and the University," a conference organized by Charles Haxthausen and John Onians and held at the Sterling and Francine Clark Art Institute in Williamstown, Massachusetts, on 9–10 April 1999, was intended to gather both curatorial and academic art historians to discuss exhibition practice from their diverse perspectives.

30. John House, ed., *Landscapes of France: Impressionism and its Rivals,* exhibition at the Hayward Gallery, London, and the Boston Museum of Fine Arts in 1995.

31. John House's polemical assertion made during the final session's panel discussion followed upon several statements by curators present that they desired a largely unmediated encounter between the viewing public and the work of art. The free engagement of

As the century draws to a close, these and many other competing views, including the current flow of race, gender, and ethnicity studies of the past several decades permeate the history of art as well as other disciplines in the humanities and social sciences. Not surprisingly, there are a diversity of views as to what constitutes a work of art, and, in some instances, even uncertainty that works of art exist: a range of views as to what might be a theory of art after the demise of idealism in a post-Hegelian world; competing views concerning the nature of an aesthetic response; divergent opinions about what constitutes verifiable assertions about a theory or of a history of art; when interpreting a work of art, contrasting views about the priority to accord different social practices; differing views of the existence of historical moments or periods and how to position objects within them; divergent opinions of the place of the artist in a societal structure; as well as uncertainty as to the role of what we have come to identify as art objects in a given society at a given time.

The abundance of competitive assertions claiming epistemological certainty suggest that although the discipline has covered considerable philosophical and empirical ground in the last century and possesses a developed awareness of the contingency of much of its acquired knowledge, art history remains a field of competing interests both within and outside the field, from the empirically based to the theoretically charged, a discipline in which politics, too, continues to raise polemical issues.[32]

---

viewer and painting was thought by some curators to facilitate the enjoyment of the work as painting and the delight of an experience generated by an aesthetic response.

32. For example: *History of Art:* W. McAllister Johnson, *Art History: Its Use and Abuse,* Toronto: University of Toronto Press, 1988; Norman Bryson, ed., *Calligram: Essays in New Art History From France,* Cambridge and New York: Cambridge University Press, 1988; Donald Preziosi, *Rethinking Art History: Meditations on a Coy Science,* New Haven: Yale University Press, 1989; Martin Warnke, *The Court Artist: On the Ancestry of the Modern Artist* (trans. by David McLintock), Cambridge and New York: Cambridge University Press, 1993; Craig Hugh Smyth and Peter M. Lukehart, eds., *The Early Years of Art History in the United States: Notes and Essays on Departments, Teaching and Scholars,* Princeton: Department of Art and Archaeology, Princeton University, 1993; Alex Potts, *Flesh and the Ideal: Winckelmann and the Origins of Art History,* New Haven: Yale University Press, 1994; Claire Farago, ed., *Reframing the Renaissance: Visual Culture in Europe and Latin America, 1450–1650,* New Haven: Yale University Press, 1995; Michael Ann Holly, *Past Looking: Historical Imagination and the Rhetoric of the Image,* Ithaca: Cornell University Press, 1996; Mark A. Cheetham, Michael Ann

Holly and Keith Moxey, eds., *The Subjects of Art History: Historical Objects in Contemporary Perspectives,* Cambridge and New York: Cambridge University Press, 1998; D. Preziosi, *The Art of Art History: A Critical Anthology,* Oxford and New York: Oxford University Press, 1998.

Art and Culture: Hans Belting, *The End of the History of Art?* (trans. by Christopher S. Wood from the German edition of 1985), Chicago: University of Chicago Press, 1987; James Clifford, *The Predicament of Culture,* Cambridge, Mass: Harvard University Press, 1988; Michael Carter, *Framing Art: Introducing Theory and the Visual Image,* Sydney, NSW: Hale and Iremonger, 1990; O. K. Werckmeister, *Citadel Culture* (trans. from the German), Chicago: University of Chicago Press, 1991; Carol Duncan, *The Aesthetics of Power: Essays in Critical Art History,* Cambridge and New York: Cambridge University Press, 1993; Martin Warnke, *Political Landscape: the Art History of Nature,* London: Reaktion Books, 1994; Chris Jenks, ed., *Visual Culture,* London and New York: Routledge, 1995; Hans Belting, *Das Ende der Kunstgeschichte: eine Revision nach zehn Jahren,* München: C.H. Beck, 1995;

Museums and Exhibitions: Ivan Karp and Steven D. Lavine, eds., *Exhibiting Cultures: the Poetics and Politics of Museum Display,* Washington, D.C.: Smithsonian Institution Press, 1991; I. Karp, Christine Mullen Kreamer, and S. D. Lavine, *Museums and Communities: the Politics of Public Culture,* Washington, D.C.: Smithsonian Institution Press, 1992; Carol Duncan, *Civilizing Rituals: Inside Public Art Museums,* London and New York: Routledge, 1995; Donald Preziosi, "In the Temple of Entelechy: The Museum as Evidentiary Artifact," *Studies in the History of Art* 47 (1996): 165–171; Amy Henderson and Adrienne L. Kaeppler, eds., *Exhibiting Dilemmas: Issues of Representation at the Smithsonian,* Washington, D.C.: Smithsonian Institution Press, 1997; Sarah Hyde, *Exhibiting Gender,* Manchester and New York: Manchester University Press; New York: distributed exclusively in the USA by St. Martin's Press, 1997.

For discussion of the museum and its responsibilities to the public from the 1970s and 1980s, see: Charles Parkhurst, "Art Museum: Kinds, Organization, Procedures, and Financing," in S. E. Lee, ed., *On Understanding Art Museums,* Englewood Cliffs, N.J.: Prentice-Hall, 1975, pp. 68–97; Ernst H. Gombrich, "The Museum: Past, Present and Future," *Critical Inquiry* 3 (1977): 449–470; John Pope-Hennessy, "The International Heritage," in Direzione Relazioni Culturali . . . Olivetti, ed., *The Preservation and Use of Artistic Cultural Heritage: Perspectives and Solutions,* New York: Metropolitan Museum, 1980, pp. 164–176; Carlo Bertelli, "Il museo domani," in Direzione Relazioni Culturali . . . Olivetti, ed., *The Preservation and Use of Artistic Cultural Heritage: Perspectives and Solutions,* New York: Metropolitan Museum, 1980, pp. 154–163; Craig H. Smyth, "Gli Uffizi ei Problemi dei grandi musee," in Paola Barocchi and Giovanna Ragionieri, eds., *Gli Uffizi: Quattro Secoli di una Galleria,* Atti del Convegno Internazionale di Studi (Florence, 20–24 September 1982), Florence: Leo S. Olschki, 1983, pp. 545–556.

For the museum as art, see: Arthur C. Danto, Review of Douglas Davis, *The Museum Transformed: Design and Culture in the Post-Pompidou Age,* New York: Abbeville, 1990 in *The Print Collector's Newsletter,* vol. 22, no. 5 (November/December 1991):183–185; Claus Kapplinger, "Architecture and the Marketing of the Museum," *Museum International* (October/December 1997): 6–9; Clare Melhuish, "The Museum as a Mirror of Society," *Architectural Design* (November/December 1997): 22–25; Victoria Newhouse, *Towards a New Museum,* New York: Monacelli, 1998; Ada Louise Huxtable, "Museums: Making it New," (review of Victoria Newhouse, *Towards a New Museum,* New York: Monacelli, 1998), *The New York Review of Books,* 22 April 1999 (vol. XLVI, no. 7), 10–15.

DISCUSSANT

DAVID FREEDBERG

IN HIS BRIEF and illuminating survey, Professor Millon accurately high-lighted the main aspects of the development of art history since the last World War. He also identified 1968 as a major turning point in art history, just as it was in the case of other humanist disciplines. Anyone who has fol-lowed the course of the humanities in the last thirty years will recognize some of the symptoms Professor Millon described: the desire for greater rel-evance to the world at large, and the belief that the academic disciplines are or ought to be capable of more or less trenchant social critique. Growing out of these positions came the sense that works of art ought not to be studied in isolation from their social context, as well as the belief that the kinds of formal criticism exemplified by the work of Clement Greenberg—brilliantly set out by Professor Millon—should be superseded by much closer atten-tion to the context in which works of art were produced. The rapid devel-opment of the study of the social construction of responses to art fitted well with the doubts cast upon the role of the author and of authorial intention by the poststructuralists and deconstructionists. The so-called "new art his-tory" exemplified such developments. Similar developments took place in other fields. In the study of both literature and music uncertainty grew about what exactly art was or was supposed to be. This led to a general insistence on the relativity of taste (though this is hardly new: there is a long tradition in art history emphasizing that taste is subjective, cyclical, periodic, de-pendent on factors that are in no way absolute). No wonder, then, that the idea of the canon became subject to severe critique. For many years we in the universities, and those of us engaged in art criticism, have had to deal with the questioning of the traditional canon. The remark that "no work of art can speak for itself" made by my English colleague John House (and cited by Professor Millon) fits right into this. Of course, the matter is not quite so simple, but it perfectly exemplifies one of the most commonplace attitudes in the humanities right now. It is endemic to the study of art, lit-erature and music in the universities. This is not the place to pass final judg-ment on such positions, though in their strongest that is, their most simplistic forms, it is hard not to lament them. They take the humanity out of the humanities. Some of the most fashionable postmodernists might not worry about this; but I do. So much, very briefly, for the similarities with other disciplines. But how, one might ask, is the history of art and architecture different from other forms of cultural history? Is there anything distinctive about it? What are the basic and essential differences as well as the accidental ones between the artistic image itself (or the building itself), and other cultural artifacts? Too often art historians forget that the good part of their task ought to be concerned with this problem specifically. But the difficulty is the following. Many semioticians, many followers of Saussure and of Pierce, have tended to conflate all cultural signs, to read them as somehow similar by nature. And this against all the implicit and explicit admonitions of the founders themselves! Such conflators often seem to regard all signs, whether verbal or visual, as theoretically identical. They insist, for example, on the arbitrary relation of the signifier to the signified as if some visual signs could never be less arbitrary than others! The consequences of so gross a theoretical conflation have not been entirely salutary. In the last few years, art historians have neglected what seems to be the fundamental issue of the differences between visual and verbal signs. What is it about the image, in the first instance, that art historians can best illuminate? What is about the work of visual art they have the particular and peculiar capacities to analyze? We have been too ready to forget what we have been best trained to do. Here I want to mention the name of the one figure who seems to have escaped Professor Millon's fine attention to the developments of the last fifty years or so. Almost more than any other, Professor Sir Ernst Gombrich has contributed to the understanding of what makes art history a distinctive discipline. He has done so by unremitting exploration of what it is about images that is different from other signs. I have long been struck by the fact that his pioneering work on how artists produce their images, how art makers stand in relation to the tradition of image-making, and how we as beholders perceive such images (work most famously represented by *Art and Illusion,* first published in 1960) has never really been taken up by art historians. Everyone recognized the importance of Gombrich's study of the nature and perception of artistic images; but almost no one took up the gauntlet. Yet it was precisely Gombrich who made clear what it was about the history of art that art historians could distinctively claim for themselves. Af-

ter all, the social history of art can just as well be practised by general historians and historians of culture and society as by historians of art. I would
claim that in recent years art historians have renounced what they are best
trained to do indeed, what they have most experience with in favor of projects that could just as well be undertaken by others. The time has come to
redefine the special and distinctive projects of art history. In his talk, Professor Elliott alluded to an issue briefly dealt with by Professor Millon: cultural dissemination in an age of globalization. Art historians ought to be ac-
tively engaged in the various ways in which culture is disseminated; and yet
the dialogue between them and between museum officials generally trained
as art historians themselves has become much thinner, if not strained, in recent years. The point of tension has been "theory": that is, the inclination of
academic art historians to theorize their work in terms of the kinds of
developments in other fields of the humanities which Professor Millon described of at the beginning of his talk. Curators in museums view most post-
modern theoretical developments (as well as more socially oriented approaches such as feminism and postcolonialism) with suspicion at the very
time that such developments and approaches have reached the apogee of
their fashion within the universities. The same applies to what passes as critical theory and cultural criticism. Dismayingly to those who still practice a
clearly defined art history, the general view in museums is that art historians in general do too much theory; while the view in the academy is that
museums are still insufficiently theorized, so to speak. This, it seems to me,
is an unnecessary tension. I would hope for some form of resolution and
reconciliation in the new millennium; but it is not yet clear what might
emerge. As I reflect on Professor Millon's talk—indeed on the situation in
the humanities in general—I realize that one further issue might be brought
to the fore. We tend to shy away from it. It has, in the broadest sense, to do
with globalization. Ironically enough, national styles within disciplines have
lately tended not to fuse or to wither away, but to become solidified. This is
the opposite of what one might have expected, prima facie. But the fact is
that by and large—and I speak very much grosso modo—the British practice a much narrower version of the social history of art than most Americans (the notion that no work of art can speak for itself still has many more
followers here than there); the French do a much narrower, object-oriented

kind of art history than one might expect in a country that produced figures such as Foucault and Derrida; while the Germans tend, on the whole, to produce rigorous, archivally based documentary research. I emphasize that I speak broadly here; but there can be question of the largely monolithic nature of national intellectual styles in art history, styles that are often at odds with those across geographical boundaries. This, it seems to me, presents a very different picture from that in the natural sciences, where to judge from the talks we have heard in these past two days there remains a certain unanimity about what can and cannot be achieved in science, and what the justifiable aims and limits might or might not be. Such is decidedly not the case with the humanities in general, and with art history in particular. It is a problem with which we will continue to grapple as the new millennium begins.

More than One Millennium: The Perennial Return of the History of Religions

ON THE STATE OF THE HISTORY OF RELIGION AND ITS RELATIONSHIP TO OTHER DISCIPLINES[*]

WENDY DONIGER

Professor of the History of Religion, University of Chicago

COMPARISON HAS always been at the heart of the history of religions. Historians of religions are themselves creatures of comparison, created, like mules, by intellectual hybrid breeding, a cross between, say, a Sanskritist and an anthropologist (I leave the reader to decide which is the horse, which the donkey), or a theologian and an African historian; they do not usually breed directly from mule to mule, one historian of religions cloning another. The modern comparative study of religion was in large part designed in the pious hope of teaching our own people that "alien" religions were like "ours" in many ways. The hope was that, if we learned about other religions, we would no longer hate and kill their followers; that "to know them is to love them." A glance at any newspaper should tell us that this goal has yet to be fulfilled in the world at large. But it fueled our discipline throughout the twentieth century, in a series of encounters ranging from the most basic sorts of dialogue (the "take a Buddhist to dinner" school) to the most ambitious universalist theorizing in the hands of scholars such as Freud, Jung, and Eliade.

At the turn of the millennium, however, the academic world, having gone beyond both of these simplistic paradigms (the dialogic and the universalist), is in danger of abandoning comparison altogether as an academic discipline, and I think this would be a terrible shame. The field of history of

---

[*] Read 23 April 1999.

religions now suffers from a post post-colonial backlash. In this age of multi-nationalism and the politics of individual ethnic and religious groups, of identity politics and minority politics, to assume that two phenomena from different cultures are "the same" in any significant way is regarded as de-meaning to the individualism of each, a reflection of the old racist attitude that "all wogs look alike." And this is due in large part to the fallout from the anti-Orientalist critique, which taught us that the British scholars who founded our disciplines had been caught up in the colonial enterprise, sus-tained it, fueled it, facilitated it. It taught us about the collusion between academic knowledge and political power, arguing that we, too, are impli-cated in that sin when we carry on the work of those disciplines.

We can no longer think without the post-colonial critique. But anti-Orientalism has led in many quarters to two different sorts of problems: on the one hand, a disregard for the philology and basic textual work that the Orientalists did very well and that still remains the basis of sound scholar-ship about cultures other than our own; and, on the other hand, a disincli-nation to compare one culture with another. Let me consider them one by one. The original anti-Orientalist-agenda was monolithic in ways that soon came to be modified, by Edward Said himself among others, and by James Scott. We have learned to see not just oppressors and victims, but oppres-sors and resisters, subverters, people who knew how to wield the weapons of the weak. Now, perhaps, it is time to reconsider the work of scholars who, though tarred by the brush of imperialism, nevertheless left us texts without which we could not do our work. (How many of the subaltern stud-ies people, I wonder, are willing to throw away the basic Sanskrit dictionary compiled by Sir Monier Monier-Williams?) . Obsessed with the nineteenth century, the post-colonial critique has forced us to look through monolithic, and hence skewed, spectacles that prevent us from seeing anything but our previous spectacles, the ones bequeathed to us by British Orientalism. It is time to stop merely looking at those flawed lenses and to try to see through them, that is, beyond them and also by means of them, this time correcting for the Orientalist distortion, to go back to them with what the philosopher Paul Ricoeur called a "second naivete": an innocence that has traveled through loss of innocence to an apparently unchanged but actually quite dif-ferent sort of innocence. There is much in the colonial scholarship on India

that is worth keeping. I am unwilling to throw out the baby with the bath—
a judgment call that depends on how good you think the baby is.

As for comparison, historians of religions have, by and large, abandoned
universalist comparative studies of the sort that Mircea Eliade once made so
popular, as had the triumvirate of Frazer, Freud, and Jung before him. Many
people think that it cannot be done at all, while others think that it should
not be done at all. Moreover, in the present climate of anti-Orientalism, it is
regarded as imperialist of a scholar who studies India, for instance, to stand
outside (presumably, above) phenomena from different cultures and to
equate them. Merely by emphasizing their commonalities, we are impli-
cated in what Rolena Adorno has called "the process of fixing 'otherness' by
grasping onto similarities." Other evil effects of simplistic comparison have
already taken their toll in some of the social sciences today (particularly political science and economics), where dominant theories like that of "rational choice," supposedly the same for everyone, have driven out the more
particularized disciplines of area studies. Psychologists, too, have until quite
recently too often assumed a universal biological, cognitive, and affective
base for human behavior, neglecting cultural factors.

But we must beware of leaping from the frying pan of universalism into
the fire of another sort of essentialism that can result from contextualizing
a myth in one cultural group. In this Kali Yuga of cultural essentialism, we
must search for something which is essential but not essentialist. And by essentialism I mean hypotheses about the unity of a group that a scholar holds
onto even when they have destructive results, like a monkey who traps himself by refusing to let go of a banana in his fist inside a cage whose opening
is big enough for his fist but not for the banana. I mean a priori prejudices
(and, as I have argued, any scholarly hypothesis must begin with something
like such a prejudice) which are not dropped or modified when members of
the target groups turn out to be different from what was expected. I want
to say to all the reductionists I know: "Let go of the banana."

The emphasis on individual cultures, when reduced to the absurd (as it
too often is), may lead to problems of infinite regress, first in the ever broadening comparisons of contexts and, ultimately, in the ever narrowing contexts themselves. This emphasis tends to generate a smaller and smaller focus until it is impossible to generalize even from one moment to the next:

nothing has enough in common with anything else to be compared with it even for the purpose of illuminating its distinctiveness; each event is unique. The radical particularizing of much recent theory in cultural anthropology, for instance, seems to deny any shared base to members of the same culture, much less to humanity as a whole. But any discussion of difference must begin from an assumption of sameness; if we start with the assumption of absolute difference there can be no conversation, and we find ourselves trapped in the self reflexive garden of a Looking Glass ghetto, forever meeting ourselves walking back in through the cultural door through which we were trying to escape.

Similarity and difference are not equal, not comparable; they have different uses. We look to similarity for stability, to build political bridges, to anchor our own society, while we spin narratives to deal with our uneasiness at the threat of difference. Either similarity or difference may lead to a form of paralyzing reductionism and demeaning essentialism, and thence into an area where "difference" itself can be politically harmful. For, where extreme universalism means that the other is exactly like you, extreme nominalism means that the other may not be human at all. Many of the people who argued (and continue to argue) that Jews or Blacks or any other group defined as "wogs" were all alike (that is, like one another) went on to argue (or, more often, to assume) that they were all different (that is, different from us white people, us Protestants), and this latter argument easily led to the assertion that such people did not deserve certain rights like the rest of us. Essentialized difference can become an instrument of dominance; European colonialism was supported by a discourse of difference. The members of a single cultural "group" may be very different and it is just as insulting to say that all Japanese are alike as to say that the Japanese are just like the French. The culturally essentialized position is, in itself, both indefensible and politically dangerous. Yet it is often assumed in "culturally contextualized" and historically specific studies: "Let me tell you how everyone felt at the fin de siècle in Europe and America." The focus on the class or ethnic group, if monolithic, can become not only boring, but racist.

My hope for the next millennium is an expansive, humanistic outlook on inquiry, one that enhances our humanity in both its peculiarity and its commonality. I am unwilling to close the comparatist shop just because it is being picketed by people whose views I happen, by and large, to share. I have become sensitized to the political issues, but I do not think that they ultimately damn the comparative enterprise. I want to salvage the broad comparative agenda, even if I acquiesce, or even participate, in the savaging of certain of its elements. I refuse to submit to what Umberto Eco has nicely termed "textual harassment."

In pursuing the multi-vocal, multi-cultural agenda, we must face the implications of the fact that we use other peoples stories for our purposes. The political problem inheres in the asymmetry of power between the appropriating culture and the appropriated. Thus, if Europe has dominated India, it is deemed wrong for a European to make use of an Indian myth. But it seems to me that there are very different ways of using other peoples's myths, some of them fairly innocuous, and that the usual alternative to appropriating a foreign text (however inadequate or exploitative or projective that appropriation may be) can be even worse: ignoring it or scorning it. Moreover, the European appropriation need not supplant the Indian version; the native voice can be heard even above the academic clamor of the foreign voice.

The gift that the post-colonial critique has given us is a heightened awareness of what we are doing, why, and the dangers involved. History of religions has also gained immeasurably by that aspect of subaltern studies which has at last made a space in which the natives speak and women's voices are resurrected. But the gift sours when the giver takes it back by excluding from the conversation the other partners who, admittedly, dominated the field for far too long: European and American scholars studying non-Western religions. We should use the post-colonial consciousness not to exclude Western scholars from the study of non-Western myths, which merely contributes to the ghettoization of the Western world of ideas, but to show how myths (and the comparative study of myths) can be used as ghetto-blasters in our own society as well as in the world at large , that is, to blast apart the ghettoes of ideology. Surely it is possible to bring into a single (if not necessarily harmonious) conversation the genuinely different approaches that several cultures have made to similar (if not the same) human problems. We must supplement the tunnel vision of identity politics with the wide screen of cross-cultural studies.

The richness and nuance of the best sort of comparison is nourished in the context of a university: a community in which a number of scholars work together on different projects in different ways. The very fact that so many people are now doing contextualized work frees the comparatist to do something else, to draw upon their work to ground new comparisons. I wish to carve out a space where, alongside the contextualizers doing their valuable work, those of us who work comparatively can do ours, too. We don't all have to do the same thing, or do it in the same way; we can stand on the shoulders of giants, or, as the case may be, pygmies, and they can stand on ours. From each, her own. My argument here is for the academy, for multi-disciplinarian, multi-cultural approaches. I would hope that the respect for "difference" (and pluralism, and diversity) which prevails in cultural studies would extend to the methodologies within the academy at large.

In order for our discipline to thrive, we must walk a tightrope between two dangers. The first is the present trend of studying only one cultural group—Jews, Blacks—or only one gender. The other is the trend of limiting those who study that group to those within the group—women studying women, Jews studying Jews—a trend which, if followed slavishly, would automatically eliminate not only my tiny, precious world of cross-cultural comparison but the more general humanism of which it is a part. This is a trend fueled, in large part, by the high moral ground assumed by disciplines, such as feminism and cultural studies, that argue, or imply, that their subject matter (racism, sexism, the class struggle, genocide) has such devastating human consequences that there is no room for error or play-fulness or the possibility of more than one answer.

But this is just one way to study the history of religions. When did scholarship cease to be a collective enterprise? When did interdisciplinary values cease to apply to comparative studies? When did the "uni" in "university" come to refer to ideology? Perhaps we should rename our institutions mul-tiversities (with overtones of multi-vocal, multivalent, multi-cultural) or Poly-versities, if not Diversities (let alone Inversities-for structuralists—and Perversities—for our academic enemies.). Whatever we call it, the academic world should never be a place where there is only one poker game in town. It should be a place where we can say, as in an ice cream parlor or hamburger joint: "Make me one with everything" (a phrase that can also be read as a pantheist prayer)

232

DISCUSSANT

HERMANN HUNGER

Universität Wien

I AM SURE you will all agree that our speaker has given us many thoughts to consider and to follow up and I'll just comment on a few of them and add a few small details. I certainly agree with your plea for really universal universities whatever the puns we may devise about them. My field is the study of ancient Near Eastern civilizations. Surely there is less danger to contribute to political injustice through scholarship by investigating such a remote past, than there is in the study of living civilizations. But let me remind you of the heated debates some years ago or maybe even now, about the question whether, as it was phrased, the Ancient Greeks stole their philosophy from Egypt. The insinuation was that this had not been noticed by Western scholars because they automatically underrated an alien civilization. In addition, it was emphasized that Egypt, as is geographically correct, is a part of Africa. In this forum the hypothesis favored present-day cultural and political dogma and it was very difficult to discuss and even more difficult to doubt it. But as Professor Doniger said, it would be a loss to throw out all the work done by other scholars just for political reasons. That some scholars had espoused political ideas that turned out to have destructive consequences does not guarantee that everything they said was wrong or was only ideology. An example from my field could be the German professor Friedrich Delitzsch who about a hundred years ago composed an Assyrian dictionary that was to be a basic tool for more than half a century, until it was replaced by a project undertaken in this country. Nobody today would share Delitzsch's anti-Jewish political views, but his dictionary was excellent.

Let me make another point about comparison in general which may seem trivial. You really have to know what you compare. Again, an illustration from my field. There is a myth about the Sumerian goddess Innana telling that she went to the netherworld and was held there temporarily. One also knew from other texts that Innana's husband, Dumuzi, was dragged to the netherworld by evil demons. All these texts were incomplete when they were first discovered. They are written on clay tablets which mostly

233

are broken when you dig them up. It was somehow natural, you will agree, to suppose that in the missing parts of the texts it would be told how Innana went down to the netherworld in order to free her poor husband. And such a story was widely compared to similar myths from other cultures. Unfortunately, when later on, the missing parts of the texts were found, it became clear that Innana had gone to the netherworld to gain control over it. She was, however, overwhelmed and detained and permitted to return to the upper world only on condition that she provide a substitute, for which role she chose her husband. Certainly comparisons of whatever kind will be different for the complete story.

Of course I do not mean by this to give advice to our speaker. She is obviously well-versed in the religions of India and maybe some of you will want to ask her questions about that field. Let me finally express admiration for Professor Doniger's wide-ranging paper, which has shown us perspectives for the history of religion and for the future of academic institutions alike.

Singularity in an Age of Globalization*

Marc Fumaroli

Professeur, Collège de France

GLOBALIZATION LIKE all those other words ending in -ism and -tion is a foul word. But the thing it stands for, under different names — evangelization, civilization, modernization, normalization — is far from new. What is brand new nowadays in this our post-Cold War era, is the scale of expectations its provokes and the rhythm of the process it commands. The global market is in sight, for the first time in history and on a worldwide scale, an almost universal network of communications makes the prospect of a homogenous interconnected public of consumers possible. On another level, a body of international and universal laws has emerged and is interpreted by emerging supranational institutions and tribunals, who set themselves up as the supreme regulators of this homogenized "new humanity." A secular arm is by way of being legitimized, outside the control of an outmoded UN, in order to enforce on a selective basis the decisions and norms of a new post-modern papal Curia whenever and wherever it encounters resistance (neither China, nor Russia or Turkey, one notes, are on the agenda).

The communicative enthusiasm which this new perspective and its incipient actualization nurtures among its innumerable tubthumping preachers, is not in itself new. Let us now take a brief look back at an earlier, infinitely less sophisticated stage in the story. One of the major arguments used by sixteenth-century Western Catholics ("Catholicism" means "universalization of the true Roman faith") to establish their superiority over the ancient pagans once and for all, was the discovery and conquest of the New World by Catholic Spain and Portugal.

---

*Read 23 April 1999.

It took a Montaigne with his *Essais* to resist this euphoria: the bloody "evangelization" of native Brazil by European Christianity was, he wrote, just as barbarous as the reciprocal warlike "evangelization" of French Catholics and Protestants in the French Wars of Religion. He also asserted that, by comparison, the ways of the Greek and Roman conquerors were far less exacting. Three centuries and a half later, Levi-Strauss with *Tristes Tropiques,* the mature fruit of his ethnological investigations in Brazil before World War II, would give us a contemporary version of Montaigne's black irony and scepticism about Western progress.

Both thinkers, at different stages in the universalizing process, became cognizant of the price which modern globalization exacted through what I should like to call the exercise of singularity. Both writers freed themselves from the triumphalist idols of their own tribe and from the human sacrifices those idols demanded in the name of universality. But the archetype of this sort of critical and ironical exercise can be traced back to Plato's myth of the Cavern. Plato's philosopher turned his back on his fellow citizens sitting enthralled by the images projected on their screen. He walked out of the cave, alone, and discovered the real world under a real sun. When he reported back on what he had seen, his discovery was greeted with less than enthusiastic acclaim.

The drive towards an at least partial "globalization" of a proponent language, and the kind of universal norms it supposedly embodies and propagates, is therefore observable in several stages of the history of the West. This universalist trend has been ignored in ancient China, Japan and India. We Westerners have a strong tradition of generalizing ourselves. There was the "Hellenization" of the known world, from the time of Alexander the Great until the golden age of the Byzantine Empire; there was a partly concomitant "Romanization" of the Mediterranean, the Middle East, and parts of Europe, from the Carthaginian wars until the collapse of the Western empire. Overlapping these two imperalisms, stemming from them and infusing them with an extraordinary new impetus, the "Christianization" of the world reached out progressively into areas of the inhabited planet unknown to the Greeks and the Romans.

The only type of "globalization" since the seventh century to rival Christianity has been Islam. It swallowed up huge chunks of the former Roman

Empire in the West and Middle East, and then the entire Byzantine Empire, while simultaneously expanding ever further into the Far East. In our own century, it has extended its hold over central Africa and continental Europe. The history of Catholic and Orthodox Europe in England, France, and the United States has been much more preoccupied than we realize with the wars in Spain and Hungary, in the Balkans, and the frontier regions of Europe, wars waged to resist the possible contraction of Christendom under the onslaught of its main universalist rival. This long, drawn-out struggle has left enduring scares and hatred, now unveiled and revived by the collapse of the last avatar of the Holy Roman Empire: Tito's Yugoslavia.

Those remote frontier struggles have not stopped the Catholic, Protestant and enlightened citizens of Western Europe, cushioned as they were from the Islamic threat by their central and southern European cousins, from increasing their hold over everywhere else outside the Continent; the conquerors waged war on each other, but the overall effect of their joint conquests was nonetheless the suppression of innumerable peoples, languages, religions, and societies. Modern anthropologists, ethnologists, archaeologists, linguists and historians have—like Christian antiquarians in the Renaissance—displayed great feats of ingenuity in resurrecting dead or dying cultures, languages and religions, swept off the map by Christian Western progress.

So there is no shortage of predecessors or models. For obvious polemical reasons, Montaigne idealized the magnanimity of the Ancients; according to him, they would have recognized the American Indians as their own soul mates. The fact of the matter is that Ancient Rome had coldly and completely buried a number of languages, like the Etruscan or Gallic ones, underneath the domination of Latin. But it is also true nevertheless, that the Romans did preserve, and eventually adopt the Attic tongue, the mother of their own literature, and they accepted into their own Pantheon many gods and goddesses worshiped by their exotic Romanized subjects. What the modern and Spanish Roman Catholics did in South America is much worse. The Protestant brand of Christian universalism has been even more successful in reducing an indigenous patchwork of Indian nations in North America to almost nothing. The reduction of diversity in the world to an ever increasing level of uniformity has been growing at an ever faster pace. Violence, bloodshed and, I might add, ethnic cleansing, have been regular traveling companions along the sad, sorry path of Western progress.

We are now witnessing a new stage in our longstanding Western ambitions. Its promising story is told and publicized daily on our television screens and on the Internet. Every evening the sound of routine bombardments illuminates the next stage in the progress of what Henry Kissinger likes to call "Wilsonianism." One-sided, short-sighted humanitarianism is called upon to persuade us that now, for once, we can feel good about bringing the post-modern Gospel of our enlightened, free and modern, English-speaking, advanced and compassionate type of commercial and legal society to the backward world.

In fact, whether we feel good or bad about it, more than ever before our goal is to complete the immense task left unfinished by the Catholic European empires: the leveling and pacification of the entire world in accordance with our latest universal criteria and self-interest. We have the moral and economic, scientific and technological superiority, not to mention the military know-how, to advance unimpeded. And since the end of the Cold War, there has been a transatlantic consensus to do just that. Euroland, a political and military dwarf, is in actual fact playing the role of nanny.

Even what we call multi-culturalism or pluri-ethnicity are, to put it frankly, merely window-dressing, sham alibis, and self-delusion. They cannot hide the ever-growing and all-enveloping standardization of the world. They blind us to the irreparable loss of cultural diversity that may still subsist on this planet. The air strikes in Serbia like the bombings in Iraq, exacerbate ethnic and confessional hatred; they hold out no promises of a happy ending through interracial marriages or festivals. The example of Bosnia, where entrenched distrustful communities are on standby ready to recommence their feuds, the example of Croatia, proud of having expelled or killed its Serbs, are ominous signs. We are much more inclined to express alarm at the loss of natural and ecological diversity in the world than we are about the corresponding doom of human ties. We have willingly let ourselves be persuaded that multi-cultural entertainment, like museums, sports teams, TV programs and the like, so popular at home, can also replace abroad, for better reasons and at lesser expense, the age-old intertwined tapestry of nations, tribes, languages, and manners that once covered the earth. They were, it is true, stridently antagonistic, but more often than not they managed to transact business with one another without selling their souls.

Today, as in the past, standardization has encountered violent resistance. The leaders are mostly desperados, latter-day Jugurthas, Mithridates or Parthians of our age. Their stubbornness and the repellent standardization they exact from their followers resembles a caricatured mirror image of the norms they claim to resist.

But the effects this has had upon ourselves are perhaps just as damaging as those it has had on foreign and so-called backward nations. Individual freedom, both private and public, for so long a source of pride for Western representative democracies, must now accommodate itself to the needs of transcendental entities that increasingly take precedence in the sphere of political representation. The global market with the homogenization of consumers that it implies, the global information network with the standardization of images and thought it introduces and, last but not least, the growing number of impersonal bureaucratic institutions to enforce the new "international laws," all largely untrammeled by any democratic control, are in the process of constructing a gigantic pyramid over the body politic. Polls tend to become a surrogate for elections. And the opinions reflected by polls are themselves reflections of mass-mediated sociological moods.

The private, thoughtful citizen, budding or mature, feels alienated and atrophied, and indeed he is. His or her means of expression or language is being eroded by a standard universal news-speak induced by the latest in communication technology. The only choice left open to him or her is a narrow range of stereotyped lifestyles. The superficiality of these apparently comfortable lifestyles, however sustained they may be by advertizing campaigns and politically correct debates, prevent too many of them from becoming personal, singular and articulate; that is, wise, loving and free.

On a sociological level, we are therefore witnessing within our own society a centrifugal movement of the "lonely" crowd, subdividing and withdrawing into closed groups or lobbies based on racial, sectarian and sexual ties or, too often for the worse, criminal ones. Virtual video-kitsch and cyberspace appeal to the young as a fake alternative for the domineering stereotypes of the mass communication market, although it too has its own share in the process. This recoiling "hot" trend demonstrates how much the "cold" universalist official creed, despite its mass media props, is divorced from the deeper needs of the souls and minds of most people. Postmodernist aesthetes try, more often than not in vain, in my view, to transform this latent schizophrenia into a creative mood. This is just as futile as if Gulliver had tried to erect an interactive "installation" on the deck of the flying fortress of Laputa.

How can singularity fit into such a world, a world so outwardly prepotent and yet so inwardly stunted? I began by saying that we what we are rehearsing, with new slogans and new means, is a very ancient Western story. We are therefore not the first to ask ourselves how not to condemn the rest of the world to our own superior model. Fortunately we have excellent mentors and friends who can teach us the arts of practicing both singularity and diversity, irony and love. Once again I should like to quote Montaigne, this time in his own words, a passage opportunely translated into English by Michael Screech:

> I do not suffer from that common failing of judging another man by myself. I can easily believe that others have qualities quite distinct from my own. Just because I feel that I am pledged to my individual form, I do not bind all others to it, as everyone does. I can conceive and believe that there are thousands of different ways of living and, contrary to most men, I more readily acknowledge our differences than our similarities. I am ready as you may wish to relieve another human being of my attributes and basic qualities, and to contemplate him simply as he is, free from comparisons, and sculpting him after his own model.

This is, I suppose, a principle of method that any urbane historian or literary critic could willingly recognize as his or her own professional duty. But it goes indeed much further and deeper than a purely academic exercise: it gauges and annihilates all moral and political pretense which today purports to level the world according to a single universal self-satisfied model, ours. It serves as a reminder that a true recognition of human diversity implies a sound knowledge of human singularity, beginning with our own. Humanist awareness and greedy humanitarian narcissism are in fact two radically incompatible attitudes. Therein lies the challenge of the next millennium.

DISCUSSANT

GLEN W. BOWERSOCK

Institute for Advanced Study, Princeton

THERE IS a kind of extraordinary coherence in the papers we have heard today and a kind of fearful symmetry in the relation between the first paper this morning and the one that we have just heard. The first speaker this morning told us that a certain word, "sovereignty," pollutes the air; this afternoon we have been told that globalization is a foul word. Through the course of the day, particularly the afternoon, we have heard a great deal about the problems of universalism as opposed to fragmentation or essentialism. Globalization is part of this whole discussion. Among the humanists here you will have heard echoes, certainly, in Wendy Doniger's paper and in Hank Millon's and, perhaps to a lesser extent in the very finely-tuned paper by John Elliott, of what is often referred to as the crisis in the humanities. I want to say that, although this expression has not been used hitherto this afternoon, the humanities have always been in crisis. I think it could be argued that crisis drives the humanities and without crisis we would not have any humanities.

With a broad reach extending back to classical antiquity and including the spread of Catholicism and Islam around the world, Marc Fumaroli has located the globalization that seems so distinctive a feature of our own time within the vast context of human history. Taking Montaigne as his guide, he sought to reclaim the many disparate cultures and languages and peoples that he sees being absorbed—Gibbon would have said insensibly—into a global community. This is a community that speaks only English, espouses democracy, worships technology and money and preaches without always practicing a lofty code of clearly western morality.

Our speaker has eloquently protested, and in general I would be inclined to agree with him. He has cunningly compared the ecological movement, with its concern to preserve the continuity and the richness of the natural environment, with the rampant devastation of the humanistic landscape. He is, in effect, appealing for something we might call "humanistic ecology." We have heard that the very multiculturalism of our own day is really a sham, diverting our attention from the loss of singularity. It is true that, as an antipode to assimilation, multiculturalism could easily become a kind of ghettoization, or isolationism within a society. We have already heard today about blacks only studying black history, Hispanics only studying Hispanic history or culture, French only French history or culture. This is a problem that is with us all the time and it is clearly not the kind of singularity that Professor Fumaroli is aspiring to. But it does, I think, point up the dangers inherent in the anti-global position, that of isolation, the loss of human rights and dignity, and—a subject of which heard so much this morning—the problem of suffering around the world. In a sense this would be the main issue that I would put to Professor Fumaroli: How to reconcile the advocacy of singularity, of diversity, of separation, with this problem that we all have to confront. And we confront it now much more than in the past because of the speed of communication, the speed with which we can get around the world, the speed with which news gets around the world. In that respect our knowledge of what is happening elsewhere is much greater and much more painful than it was in earlier generations.

I should like to take one example from my own field of the Roman Empire to see whether there is some way around this problem. It is true, as the speaker said, that the Romans eliminated a lot of languages and local cultures, particularly in Italy. But in the case of the Eastern Mediterranean world, the Romans were quite remarkable in supporting the Greek culture that they found. They clearly admired it, they allowed the language and the culture to continue and to grow, and it provided a kind of glue in the Eastern Mediterranean that permitted people with different cultures—Jews, Arabs, Egyptians, Cappadocians—actually to talk to each other, to communicate with each other and to put down in some kind of endurable form what they had in the way of local traditions. So, it seems to me that maybe this kind of thing is a way of combining globalization, which is certainly in terms of the ancient world what we see in the Roman Empire, with the preservation of singularity. Is this kind of thing imaginable in a modern context? Because of the speed of communication and the shared technological advancements around the world, I think that globalization, even with the national organization which was so eloquently mentioned this morning is simply not going to go away. So we have to deal with it in the best way we can, and I wonder whether or not the appeal from Wendy Doniger this afternoon for comparative studies may not guide us to a kind of reconciliation of these objectives.

CLASS V

THE PROFESSIONS, ARTS AND AFFAIRS

One Hundred Years of the Renaissance*

HANNA HOLBORN GRAY

Professor of History, University of Chicago

Good Morning. My name is Mrs. Rip van Winkle. Some time ago I left my profession of what was then known as Renaissance history for a period of academic administration. When I woke up many years later, it was to find that the field had been radically deconstructed during my absence. Back on the faculty, I innocently announced course titles containing the newly forbidden name and was sternly informed that I was now attached to Early Modern Europe, unless I wished to be taken into the Middle Ages. The dividing barrier between these two appeared to blot out the space for what I had grown up with for half a century as "Ren and Ref."

At the same time, people who kindly asked what I might be doing now exclaimed, as they had always done, "Oh! The Renaissance! Such an *exciting* time!" They seemed to assume that one had gained the luxury of inhabiting a golden age of extraordinary genius, splendid art, heroic optimism, noble ideas, fantastic discoveries and remarkable literature in which even evil showed a face of beauty, a time immortalized by the indelible sight of Charlton Heston on his back with his paint brushes beneath the Sistine ceiling. A deeply embedded and diffuse view, remotely linked to but simplistically distorting Burckhardt's vision of the Renaissance, continues to prevail, whatever may be the findings and arguments and reinterpretations made by recent scholarship. Whether in school texts or in the scripts of tourist guides, the beat goes on. The image of Renaissance Man, of an age expressing in the different dimensions of its life a spirit of secularism and individualism, a pursuit of worldly ambition and fame, a commitment to freedom and creativity, and the conclusion that the Renaissance had helped bring into being

---

*Read 24 April 1999.

those fundamental elements that distinguish the modern world—these retain a seductive hold.

That a considerable distance should separate scholarly interpretation from the abiding stereotypes of history is nothing new. Yet the problem of the Renaissance represents a particularly acute instance of that phenomenon. It seems impossible to abandon the dreaded "R" word altogether and equally impossible to agree on what it might mean now or ever. In addition, the Renaissance exists as a kind of business, too, a not-for-profit corporate shell, with a highly articulated network, culture, and set of practices and rituals that cannot easily be disturbed. There are innumerable regional Renaissance conferences (southeast, northwest, central mid-West, New England, and so forth), and constantly proliferating Renaissance seminars and centers. Students of the field know that spring has arrived when, in every province, town, university, research library, and museum, there convenes the annual Renaissance meeting. Renaissance men and women can be seen criss-crossing the country in a restless flow of migration to offer papers, discussions of papers, comments on papers, discussions of comments on papers, concerts of early music, exhibitions, banquets of Renaissance delicacies, and sharply conflicting views as to whether in fact there was a Renaissance at all. The eponymous idea is on the defensive, yet it still defines the event. Over time and, I found, especially during my hibernation, the papers have expanded enormously in number and in subject matter. So, for example, presentations on "Grace and Faith in *Paradise Lost*" jostle for attention with "Foot Fetishism in Milton's *Comus*," and "The Coronation of Charles V" with "Lactation, Language and Empire in Early Modern Spanish Texts." Parenthetically, I noticed the other day that the most recent issue of the magazine *Civilization*—an apt title for our purposes—has on its cover a come-on headline: "The Renaissance and Dr. Ruth."

The idea of the Renaissance as a distinctive and coherent period of European history has a long history of its own, one certainly not confined to Jacob Burckhardt's *Civilization of the Renaissance in Italy*. But it is astonishing how a single book, even when long set adrift from its philosophical moorings, should have inspired the fundamental terms of question and debate for the entire century in which history took root and flourished as a professional discipline in the U.S. In considering, refuting, modifying, transforming or even attempting to shake off Burckhardt's characterization of a Renaissance civilization that ushered in the modern world and that displayed in its diverse manifestations a core unity of large historical consequence, the Renaissance battles became wars over the validity and nature of periodization in history, over the origins and meanings of modernity, and over the subjects and methods appropriate to historical understanding more generally. The state of the problem of the Renaissance has thus always reflected something basic about the state of the discipline itself and about the varying shifts of direction it has taken. And the Renaissance has been our equivalent of the Polish Question; no topic associated with the age, however minute or specialized, can fail to be referred finally to what it illuminates about the problem of its periodization.

To think, then, about one hundred years of the Renaissance is to think about much wider issues of historiography. One may observe a trajectory running from the beginning to the end of the century. At first, the Renaissance was conceived as a major key to identifying a clearly marked path within the terrain of European history. Now, it is seen as no key, or only a minor one, in mapping a landscape that contains no single or obvious pattern. Between these points, historical research, its priorities and fashions, have shaped plural Renaissances and different histories.

Among current narratives of the Renaissance, there has emerged a story about its study, and the role of such study, in twentieth-century America. This account describes an early phase in which a conviction that history should serve the understanding and affirmation of American civic ideals and that a paradigm of "Western Civilization" should be the focus for education and for the study of European history dominated the development of Renaissance scholarship. It posits a second and later thrust dominated by the critical influence of emigré scholars from central Europe. This group is seen as inspired, at least in part, by an agenda born from the experience of European catastrophe in the 1930s. It is thought to have re-invented the Renaissance as an interdisciplinary field of study, one centered in a broadly humanistic and deeply learned tradition of trans-Atlantic origin, its disparate emphases united by a belief that the Renaissance existed in thought and institutions, in literary and artistic style, and that it represented an enduring and still vital foundation for understanding how the critically endangered modern world had come to be.

This part of the newer history of Renaissance history interprets the work

249

of the emigrés and their successor generation of American scholars as constituting the peak of Renaissance studies in this past century. It then goes on to trace the disintegration of an aging historical faith. I would argue that this is an incomplete history. One cannot so easily read the emigrés' work primarily as a direct response to contemporary ideologies or, as another commentator has rather oddly put it, as a "strategy of escape." It should be noted also that the Europeans were not in their time the only students of Renaissance studies in this country, however important the influence they exercised. At the *fin de siècle* the history of the Renaissance in the twentieth century is being written from a vantage point that sees those scholars as important, but a bit out-dated; productive, but limited in their perspective, supporting the rationale of historical periodization while caught in the need to assert and defend a tradition under siege. Needless to say, our excellent commentators—for they are indeed excellent historians—have repudiated much of the faith and come to view much of the tradition as blindered and time-bound. They have participated in the past decades of changes of direction in historiography that challenge once accepted assumptions about historical truth, the nature of past cultures and the means to their study, the areas of historical investigation most worth pursuing. They do not fail to acknowledge indebtedness to their predecessors. The strength and sophistication of Renaissance scholarship they have inherited and have built on are never in doubt. But history itself has been transformed, and with it, the Renaissance as well, whether submerged in the field of early modern or surviving on older life–support systems.

The grand schema of western history, with the Renaissance in a starring role, has failed many scrutinies of revisionist competition. It is confronted in the first instance by the globalization of history; in the second, by the effects of a deepened recognition that whole areas of the past, its economic and demographic conditions and cycles and its forms of social structure and evolution, move along time lines of crucially varying speeds. The newer forms of cultural and social history have unraveled the idea of eras knit together by the unifying commonalities that older periodizations insisted were surely to be found. The diversities and singularities of historical existence, their tensions and oppositions and contradictions and discontinuities, the erratic and uneven movements of historical time, the sustained life of ingrained and obstinate habits of attitude and practice in the face of apparent change: all this has moved to the forefront of attention and interest in many areas of historical investigation. The project of laying out its dense particulars has replaced the hope of finding coherent patterns in the complex experience of the past. Skepticism about achieving any real knowledge of or objectivity in explaining that past, certainty that all historians, or at least all previous historians, have been to some degree captive to ideology and its aims, credos that attack the "elitism" of studying high rather than popular culture, and the radical questioning of so-called modernity, its definitions and values—all this has struck at the heart of a long, though never monolithic, tradition of Renaissance history. New styles of interpretation, whether associated with subject matter, theory, or other disciplines such as anthropology, have had a profound effect on the kinds of history thought to be valuable and acceptable. The new historians have brought significantly new questions and made enormous contributions to understanding what were frequently unexplored areas of the centuries we now call early modern Europe, finding more evident continuities over the longer span or more evident singularities in studying a particular phenomenon or community.

And yet the framework of the Renaissance hangs on, not only in such areas as intellectual and institutional history, but even in the work of historians who dispute its existence. The language of "Early Modern," after all, can scarcely offer neutral territory, for it immediately raises the spectre of the "modern."

In speaking of European history today, two things have become politically incorrect: one, any suggestion that western history should be, in today's phrase, "privileged," and two, falling into what is perceived a closely connected fault, that of constructing this history from the position of modernity—both because that incurs the sin of "presentism" and because it creates a false "teleology" in which the modern, or the values of the modern, become the goal or culmination of a selective history of progress and are implicitly assigned some superior virtue.

Prosecutors in jurisdictions that have put the Renaissance on trial have brought some pretty serious charges: that the field is incorrigibly western, even if its scope embraces the age of discoveries, including the discovery of the "Other;" that it is directed to uncovering the origins of the modern world and so falls into the presentist and teleological fallacies; that its adherents assume that some more or less verifiable reality attaches to this epoch of transition and to the essential elements that characterize its universe as opposed to that of the Middle Ages; that elitist historians have neglected all those diversities and hidden populations and cultural expressions that were the vital constituents, lying beneath the thin facade of high culture, of a society very different from that usually depicted.

What of the defense? To argue the case for the Renaissance, one must at the outset concede a chastened and far more modest version of its character and impact, a far more pluralistic description of the age, and a far more generous appreciation of the unequal passages of time and characteristics of place than those who believe a period should represent a neat and fully accessorized package might once have thought. (Of course this formulation caricatures the thinking of most Renaissance historians of any time.) The defense will then rest on two major arguments: first, that it is the understanding of modernity, rather than of the Renaissance, that has undergone the greatest upheaval; second, that to define the Renaissance as a distinctive age in intellectual history, in directions and habits of thought (and in the history of art and literature, too) has continuing merit and validity.

At the end of the century, it is not only new modes of history and new critiques of the possibilities of historical knowledge that have altered the landscape. The deconstruction of the Renaissance reveals a deeper current of change: that the modern world is not what it used to be, or was thought to be earlier in the century, that the present may be already a post-modern world with its repudiation of older symmetries, over-arching truths, or reasonably, if not absolutely, objective methods and standards of achieving sustainable conclusions in historical argumentation.

Talk about presentism! Today's critics, as their own theories would predict, are as capable of projecting the present on the past as are those whose errors they condemn. The odd result is that an age seen as irredeemably foreign in its contours can become strangely familiar as it is re-presented, and that the study of a past which presents mainly images of otherness can become a mirror of self-presentation even as the historians question whether there is a here here or a there there. Does this necessarily descend to mere subjectivity? I think not. It may sound naive, but it is still worth recalling the simple words of Cicero, who said that not to know what happened before you were born is to remain always a child, in order to reflect on the function that history is asked recurrently to perform: namely, to arrive at some greater illumination of our own condition, and that of our own world, by engaging with the past, to reappropriate that past, however imperfectly, from a great distance. To say that is to demand no higher value for one time or one goal than another, nor is it to deny the diversities, tensions, contradictions and unfulfilled possibilities that mark all times. It is to acknowledge what is always a continuing process of two-way engagement.

Intellectual history, as opposed to a broader cultural history, does study a subset of humanity: the intellectuals. There is nothing elitist about this, unless one wished to embrace the unlikely thesis that only intellectuals matter or that they actually exercise the powerful influence they might like to imagine. But the thought and writing of intellectuals do matter. Education, its institutions, content and aims, also matter. To study the clash and evolution of ideas, their relation to the social and political environments in which they are forged and argued, the purposes to which they are directed and the successive re-interpretations and mis-interpretations to which they are subjected, remains a vital dimension of historical inquiry. The debates over the right methods and questions of such inquiry remain a lively sign of the health of the discipline. The ground of the Renaissance remains fertile space for these reflections and controversies.

It was an era in which, over a long period of time, a self-conscious group of intellectuals, later to be called humanists (today they might be seen as the first public intellectuals) attacked the high culture that they complained was dominant in their day, turned their backs on what they saw as an age of cultural darkness, and invoked the models and spirit of antiquity as the foundation for a new and humanly centered ideal of knowledge and education located in a tradition of the liberal arts. They developed assumptions and conclusions about learning and its uses, about the social and political order, about history itself, that entered into the mental baggage of educated people well beyond their time. Never, outside its core consensus, a single movement of thought when applied to its questions of interest, and never an exclusive or singly triumphant strain of sensibility, its influence was pervasive even where it was at least partially opposed. Something had happened, something that the humanists came to hail as the dawning of a new era. We need not accept at face value their conviction that they were living a renaissance, but we need to understand it, and its enduring impact, as a critical shift in intellectual history.

There is a great deal of good new work going on in this field, and it, too, has been enriched by the other histories I have cited. For the future—and here I am at risk, for historians are meant to be prophets of the past—I foresee a renaissance of the Renaissance within the more limited boundaries I have sketched, a Renaissance not dependent on some historical metaphysic but on a respect for the claims of reading its intellectual history to the greatest possible extent in its own terms. To do so does not mean to ignore questions whose urgency may derive from the present. And we must recognize that the present, and therefore both the modern and the early modern, will represent a constantly moving target.

Members of the jury, you may finally throw up your hands and choose to render a verdict of mercy. After all, given the volume of resources already invested in the Renaissance business, it would be quite awkward and certainly very costly to change the logo and replace the tee shirts. Perhaps we should just print up new ones for the new century in anticipation of the next stage in the history of Renaissance history. We could start with one that says "The Renaissance loves Dr. Ruth—she thinks it's *so* exciting!"

DISCUSSANT

WILLIAM J. BOUWSMA

University of California, Berkeley

PROFESSOR GRAY'S talk began with a typical example of the decadence of the subject under discussion. I think, however, that she and I are in agreement that the Renaissance and Reformation never constituted by themselves an age in the past, whatever that might mean. The two of us came out of the same shop, I a few years earlier than she. We had the same teachers, read the same books and, I suspect, had the same rather personal interest in choosing to study the movements to which these grand names pointed. And we were also aware that there was much during the period between the fourteenth and eighteenth centuries distinct from, and even opposed to, what we included under these rubrics—notably developments in scientific thought and formal philosophy. We were also aware that European universities were, on the whole, not hospitable to the thought of Renaissance humanists or religious reformers, whether Protestant or Catholic.

I share what I took to be Professor Gray's initial distress at the virtual disappearance [of the Renaissance] as a major identifiable field of European history although she seems to have modified that impression in the course of her paper. I agree with nearly all she has said, but for her suddenly returning to this field after a quarter of a century of exile this recognition was in some degree a shock, though rapidly absorbed, evidently. For me, it had been a long and slow process of recognition and depression, which perhaps explains my greater pessimism about the future of this field.

I have had, therefore, plenty of time to think about it and especially about why it has occurred. Part of the explanation lies in what has happened to college teaching in general during the last few decades and to the presentation of the past to students. My own teaching career coincided, after World War II, with the enormous expansion of higher education, a development, if I am not mistaken, the public universities, of which I have now mainly taught, experienced more than private colleges, especially the increases of the sheer numbers of faculty required to deal with huge numbers of additional students. Existing graduate programs were much expanded and new ones were established, often, I suspect with inadequate resources where they had not previously existed.

I feel somewhat insecure, however, in trying to evaluate the quality of graduate training in this emergency situation, partly because I have some doubts about its effectiveness earlier. I do recall that many years later, when I was teaching at another institution to whose jubilee its sons are supposed to throng, members of my department sometimes congratulated themselves that its graduate students were so good that they required little faculty attention. The faculty, therefore, could concentrate on what they considered their own work. I hasten to add that this sentiment was not universal. But the major problem in this huge general expansion as I now see it, was that it took no account of the changing needs of the undergraduate students that these newly-minted teachers were supposed to teach. Graduate programs in history, perhaps especially in institutions where they had not previously been important, competed to demonstrate their rigor and professionalism by adopting the same requirements as the older universities, notably the requirement of a doctoral dissertation based on "original re-search" as only then could these products qualify to teach graduate students much like themselves—there would be constant replication of the same sort of teaching for a totally different student body.

This requirement, the value of which for undergraduate teaching might have been more thoughtfully reconceived, usually meant that the disserta-tion had to be limited enough to be completed competently in a finite length of time by a relative beginner. The results, of course, were to give further impetus to the fragmentation of historical study. History, already underway in many dissertations and a shift from cultural intellectual sub-jects to concrete projects in social and economic history, often aided by computers. I mention this not of distaste for such work but because I think it has contributed to the shift we are now describing. Research has tended to replace reflection about the past. It was often now quite literally true that the training of teachers of history reached a climax of knowing more and more, ideally everything, about less and less.

Another result inimical to the kind of thought required for study of the Renaissance and Reformation was that dissertations became manageable in the degree to which they were limited geographically. A major, and I think deeply unfortunate consequence, was to strengthen a tendency to identify students, even to the time when national identities were, at best problem-atic, with particular national states. Larger questions of European resonance were less and less likely to be considered. In short we were now giving in-creasingly specialized training to students, most of whom, at first and many during their entire teaching careers, were supposedly being prepared to in-troduce undergraduates to what it meant to think about the past. Under such conditions, larger questions, for example about the so-called Renais-sance and Reformation received less and less attention.

This then is one element in my sense of what has happened to the Re-naissance and Reformation. History has become increasingly specialized and compartmentalized. Fundamentally, I suppose because historians them-selves like it this way, feel more comfortable about smaller problems about which their conclusions are less likely to be attacked. It is to me especially curious that at a time when nationalism is more and more dimly regarded, its disappearance sometimes even predicted, historians have tended in-creasingly toward the formation of smaller groups according to the nations of their choice but intellectual and cultural history cannot be effectively studied in such terms.

There also seems to me an even more serious obstacle to the rebirth of the Renaissance and Reformation to anything like their former stature. For such conceptions were a crucial element in a scenario, a vast myth in the more serious sense of that term, that once dominated historical thought but has essentially collapsed since World War II. This was the belief that all human history, the West showing the way, has been and will continue to be an indefinite advance toward the only vaguely imaginable goal of universal prosperity, peace and perfection, which dependant on the cultural and religious freedoms initiated by the Renaissance and Reformation. The West leading the way was not exclusive as it was showing that way to the rest of the world.

This is essentially what I was taught in History I at Harvard sixty years ago. I remember vividly one of the senior lecturers who collaborated in teaching the course that introduced freshmen to history. I remember him admitting in deep seriousness—World War II had just begun—that occasionally in the genial procession of history, it is necessary to take one step back in order to advance two steps forward. This was the only qualification of the conviction of progress that I can recall from my freshman year. I suspect now that this vision motivated my own decision to study the Renaissance and Reformation. In fact my interest in these subjects has survived the loss of it although perhaps what has really happened is that what was once a conviction about the destiny of the human race has become for me a matter of essentially personal interest. I continue to love and rejoice in the complementarity of the Renaissance and Reformation though perhaps a much further fragility of what they represent, especially as they're increasingly trivialized in the Renaissance conferences to which Professor Gray has alluded.

I therefore welcome Professor Gray's return to a kind of scholarship in which in her distinguished career she early displayed insights of extraordinary interest. Thank you.

Race and Admission to Universities*

DEREK BOK

University Professor, Harvard University

FOR SIX MONTHS, I have been a somewhat reluctant participant in a great ideological struggle that has been going on in America for the past 25 years. The struggle to which I refer has to do with the role of race in university admissions. The stakes are high, and feelings on both sides are intense.

For minorities, universities are the gateways to comfortable incomes, interesting careers, power and influence in society. Blacks and Hispanics are still woefully under-represented in the professions. If they are to improve their position by continuing the gains they have made in the past two decades, it is essential that selective colleges and professional schools go on taking account of race in deciding which applicants to admit. Abolishing racial preferences would cut the number of blacks in law school in half; at leading schools, the numbers would decline to less than half of one percent. In medicine, according to the journal *Blacks in Higher Education,* only seven blacks in 1995 would have qualified for the top ten U.S. medical schools if admission were determined by college grades and test scores alone. So the consequences for minorities of abandoning current admissions practices would be serious indeed.

Conservatives see the problem entirely differently. To them, preferential admissions are clearly wrong. Most conservatives do not oppose current admissions policies out of bigotry or prejudice. In their view, race preferences are a misguided bit of liberal social engineering that do not help the intended beneficiaries and are grossly unfair to those who work hard and do well in school.

---

*Read 24 April, 1999.

259

Both sides have argued passionately for their position. Supporters of racial preferences insist that it is only fair to give minorities a helping hand after generations of oppression. To them, standardized test scores are irrelevant. They are biased against minorities. Moreover, universities have traditionally given preference to other groups with low scores, such as athletes and alumni children; why should they not do likewise for blacks and Hispanics who have been held back so long?

Conservative opponents reply that preferential admissions only hurt those they claim to help. Minorities can't compete if you put them in colleges with better qualified whites. That is why their drop-out rates in selective colleges are consistently higher than those of whites. Moreover, minorities will never learn to work hard at their studies if they can get admitted to good colleges and professional schools without achieving as much in school as whites. After they graduate, they will be stigmatized in later life, since employers will assume that they gained admission to selective colleges only because of their race.

Universities, oddly, have contributed very little to the debate. Although their own policies are under attack, they have rarely tried to convince the general public that their methods are fair and proper. By and large, they have simply continued to repeat that racial diversity is good for everyone's education.

It is interesting to note that although most of the arguments on every side are based on assertions of fact, there has been almost no serious effort to test whether the assertions are true. Even universities—the nation's leading centers of research—have never tried to demonstrate what the effects of preferential admissions have been or whether they have had the beneficial effects on education that their presidents and deans have so often claimed.

It was in these circumstances that Bill Bowen and I undertook to study the effects of race-conscious admissions. To us, it seemed tragic to resolve such an important issue without first ascertaining the facts about how the disputed policies had actually worked. Fortunately, we had the benefit of a huge body of data compiled by the Andrew W. Mellon Foundation based on some 60,000 students who had attended 28 public and private colleges under race-conscious admissions policies. The students involved were of all races. Half of them had begun college in 1976 and hence had had some 15 years of experience following their graduation by the time we surveyed them. The other half had entered college in 1989 and thus could provide a reasonably contemporary view of college life.

In studying the experience of these students, we were particularly interested in answering three questions. First, we wanted to know whether the minority students in our sample were truly qualified to complete the academic program successfully. Unless they could do so, neither they nor their colleges would benefit by having been admitted. The second question we investigated was whether the existence of a racially diverse student body enriched the education of all students by helping them learn to live and work more effectively with members of other races. Finally, we wanted to determine what had happened to the minority students after they graduated. One important reason for race-sensitive admissions was to prepare larger numbers of minorities who could enter the professions, help build a larger minority middle class, and assume positions of influence and leadership in their communities and professions. After 30 years of experience, it was important to determine whether the universities involved had succeeded in this effort.

What did we learn about these questions from examining the history of the 60,000 students in our study? First, we learned that even though most minority students attending selective schools would have been rejected under a strict race-neutral regime, they seemed to have been qualified academically to complete the academic work of the institutions that admitted them. It is true that most of the blacks in our study received lower grades than their white classmates and graduated at slightly lower rates. The reasons for these disparities are not fully understood, and selective institutions need to work harder to help minorities improve their academic performance, as a few universities have already succeeded in doing. Still, 75 percent of the blacks and 81 percent of the Hispanics in our study graduated within six years from the college they entered, a figure well above the 59 percent of whites and 40 percent of blacks who graduated from all Division I NCAA schools. (It is important to note that some of the students who did not graduate in six years transferred to other schools or finished college at a later date.) Moreover, minorities did not graduate at these high rates by majoring in easy subjects. Black students selected substantially the same concentrations as whites and were just as likely to choose difficult majors such as those in the sciences.

How much does diversity add to the learning experience? Have blacks and whites learned to get along better or has diversity resulted in self-segregation and greater tension? Undoubtedly, minority students often spend time together (as do hockey players, campus newspaper editors, and members of other student groups). But much racial interaction also occurs. Eighty-eight percent of blacks who entered selective colleges in 1989 report having known well two or more white classmates, while 56 percent of their white classmates say that they knew at least two black classmates well. How many older Americans can make that claim?

Substantial majorities of students of all races in our study feel that learning to live and work effectively with members of other races is important. Large majorities also believe that their college experience contributed a lot in this respect. Consequently, almost 80 percent of the white graduates favor either retaining the current race-sensitive admissions policies or emphasizing them more. Their minority classmates support these policies even more strongly.

Some critics allege that race-sensitive admissions policies aggravate racial tensions by creating resentment among white and Asian students rejected by colleges they hoped to attend. Although we could not test this possibility definitively, we did examine the feelings of white students in our sample who were rejected by their first-choice school. Significantly, these students were just as supportive of race-sensitive policies as were those who were admitted by their first-choice school.

Finally, we found that the black students in our study have succeeded very well in what athletic coaches often refer to as "the game of life." (Their Hispanic classmates have probably been successful as well, but too few were enrolled in the class entering in 1976 to allow reliable analysis.) Fifty-six percent of the black graduates who entered these selective schools in 1976 went on to earn advanced degrees. A remarkable 40 percent received Ph.Ds or professional degrees in the most sought-after fields of law, business and medicine, a figure slightly higher than that for their white classmates and five times higher than that for all black BAs nationwide.

By the time of our survey, black male graduates who entered these schools in 1976, though typically less than 40 years old, were earning an average $85,000 per year, 82 percent more than other black male college graduates nationwide. Their black women classmates earned 73 percent more than all black women BAs. Some readers may suspect that these figures simply indicate that blacks continue receiving preferential treatment after they leave the university. Our findings suggest a different conclusion. Comparing black and white men with similar qualifications—same colleges, same grade averages, same test scores, same majors, same socioeconomic backgrounds, same sector of employment, and so forth—we found that blacks earned $8,500 per year less then whites. This result indicates that, on balance, black men continue to experience more discrimination than favoritism in the workplace. Comparing black and white women who have the same records, we find that average earnings were identical—again, no evidence of favoritism.

Despite their high salaries, the blacks we studied were not simply "looking out for number one." In virtually every type of civic activity—from social service organizations to parent-teacher associations—black men were more likely than their white classmates to occupy leadership positions. Much the same pattern holds for women. These findings should reassure black intellectuals, such as Henry Louis Gates and Cornel West, who have worried that blacks—especially black men—would ignore their social responsibilities once they achieved financial success.

In addition to assessing the positive results of race-sensitive admissions, we were also able to test a number of the arguments made by proponents and critics of these policies. For example, many defenders of affirmative action criticize the use of standardized tests, such as the SAT, arguing that they are culturally biased against minority students. If this were so, one would expect to find that minorities do better in college than their test scores predicted. Our findings, however, showed the opposite to be true. Minority students consistently performed less well in college than one would have expected from their test results.

We also examined the argument made by critics to the effect that minority students are demoralized by having to compete with whites with higher high school grades and test scores. Was it true, as Dinesh D'Souza asserts, that "American universities are quite willing to sacrifice the future happiness of many young blacks and Hispanics to achieve diversity, proportional representation, and what they consider to be multi-racial progress"? The facts are very clear on this point. Far from being demoralized, blacks from the most competitive schools are the most satisfied with their college experience. Among blacks with similar test scores, the more selective the college they attend (that is, the higher the average test scores of their white classmates), the more likely they are to graduate, earn advanced degrees, and receive high salaries.

Finally, we were able to determine whether minority students were stigmatized in later life by having been admitted under an affirmative action admissions policy. If such a stigma existed, one would expect to find a greater gap in earnings between the black students in our study and their white classmates than the earnings gap between black and white students attending colleges without a race-conscious admissions policy. In fact, however, the earnings gap among black and white students in our study was substantially smaller. In other words, far from dampening the earnings of black students relative to whites, race-conscious admissions improved them. Moreover, if such policies created a stigma, the black students involved certainly did not know it. Looking back, the blacks who entered selective colleges in 1976 were as satisfied with their college experience as their white classmates. Only 7 percent of these black graduates said that they would not attend the same selective college if they had to choose all over again.

Having compiled all these findings, what is the bottom line? Have we resolved the dispute over race-sensitive admissions? Certainly, our findings have accomplished something. We have demonstrated that universities have succeeded fairly well in accomplishing their goals. We have laid to rest several spurious arguments from the left and the right. We have also defined the stakes involved by demonstrating fairly precisely what the consequences for minority enrollments would be if race-blind admissions were required. Even so, after the dust has cleared, we are still left with a fundamental dilemma that facts alone will never resolve.

On the one hand, are we prepared to have a society in which one-third of the population are black and Hispanic but almost all the positions of influence are held by whites with a sprinkling of Asians? Consider for a moment what the effect on the law would be if we eliminated racial preferences. Less than 1 percent of the students in the top half of all law schools would be black. Virtually no blacks would be recruited by established law firms, since they almost never recruit from schools in the bottom half. The pool of potential black judges would be cut by more than half, and almost none would have attended better than average law schools. What would these results mean for the credibility of our justice system to minorities? What would they do to the pool of future black leaders for the bar, for the community, for the government?

Unfortunately, the alternative is not easy to accept either. How comfortable are we with allowing important decisions for young people to turn on color of their skin? It may be relatively easy to contemplate such policies for a brief period of time. But no one can predict how long it will take before the current test score gap is eliminated. Although the gap has diminished by one-third since the early 1970s, it has not narrowed for the past decade and no one is predicting that it will close completely anytime soon. How does the prospect of indefinite racial preferences fit with Martin Luther King's ideal of a world in which advancement is determined not by the color of one's skin but by the content of one's character?

What can we do in face of this dilemma? At present, most Americans do not acknowledge the dilemma. Seventy-five percent do not want college admissions influenced by race. But 75 percent do want racially diverse student bodies. Most people do not know enough yet to appreciate the difficulty in reconciling these two aspirations.

Conservatives argue that the answer lies in reforming the schools and that preferential admissions distracts us from that essential goal. No one disputes the importance of improving our schools. The problem is that no knowledgeable person expects this to be done in the foreseeable future. What do we do about university admissions policies in the interim? Far from claiming that these policies interfere with reforming the schools, most observers believe that effective school reform will be more difficult to achieve without the help of well-trained minority educators, many of whom will be beneficiaries of preferential admissions.

A few commentators have argued that we should resolve our dilemma by admitting students on the basis of class, not race. Their argument is beguiling. Since minorities are more heavily represented among lower income groups, proponents claim that a class-based policy would reward students for overcoming adversity, achieve greater racial diversity, yet never explicitly take race into account.

Class-based admissions purport to provide us with a neat way around the dilemma. Unfortunately, the proposal cannot work. There are simply too few minorities who are both poor *and* capable of meeting academic standards of selective colleges. Among all students in America who come from families with incomes below $15,000 and who have an SAT score above 1000, only one in six is black or Hispanic. Thus, even if universities took only poor students (which would be impossibly expensive) they would still not achieve greater racial diversity than they already have.

Politicians have come up with yet another solution. In Texas, a Republican governor and legislature have voted to abolish tests and simply admit the top 10 percent of every high school class. California regents have recently adopted a similar approach.

Such a policy avoids explicit racial preference, since every student is admitted by achieving the same rank in class. Unfortunately, however, the equality is only cosmetic, because high schools are so uneven in quality. In many schools, especially those that are predominantly minority, even top 10% students are not at all prepared for a selective college.

Meanwhile, in very good high schools, especially those that are predominantly white, many students who are not in the top 10 percent are perfectly well prepared. Hence, the 10% solution will cause the quality of both minority and non-minority students to decline. Far from achieving more equality among students admitted to selective colleges, racial differences in board scores will increase. This seems a high price to pay for the appearance of racial neutrality.

If none of the proposals made thus far will allow us to achieve racially diverse classes without awarding racial preferences, how will we resolve the underlying dilemma? My personal opinion is that Americans will not allow diversity to disappear in selective colleges and professional schools. What Texas and California have done reveals how far we will go to avoid this result. Still, the problem remains that simply abolishing standardized tests is not a good answer, since it will widen the gap between white and minority students and diminish the academic qualifications of both groups.

In my view, the best solution would be to allow preferential admissions to continue. This is the only solution that achieves diversity by admitting the best qualified minority students. It also respects the autonomy of universities—or, to make the point more clearly, it bears out Justice Frankfurter's observation that we will have better universities in the end if we leave educational decisions to educators by respecting the "four essential freedoms of a university—to determine for itself on academic grounds who may teach, what may be taught, how it should be taught, and who may be admitted to study." Finally, giving discretion to selective universities avoids the accumulation of rules that will develop if courts and government officials are drawn more and more into deciding what race-blind admissions really means. What appears to be a clear-cut standard will in fact result in recurrent controversy. Does race-neutral admissions mean that no special efforts can be made to recruit minority students? Does it rule out minority scholarships? Does it preclude special efforts to work with minority high schools? As these questions wend their way through the courts and administrative agencies, a tangle of rules will emerge which, I predict, will not improve the quality of the admissions process.

Even if universities retain broad discretion over admissions, however, the awkward question remains—will there ever be an end to racial preferences? The flip response is to say that racial preferences will end when legacy preferences, geographic preferences, and athletic preferences end—or when racial discrimination in the society ends. But this is not a sufficient answer, nor will it satisfy open-minded critics. At the very least, there needs to be some expectation that preferences will end and that universities are doing whatever they can to hasten their eventual demise.

In fact, I do see some hope of ending preferences—or at least, I can perceive some tangible steps that universities could take to try to end them more quickly. The first step would be to undertake intensive research on why racial differences in board scores and academic performance persist. We are quite sure that these differences are not innate. But we don't know why they exist. For decades, the subject has been considered too explosive to investigate. This is tragic. We do minorities no favor by ignoring this question, for only when we understand the reasons for the test score gap can we hope to solve the problem.

The second step is to build on what we already know about improving the academic achievement of minorities, many of whom are not performing up to expectations. A few universities have already made substantial progress along these lines. In every case, certain key ingredients enter into the successful programs. The university must establish high expectations for the students involved; the programs must not be perceived as remedial. Participants should be encouraged to work closely together and support one another in pursuing academic success. They should all receive adequate financial aid. And they should have ample counseling from academic advisors and from mentors who have succeeded in the professions. Such efforts should be available to all students who perform below expectations, but minorities are likely to be prime beneficiaries of such efforts.

The third step should be to search for new ways of identifying talent that don't rely on grades and scores but look for other evidence of ability to do well in college. One or two programs of this kind already appear to be succeeding. For example, a foundation in New York selects inner city students of all races, not by grades and scores but on the advice of teachers, counselors, and principals for the students qualities of character, perseverance, and leadership. Those selected receive special training on Saturdays throughout their senior year, not only in academic preparation but in how to reach across racial barriers and serve as positive leaders in their college communities. Following this training, they go off in groups to participating private universities. The results thus far are most encouraging. Fewer than 8 percent have dropped out, and several have risen to positions of leadership on their campuses.

Whatever the answer, how the controversy over admissions is resolved will have a lot to do with the future of our profession. Thus far, alas, the debate has generated much more heat than light. Ideologues on both sides have made irresponsible arguments and displayed more certainty than their actual knowledge of the facts could possibly warrant. Voters have had an unrealistic notion that universities can abandon racial preferences but still preserve diverse student bodies. Universities have failed to do enough to educate the public about their admissions policies or to improve the academic achievement of minorities and other underperforming students.

Fortunately, no permanent damage has been done—at least, not yet. The real challenge lies ahead. If we lack imagination and wisdom, we could either perpetuate indefinitely a system of racial preferences that leaves most Americans feeling uncomfortable or we could ensure a stratified society that will seem less and less appropriate for an increasingly diverse society that will include one-third blacks and Hispanics within the working lives of today's college students.

With sufficient energy and creativity, however, it is still possible to meet the challenge with solutions that will improve our student bodies, enhance the quality of their education, and enrich the future leadership of the professions and the nation. Only time will tell which road we choose. Meanwhile, those of us in higher education can take satisfaction from the fact that over the past 30 years, our admissions policies have allowed us to prepare thousands of minority lawyers, doctors, business executives and other professionals who are building a larger black and Hispanic middle class, playing constructive roles in their community, and helping to overcome the extreme racial stratification that characterized our society only three short decades ago.

DISCUSSANT

DAVID GARDNER

I AM NOT clear whether Derek, by referring to "race-conscious admissions," means race-sensitive admissions or race-determinative admissions. These differences are not of degree but of kind; and, as with so much of this problem, the difficulty lies less in the articulation of broad policy and in the sketching of general practices, than it does in the nuances, subtleties, and definition of the terms employed when discussing and debating this issue; and the terms, it seems, are as often ambiguous as they are singular in their meaning.

2. Race, as with other broadly described categories of peoples is subject, in its application to individuals, to substantial interpretation. This is especially true in a society marked by an increase in racially mixed-marriages, in children out-of-wedlock, and in-migration from racially mixed societies, not to mention the misrepresentation and outright fraud that self-identification questions on admission applications invite. This is a matter not sufficiently considered either in policy or in the administration of affirmative action programs, at least it seems to me.

3. The term "minority" has different meanings depending on where one lives in this country. Not since 1992, for example, has there been an ethnic majority in the university's entering class at the eight campuses of the University of California enrolling undergraduates, only a plurality. In UC's entering freshman class of last year for California resident's, Asian-Americans were a plurality at Berkeley, UCLA, Irvine, and Riverside as were whites at Davis, Santa Barbara, San Diego, and Santa Cruz. Not only Blacks, who were

the object of *The Shape of the River,* but also Hispanics, Native Americans, South Pacific Islanders, Filipinos, Asians, and others are also part of the Affirmative Action equation in many states, and especially in California. And the term "underrepresented" is also an interesting one, in common use as it is, for seeking to define our target populations: underrepresented compared to what or to whom; how do we calibrate or count it all up? Do we do so numerically or proportionally and, if that is settled, as measured against what cohort: undergraduate enrollments at a given institution; high school graduates in a given year for a particular state or region; the applicant pool in particular or general; the state's population generally; the age of the college-going population, and so forth?

4. There are also differences in law and custom between the public accountability of private universities and public universities, including admissions. The private nature of admissions at the privates is a protection for institutional practices whether defensible or not; the public nature of admissions at the public universities render them vulnerable to unrelenting attack whether such policies or practices are defensible or not;

And, in closing, a brief personal recollection very much pertinent to this discussion. In 1990, I had scheduled a full day meeting of the University of California's Board of Regents to discuss the university's affirmative action plans and programs in purchasing, contracting, personnel, and admissions. At the end of a very difficult and frustrating day—at least for most Regents—one Regent in sharing his frustration with me said, "Dave, there must simply be a solution to this problem, especially as to the University's admission's policy." I remember responding roughly as follows:

"Regent—for those of you who believe there is a solution to this problem, you do not comprehend the problem; and for those of us who work daily with this matter and who do comprehend the problem, there is no solution. We are doing the best we can, all things considered." Derek, in a way I think you are saying the same thing, but, as you also point out, we need to keep thinking about it, debating it and working to find more agreeable outcomes than settling for programs that pit one race against another on the one hand or pretending that this matter will simply resolve itself on the other.

Health Care in a Democratic Society*

REMARKS TO THE
AMERICAN PHILOSOPHICAL SOCIETY

NANCY KASSEBAUM BAKER

Senator from Kansas, 1978–1997

SINCE 1743, the American Philosophical Society has followed Benjamin Franklin's advice and "improved the common stock of knowledge" in the most distinguished way. Through the years the skills of many prominent members have enhanced our health and our quality of life.

In reflecting this morning on the extraordinary challenges facing health care today, I would like to start with someone who would never have qualified for membership in the American Philosophical Society.

In the late 20s, my home state of Kansas gave rise to one of the more colorful figures in American history, the "goat gland doctor," John R. Brinkley. Doc Brinkley was a masterful con, selling "remedies" including goat gland implants for everything from impotence to baldness. He founded the first radio station west of the Mississippi, KFKB, which stands for Kansas First Kansas Best, and used its powerful signal to peddle his wares across the prairie. He was pursued by the American Medical Association and the Federal Radio Commission that eventually took his license away from him in 1930. He ran for governor and came very close to being elected. He finally moved to Texas where he reestablished a successful radio program and clinic. Eventually he was charged with mail fraud.

Doc Brinkley made his fortune and found his place in history not through the strength of his medicine but through the power of his message. He built an empire by distorting the truth and persuading thousands of people to believe in his distortions. Doc Brinkley took full advantage of the intersection

---

*Read 24 April 1999

of two powerful forces in American culture—the desire we all have to cure our ills and the power of mass marketing to shape public opinion.

Today, we are not confronted with goat-gland charlatans. But we still want to cure our ills, and we still are bombarded with promises of new breakthroughs, some real and some fanciful. In the haze of competing claims and promises, finding the truth is more difficult than ever before.

At the same time, the issues themselves have become more complex. We face difficult decisions as a society about how to reconcile the rapidly growing promises of medicine with the costs of treatment that are rising equally quickly.

We face financial questions, ethical questions, legal questions, and human questions. We face issues of privacy, regulation, and the proper role of government. All of these are serious. All of these are difficult. And, unfortunately, none of these can be resolved so simply as by sending federal agents to run off the quacks.

We must face these issues in the only way we know how—one by one, within the decision-making framework of our democratic society.

But is our government up to the task today? Are we able to settle the difficult questions of health care in the new century through our traditional institutions? Or must we reshape our democratic institutions for the new century? This is the fundamental question I propose to consider today.

Just as technology has complicated our health care, so it has complicated our democracy. Communications technology has brought our democratic republic to a crossroads. Our founders established a republican form of government not only because they favored it philosophically but also because the realities of their time demanded it. The population of eighteenth-century America, consisting largely of rural citizens widely dispersed among thirteen colonies, made direct democracy impossible.

But today, through the power of communications technology, we could. Television, radio, telephones and the Internet bring ideas into our home and carry our ideas out to reach others.

C-SPAN brings every debate of our elected representatives in Congress into our living rooms.

Could we not pose the questions of the day to all of our citizens instead of only an elected few? Could we not watch debates in Congress from the comfort of our easy chairs and then vote all together as a nation, from our homes, with the touch of an armchair button? Could we not govern America, in effect, as one giant Internet chat room?

The answer is, of course, we could. The technical ability to make any such change in our institutions of government is within our grasp. And so, unlike our forefathers, we no longer have the luxury of accepting republican government by default. For the first time in Western Civilization since the small city-states of ancient Greece, direct democracy is possible. The question for us is not *can* we exchange representative democracy for direct democracy. The question for us is, *should* we?

That question is difficult enough when confronted as an abstract notion in a college classroom. It is far more difficult when confronted in the context of real decisions that affect people's lives.

I believe the issues surrounding health care bring into focus the tension between direct and representative democracy. These issues are inherently personal to each of us. Health care affects us all in our lives and our families, and so we all have an incentive to want the best and most health care that technology can provide.

At the same time, health care touches every aspect of our public lives. It is intertwined with almost every domestic issue in America. One-seventh of our country's economy involves health care matters. Our country incurs opportunity costs every time we expand our health care system.

We need focused, objective leaders to sort through the bombardment of competing interests on public policy decisions about health care. Could a direct democracy, in which each of us is both patient and decision-maker, provide that sort of objectivity?

During my time in the Senate and in the years since, I have seen this issue arise time and again. Let me offer some examples:

Example 1: While I served in the Senate, the Clinton administration proposed a far-reaching program to vaccinate every child in America against childhood diseases. There was room for reasonable people to disagree about the merits of this proposal—on the basis of cost, or on the basis of science—and there was vigorous debate in the Senate.

But the public debate became terribly distorted. Rumors that this vaccination plan was in fact some sinister plot to give government control over our lives and to shift power from parents to bureaucrats spread rapidly among people with anti-government leanings, particularly over the Internet. I received hundreds of letters, telephone calls, and postcards from people who believed this vaccination program would somehow imperil our freedoms.

If we had chosen through a direct vote of the people, would this program have been enacted? And would most people have had the benefit of full debate from all points of view? Or would the public have been swayed by distorted arguments of a vocal few?

Example 2: The headlines today are full of news about the drug Viagra. One difficult question is who should pay the cost? The Veterans' Administration, for example, has decided to cover Viagra, while the debate continues about whether Medicare should pay for it.

In our system, these sorts of decisions about whether specific drugs are to be covered by public health benefits are made through a deliberative process. There are hearings, evidence is collected, and, yes, political forces are weighed.

But how would this process work if we had a direct democracy? Would we ever find a drug whose cost should not be covered, or would there be an incentive to vote to cover every drug that came along—particularly a drug that gets good press, as Viagra does, or a drug that is wanted more than it is needed.

On the other hand, might a direct democracy—with true majority rule—exclude from coverage little-known drugs that few people need? One of the pieces of legislation I was proud to introduce in the United States Senate was the Orphan Drug Act, which established incentives to make available life-enhancing medicines that were in such low demand, for instance, Huntington's disease, that, for financial reasons, drug companies would not produce without government assistance. What would we tell those few Americans who need these low-profile drugs when an overwhelming majority of the voters cast their ballots not to pay for them?

Example 3: Our system for allocating transplant organs also illustrates the tensions between direct and representative democracy. There is a long-standing fight in Congress and in the administration over how to allocate organs for transplant. Should we use a regional system, in which organs are first made available for potential recipients in the region where they are donated, or should allocation be conducted nationally based solely on absolute need? If we had a direct democracy, the voice of those regions with the greatest population would inevitably carry the most weight. The delicate constitutional balance that gave each state two votes in the Senate would be gone. And, with it, the system of regional allocation of organs likely would vanish as well—with real consequences for real patients.

Example 4: The tension between the unstoppable advance of science and the unavoidable constraints of the federal budget also would put a direct democracy to the test. Science—particularly medical science—is marching ever forward. New treatments for cancer are in trials, and others are on the horizon. A new generation of artificial organs is under development. There are a thousand new breakthroughs—and there is no doubt that many of them have the ability to extend and enhance life for many people.

But they are expensive. And although we do not like to accept that cost sometimes limits what treatments a patient can receive, the fact is that expensive new technologies raise difficult questions. There will always be tradeoffs, consequences and risks for the decisions we make.

We have struggled with this issue for decades. The Medicare Commission recently released its recommendations to keep the system afloat, although that report was deeply divided over coverage of prescription drugs—as, of course, is the public at large. We continue to seek ways to insure every American. While I chaired the Senate Labor Committee, I joined with Senator Kennedy to pass focused legislation that ensures portability of health insurance and protection for pre-existing conditions when people change jobs—and now, even that limited accomplishment is under assault in Congress.

Example 5: As close to a controversial issue as I can illustrate, and an example of direct democracy at work, took place in Oregon in 1994. An initiative was placed on the ballot which legalized physician–assisted suicide. It was called the "Death with Dignity Act." It sprang from the grassroots and was an emotional debate on both sides. It was approved 52%-48%. An injunction was sought in the U.S. District Court and went up to the Supreme

275

Court, which refused to hear the case. In 1997, on the ballot again was an initiative to repeal the legislation—which was defeated 60%-40%. By March 1998–90 pages of guidelines have been completed.

Example 6: Medical decisions cannot be made in a vacuum. There are questions of ethics and morality that invite regulation. There are questions of individual rights and privacy that invite regulation. We all say; we want to leave doctors alone to attend to the ill; the reality is, we never do and we never can. Health care decisions inherently raise questions that go well beyond medicine, and as medical science advances, that will become even more true.

For example, the State of Kansas recently filed suit to stop a company in Washington state from selling Viagra and other prescription drugs over the Internet. The sales were made with little or no fact checking to ensure that the person making the purchase had a legitimate medical need for the drug. In fact, drugs often were sold to minors impersonating their parents online. Although doctors in Washington state were involved in dispensing the drugs, the State of Kansas was not convinced that those doctors had sufficient contact with the Kansas patients—whom they never actually met— to permit the sales to proceed.

Is that an unjustified intrusion of government into medicine? Or is that a legitimate exercise of the state's police power to protect its citizens against the improper practice of medicine? Eventually it will be the courts, not the doctors or the politicians, who decide these questions. And that's not so different, I suppose, from how the Doc Brinkley controversy finally was settled.

Example 7: Genetics raises a special set of challenges for proponents of direct democracy. Currently, at the National Institutes of Health, the Human Genome Project is mapping the entire human genome. With each new discovery on the path to completing this massive project, we enhance our ability to detect diseases that previously were beyond detection. Through genetic testing, scientists now can peer into our medical future, in part by studying our family's medical past. They can predict the likelihood that we will develop, or not develop, various ailments. But do we want to know? Should we be compelled to know? And if we choose to know about our own genetic makeup, should we be compelled to tell others, such as our insurance companies?

The emerging abilities of scientists and others to grow human tissues raise yet another challenging set of issues. We now have the ability to grow replacement body parts—from thumb bones to skin cartilage. And that ability will become even greater in the future.

But should we use it? When? How? If the American people voted on those questions, would they reach the same conclusions as their elected representatives? And what if they knew that certain genetic advances were made possible by research that is politically controversial, such as research using fetal tissue of experiments conducted on laboratory animals? How would a direct democracy address difficult questions of bioethics and privacy? Would a direct democracy or our representative government reach better answers to these difficult questions?

When these matters are debated in Congress, the outcome is influenced, at least in part, by organized interest groups—disease-specific groups, senior citizens' groups, groups that care about the effect of health care spending on the federal budget, religious and social groups. The doctors have their organization, the nurses have theirs, the anesthetists have yet another. The insurance companies are organized. The hospitals have an association.

James Madison foresaw the power of the "factions," but concluded in *The Federalist Papers* that they would cancel each other out. That was the brilliance of our representative form of government.

But in a direct democracy, the influence of a small number of powerful, well-financed factions is amplified. And there may be little ability of opposing points of view to make themselves heard by the great majority of Americans. We witnessed this when opponents of the Clinton health care bill created "Harry and Louise," an advertising campaign which did more to doom that legislation than all the critical analyses of all the think tanks in Washington. But do we really want public policy shaped more by advertising genius than by policy analysis?

I think not.

Today, the threat of a shift toward direct democracy is not an academic issue, and it is not far-fetched. While we are not on the verge of installing voting buttons in every living room in America, there is little doubt that we are moving away from deliberative decision-making and toward mass influence on public policy.

In our democracy, we very much personalize issues. Without the civil give-and-take of a legislative process, it becomes easy to carry issues to extremes. And in a society where we are constantly bombarded by so much information that no human can process it all, the natural reaction of most of us is to hear only what we want to hear.

In the Senate, I often would receive postcard campaigns from my constituents on this issue or that issue. And I was amused when people would call to ask how many cards I had gotten on each side of an issue, as if I was obliged to vote based on whose voice was loudest.

The trouble with that "tally 'em up" approach is the lack of any mechanism for measuring fullness of thought or intensity of feeling, no allowance for weighing other considerations. Are 1,000 pre-printed postcards, which involved little thought by the senders, worth any more than one well-thought-out letter? I always believed that the power of an argument, not its volume, was what ought to matter.

If our country is to successfully sort through the increasingly complex issues that science and technology lay at our feet, I believe we must affirm our commitment to representative democracy. We must reconfirm our belief in the deliberative process that has served us well for more than two centuries. There are no easy solutions.

In conclusion, I would offer this observation—in the book of Proverbs there is the acknowledgment that knowledge is the important thing—therefore get knowledge. But with all thy getting get understanding. We must take the responsibility to be an informed public so that we may then better understand the complexity of the decisions to be made.

DISCUSSANT

FRANCISCO J. AYALA

University of California at Irvine

SENATOR KASSEBAUM-BAKER has set the stage for a wonderful discussion. Noting that health care questions raise difficult issues—financial, legal, ethical and human issues, as well as issues of privacy, regulation and the proper role of government, to use her terms, she asks: "Is our government up to the task . . . Or must we reshape our democratic institutions for the new century?"

Representational democracy, she notes, was established by our founders, "not only because they favored it philosophically, but also because the realities of their time demanded it." But it is no longer so, she notes. Communication technology brings every debate of our elected representatives in Congress to our living rooms. We, all citizens, could vote together as a nation from our homes, governing all America as one giant Internet chat room. God forbid, she added. (That was not in the manuscript, if my recollection is right.)

But we should know, the Senator argues, that direct democracy is possible but is not desirable. She has used six health-care examples as a sustained argument for the continuation of the representative democracy form of government that we received from the Founders. She points out dangers of direct democracy and concludes that we must press ahead with our time-tested process of representative democracy.

Senator Kassebaum-Baker's conclusions seem to me unobjectionable. But I wonder whether libertarians of certain kind, those who want the government off our backs, would agree? The alternative would be not the kind of rule of the mob that might come to be with direct democracy. Rather, the argument might come from the other side, from those who, like Robert Nozick in his book, *Anarchy, State and Utopia,* would claim that "No state more extensive than the minimal state can be justified."

Let me make clear that such is not a form of libertarianism that I hold. But then there are, again quoting the Senator, "questions of ethics and morality which invite regulation . . . [and] questions of individual rights and privacy which invite regulation." The problems can be many, even with our form of representative democracy.

In my field of genetics the issues of genetic engineering are becoming close to the fore, particularly, again as the Senator noted, as we come close to obtaining the secrets of the human genome. Let me sketch some issues.

I will first distinguish between genetic "therapy" (which seeks to cure diseases and disabilities) and genetic "enhancement" (which seeks to improve the genetic make-up of individuals, whatever "improving" may mean here).

It is now possible to practice gene therapy using molecular biology methods to cure some diseases, and the methodology is improving quickly. Some people are opposing this technology not for therapy purposes, but only when it is used for genetic "enhancement," that is, for improving the human genetic makeup.

Now, genetic therapy and genetic enhancement can be done not only on the individual, *somatically,* but also in the *germ line,* so that the descendants will carry the new genetic makeup and not only the individuals in which it has been practiced. The question is: are these matters to be decided through the representative democracy way of government? Some will ask, rather, should they be regulated at all by the government? It might seem best to leave these matters to the individual's decision. But then, genetic engineering in the germ line has consequences for future generations; it has social consequences. And there is the issue of allocation of limited resources. Do we set up priorities or do we leave genetic engineering as a free-for-all, dependent only perhaps on the ability of individuals to pay for it?

And then, what about cloning of individual humans? Let me here make a brief parenthesis. As my fellow population geneticists, at least, are quite well aware, one cannot clone human individuals. Contrary to what has been said in the press and elsewhere, you can clone the *genome* of a human individual but not the individual as such. If somebody were to clone my genes, the new individual would have a physical resemblance to me at the same age, but in matters of intelligence, character, tastes, preferences—all the things that determine personality—this individual would be completely different from me. Indeed, there are not serious grounds to think that the individual developed from my cloned genes would be more similar to me than to others among his peers, that is, to other individuals of his generation, with respect to these matters of personality. My genetic clone would have been exposed to a very different familiar, cultural, and sociopolitical context. He would not grow in the same family I did, experience growing up in Spain under General Franco's dictatorship, go to the same schools, or migrate to the United States to study at Columbia University, and so on and on.

The well-publicized case of the sheep Dolly has brought the possibility of cloning a human genome to the forefront. President Clinton has proposed a five-year moratorium for exploring and public debate of the issue of human cloning from all relevant perspectives. Is this issue of human cloning ultimately one that we want to be regulated by the government?

And what about therapeutic abortion? Or any kind of abortion, for that matter. For some, any form of abortion is murder, independently of whether the embryo is at the four-cell stage of development or in the sixth month of pregnancy. For others, any limitation of abortion rights is an intolerable invasion by the government of the rights of the individual—the mother-to-be. Still others want to take into account the stage of development of the fetus and whether there are health issues concerning the mother or the child to be born, and the like. As the Senator has pointed out repeatedly, these are very complex issues that are multidimensional.

I will not proceed further but simply say that Senator Kassebaum-Baker, with an eloquent and thoughtful presentation, has opened up a full chest of issues, which are not new but surely deserve exploration and debate, as I hope it will now happen.

Culture and Democracy in America*

SHELDON HACKNEY

Professor of History, University of Pennsylvania

T̶HE ARGUMENT about the propriety of government sponsorship of cultural activities in the United States is really an argument about what kind of society we want to be. In particular, it is a conversation about the relationship between individualism and community in our democratic culture, a recurrent theme of the national dialogue from the beginnings of the republic.

True, in its current form as part of a "culture war," it burst forth in May 1989 when Senator Jesse Helms, using information provided by the conservative Christian American Family Association, condemned the National Endowment for the Arts (NEA) for providing funds for Andres Serrano's "Piss Christ," which he took to be sacrilegious.[1] This was followed closely by the controversy over the retrospective of the photographs of Robert Mapplethorpe, some of which were homoerotic. That exhibit was organized here in Philadelphia at the Institute of Contemporary Art, part of the University of Pennsylvania, where it showed without incident. It was canceled, however, by the Corcoran Gallery in Washington under pressure from Senator Helms, who objected to tax dollars being used to support what he judged to be pornography and what he assumed would offend the sensibilities of a large number of tax payers. Since then, the war has raged episodically. The most recent skirmish occurred this spring when the NEA suddenly announced, soon after reporters began inquiring about the project,

---

*Read 24 April 1999.

1. Cynthia Koch, "The Contest for American Culture: A Leadership Case Study on The NEA and NEH Funding Crisis," Penn National Commission on Society, Culture and Community, September 1998, unpublished, but available on-line at WWW.UPENN.EDU/PNC.

that it had withdrawn the subsidy for the publication in English of a children's book written by the Zapatista leader, Subcommandante Marcos.

In its most virulent form, this culture war is designed to roll back the shifts in moral values that conservative critics trace to the "counterculture" of the 1960s, to resist the radical relativism and intellectual indeterminacy that is known variously as poststructuralism, deconstruction, critical theory and postmodernism, or perhaps even to stem the tide of change flowing from modernity itself (the intellectual revolution originating in Renaissance humanism, the ongoing scientific revolution, Enlightenment rationalism, and the triumphant ideas that humans can understand and control the natural world in which we live and that the application of human reason will result in material and eventually moral progress).[2] Religiously-based cultural conservatives have as allies in the culture war libertarian ideologues and political conservatives whose objective is, in the words of art critic Robert Hughes, "to defoliate the liberal habitat."[3]

The climax of this battle came in the aftermath of the revolutionary election of 1994 that brought Newt Gingrich to power as the Speaker of the House of Representatives, at the head of a majority dominated by "New Republicans." Moving quickly to accomplish as much as possible of their "Contract With America," including the elimination of NEA, the National Endowment for the Humanities (NEH),[4] and the Corporation for Public Broadcasting (CPB), the new majority sought to make the federal government smaller. It would be a mistake, however, to think that their budgetary

---

2. See my fuller discussion of the culture wars in the context of higher education, "Higher Education As A Medium for Culture," *American Behavioral Scientist* (March 1999), pp. 987–997.

3. Robert Hughes, "Pulling the Fuse on Culture," *Time,* August 7, 1995.

4. The National Endowment for the Humanities is an independent federal agency that makes grants to nonprofit organizations for projects that "insure progress in the humanities." In the authorizing legislation, the humanities are defined by a list of disciplines, such as History, Philosophy, the study of Literature, the study of Religion, etc. I think of the NEH as funding three categories of activities: the creation and preservation of knowledge in the humanities; the translation of that knowledge into educational experiences for both formal and informal settings; and public programs that make humanistic knowledge available to as broad an audience as possible.

attacks on the NEA, NEH, CPB, and the Institute for Museum Services had a lot to do with saving tax dollars. Those agencies were under fire because they were thought to be dominated by the "cultural elite," the newly named specter that religious and cultural conservatives claim is stalking heartland America.

All of the targeted agencies suffered budgetary recissions in FY 95 and serious reductions for FY 96—but they survived. They survived more because of the popularity of Big Bird, and the grass roots advocacy of enthusiasts of the arts, humanities, and public television, than because of any of the powerful rational arguments that people like me kept making. Nevertheless, they survived, and therein lies a tale.

Before the creation of the NEH and NEA in 1965, federal support for cultural activities had been not only sporadic but had also been camouflaged. The creation of the Library of Congress in 1800, arguably the first act of cultural support, was a hotly debated issue, in part because it was done by purchasing Thomas Jefferson's library. The Library of Congress continues to masquerade as a legislative reference service for Congress, whereas it is actually an incredibly valuable research library and an extremely active cultural institution. The Lewis and Clark expedition, which was a knowledge-gathering foray, was presented instead as a search for a commercial route to the Pacific. When John Quincy Adams in 1825 proposed the creation of a national university, the idea was killed by arguments against "centralization," an argument that is still potent and prominent in a culture that prefers that power be widely dispersed. The chartering of the Smithsonian Institution in 1846 was simply taking advantage of a private benefaction, and it enjoyed the cover of appearing to be about practical scientific knowledge. Providing tax deductibility for gifts to cultural institutions began almost unnoticed in 1918. The Department of Commerce subsidized the production of movies in the 1920s in the guise of supporting an export industry. The New Deal ran the Federal Theater Project and the Federal Writers Project, and it subsidized artists in various ways, but all of that was done as a temporary relief measure. During the Cold War, the government created the new position of Under Secretary of State for Cultural Affairs in order to promote American culture abroad under the theory that "soft power" could be deployed in the service of American strategic interests. Most cabinet departments now support cultural activities within their domains in one way or another, not to mention the Library of Congress, the Smithsonian, and the National Gallery of Art.[5]

Yet, none of these activities has ever risen to the level of a national cultural policy. In fact, even after 1965, when the NEH and NEA were created, we can not be said to have a national cultural policy. We have simply a conscious policy of supporting cultural activities of various kinds. Why this coyness?

It has to do with the American Identity. Beyond its common core of civic nationalism, a commitment to democracy and the political values expressed in the Declaration of Independence and the Constitution, the American Identity can be located in part in the dialogic relationships between the opposing elements of a number of dichotomous pairs: liberty and equality; individual and community; self-reliance and corn-husking, barn-raising cooperation; common-man humility and glittery celebrity; materialism and religiosity; hard work and get-rich-quick schemes; and so on.

Primary among these mutually modifying values is the interplay between liberalism and republicanism, which is a first cousin to the relationship between individualism and community. Even though it has been popular to say that we are all Jeffersonians, and even though the rhetoric of individualism is more evident and seems to have more authority than that of community, our civic ideals are actually a mixture of classical liberalism and classical republicanism. What I find interesting is the covert nature of civic republicanism, the apologetic way that arguments in favor of shared goals and collective well-being are made.

That is so because the myth of individualism has such a firm hold on the American imagination. For instance, the lonely hero of Hollywood westerns dominates the silver screen. Between 1924 and 1967, 24 percent of all movies made in Hollywood were westerns. In 1995, John Wayne, the leading western hero of all time, was ranked number one in polls as the public's favorite male movie star, even though he had been dead sixteen years. As Garry Wills writes, Wayne "embodies the American myth. The archetypal American is a displaced person—arrived from a rejected past, breaking into a glorious future, on the move, fearless himself, feared by others, a killer but

---

5. Michael Kammen, "Culture and the State in America," *The Journal of American History* (December 1996): 798.

cleansing the world of things that 'need killing,' loving but not bound down by love, rootless but carrying the Center in himself, a gyroscopic direction-setter, a traveling norm."[6]

In this myth, the authentic American appears out of nature, not out of books or the accumulated artifacts and wealth that represent civilization. We like our heroes natural, not cultivated. This is the root of both our Jeffersonianism and our anti-intellectualism. We admire close contact with nature; we distrust all concentrations of power, both public and private; we think dignity is achieved by performance rather than by status; and we are skeptical of experts.

Something of the Yin/Yang mechanism that is at work here is suggested by the fact that the real story of the West is more the story of the American army, large and cooperative groups traveling together in covered wagon trains, and federally subsidized railroads than it is the story of isolated mountain men, single explorers, or lonely cowpokes. John Wayne looms large in our fantasies, but the national genius is for large scale organization—the Union Pacific Railroad, Western Union, U.S. Steel, Standard Oil, General Motors, IBM, Microsoft, D-Day in Normandy, putting a man on the moon, the Gulf War—the coordination of individual efforts and the application of technology on a massive scale. We hide this fact from ourselves by worshipping the unbounded individual.

Seymour Martin Lipset in his book, *American Exceptionalism,* reminds us that the United States is the most individualistic nation in the industrialized world, as well as the least taxed, the least regulated, and the most afflicted with social pathologies."[7] Perhaps for this reason, our commitments to community are hidden. You have to look closely for them. The price for sending a first-class letter across town is the same as it is for sending it across the continent, thus subsidizing a lot of folks who live in remote locations. Our regulators prevent the exclusion of high-risk demographic groups from insurance pools. High hospital rates paid by the wealthy and the insured cover the costs of treating indigent, uninsured patients. Before the breakup of the Bell system, long-distance rates subsidized local rates, and various

6. Garry Wills, *John Wayne's America* (New York: Simon and Schuster, 1998), p. 302.

7. Seymour Martin Lipset, *American Exceptionalism: A Two-edged Sword* (New York: W. W. Norton and Company, 1996).

other kinds of cross-subsidies operated to make phone service more widely available, and to support a lot of world-class basic research at Bell Labs. Such practices act out our moral commitments to each other in unnoticed ways.

Significantly, the most important of these invisible bonds of community are being attacked by the hyperindividualistic cultural conservatives. The public school system, the last best hope of the poor to see their children gain a chance to succeed, is being undermined by the private school voucher movement. Proposed privatization plans for Social Security would retreat from the most popular income redistribution system the federal government runs, a system in which current workers pay for the retirement of past workers, and the less well-to-do are supported by the more-well-to-do. Though the terms of the debate don't reflect it, contemporary political battles are about individualism and community.

One of the most interesting facets of the current debate is that it cuts across the usual political alignments. The classical liberal tradition thus embraces people both on the left and on the right. Its central thrust is that the government should remain neutral in the choice of values and in determining what is the good life. "Process liberalism" this is sometimes called. According to process liberalism, society is thought to consist of freestanding individuals who pursue their own interests and choose their own values and identities. They are thought of as self-regarding and self-actualizing individuals. The government must, of course, furnish common goods, such things as national defense, clean air and pure water, police protection, perhaps roads and bridges, things that are indivisible so that either everyone has them or no one has them. The market cannot distribute them in the same way it distributes individual goods. Beyond common goods, however, the government is merely to protect the rights of citizens so that individuals have maximum freedom to choose their own values, their own identities, their own idea of the good life. There is no such thing as the common interest that is separate from the aggregation of the individual interests of the citizens. In practice, this framework can lead to rights-based liberalism, such as one sees in feminism or the ACLU, or to a libertarian brand of conservatism.[8]

---

8. Michael J. Sandel, *Democracy's Discontents: America in Search of a Public Philosophy* (Cambridge: The Belknap Press of Harvard University Press, 1996).

Classical liberalism was not the only philosophical tradition to have survived the American Revolution, however. Civic republicans, with roots in Aristotelian philosophy and Renaissance humanism, believe that the purpose of government is to produce good citizens. That requires a judgment about what the good society is, so that the government can inculcate appropriate values in inhabitants through education, exhortation, and policies expressed in law. Freedom in such a regime consists in participating in self-governance (rather than in being maximally free of external constraints). The success of the society depends upon citizens behaving virtuously, and the highest virtue is to set aside one's own self-interest in order to pursue the common interest of the society as a whole. One hears echoes of this strand of republicanism more and more these days from virtuecrats such as William Bennett, and perhaps the religious right that wants government to inculcate correct moral values, but also from communitarians on the Left such as Amitai Etzioni.

The problems with these two strains of public philosophy in their pure form are obvious. The civic republican notion might work wonderfully if the elite were always virtuous and clear-headedly aware of their own motivations, but they are not. In practice, it is very hard to tell the difference between policies that the elite insist are for the good of the society as a whole and policies that serve the selfish interests of members of the elite themselves. The opportunity for oppression concealed as virtue is enormous. It is also true that civic republics are subject to the temptation to vest full citizenship in select groups, because the well-being of the republic depends upon the ability of individual citizens to deliberate and choose the best course of action for the community as a whole. It is always tempting to think that some kinds of citizens and some groups are better qualified for that kind of deliberation than others. Most important, in this cynical age, one cannot rest a public philosophy on altruism.

Liberal theory assumes that we all can start our "life of choosing" unencumbered by outside influences, but that is impossible. We are born into particular families in particular locations and at particular times, and all of those contingencies shape our choices. There is no escaping our context, so our choices are never completely free. We also cannot choose options of which we are not aware, nor can we achieve what our childhood has not prepared us for. Our possibilities are filtered through our cultural situation. It is also true that the radical focus on the individual obscures the degree to which the fate of the community determines the fate of individual members.

Fortunately, there is a way out of this dilemma, a dilemma posed by the deleterious effects on society of selfishness on the one hand, and our lack of faith in altruism on the other! We all must ask at every turn the crucial question, "What kind of society do I want to live in?"

Asking that question makes us realize that we have a self-interest in both the economic and the cultural opportunities of our neighbors. Immunization is a useful, though inexact, metaphor. There is a sense in which ignorance and cultural deprivation are like the measles. We can't "catch" them, but we can catch the things they spawn: violence, deviance, and poverty of the spirit. Do we want to live in a society characterized by huge disparities of wealth or education? Do we want to have to fend off desperate beggars every time we walk down the street? Do we want to live with an underclass that is so hopeless that its members engage in self-destructive behavior and also prey upon those who have more? Do we want to live in a society in which a majority cares little for the preservation of the cultural heritage in whatever form it appears, and in which the human need to make sense of life, to figure out who we are and how we are connected to others, to find some meaning and inspiration in human experience is pursued at a depressingly low level? In such a society, the pursuit of happiness will be painfully hobbled.

Education may be the clearest example of the mutually modifying nature of our dual commitments to individualism and to community. We are currently having a great debate nationally about whether education is an individual consumer item that can be privatized or a common good that needs to be provided to everyone. It is clearly both. The individual benefits from education, certainly, but so does society at large. That is why we have compulsory school attendance laws, and that is why for higher education we have traditionally split the costs between the individual and the wider society in both public and private institutions. The critical thing to realize about education, as about the sorts of broadly available cultural activities funded by the NEA and NEH, is that each of us will be better off if our neighbors have it.

Let me assume here that we all agree that the humanities are good for individuals, and that there is also a civic component to their "goodness," especially in a democracy. The culture wars pose the classical liberal question, why should the humanities be sponsored by the government? Indeed, the toughest argument to answer is the argument that we should simply privatize all cultural activity. If the public wants it, say the individualistic critics, they will find a way to pay for it, either through ticket sales, commercial sponsorship, or private philanthropy.

Well, cultural opportunities can be privatized to some degree, though there are important cultural treasures and cultural activities that cannot be funded through any kind of market mechanism. We understand intuitively our common interest when it comes to national parks, or perhaps such historic battlegrounds as Gettysburg, but without public funding countless other cultural experiences would not be available to the general public because there is no individual incentive to fund them and there is no mass audience able to pay for them through ticket sales or commercial sponsorships.

One important category of humanities activities that would suffer grievously from privatization are those whose beneficiaries are located so far away in time or space from the creator of the "product" that they can not be identified, and so required to pay. The beneficiaries of the collected papers of "great" people are the teachers and students who will use them into the indefinite future. The beneficiary of an NEH fellowship is not the individual scholar so much as the other scholars and teachers and students and text book writers and the general public who will use his or her work in the future. The beneficiary of an NEH preservation grant is not the receiving institution but those in the distant future who will be able to read the threatened texts and see the deteriorating historical artifacts that otherwise would be lost.

A second category includes activities that have an immediate and identifiable audience, but an audience that cannot pay. I am thinking here of high quality historical documentary film, or perhaps the production of educational programs or museum exhibits that are rich in content. Sponsors do find these programs to be good vehicles for helping to carry a commercial message, but they won't pay for the full costs to produce high quality because they can get their message out more cheaply with less costly (and lower quality) programs. Frequently it is the NEH grant that provides the seed money and the authentication that attracts a commercial sponsor.

These and other cultural activities have few patrons other than the federal government, and their availability to the general public enhances the quality of life for everyone while it helps to produce the sort of society that most of us want to live in.

Given the privileged rhetorical position of atomistic self-reliance, it is also critical in these contentious times that the funding choices of the NEA and NEH be defensible in politically neutral terms. The NEH accomplishes this by a clear policy position that says in effect, "We do not fund partisan activities; we do not fund activities that are designed to convert an audience to a particular point of view; we do not fund activities that are merely celebratory; and we will insist on scholarly balance in everything that we support." This does not guarantee that the NEH will not draw political lightening, but it makes it much harder for critics to find a complaint that can be used to demonize the agency.

Meanwhile, we should avoid the dead-end argument between selfishness and altruism. We should keep asking instead, "What sort of society do I want to live in?" My conviction is that it is a society with a rich cultural life available to all, a society whose individualism is expressed in a common commitment that every individual should enjoy the maximum opportunity to lead a fulfilling life illuminated by the wisdom, beauty, and self-knowledge only achievable through an active cultural life. In such a wholesome democratic society, there is a useful role for the government to play.

DISCUSSANT

JOHN D'ARMS
American Council of Learned Societies

JUST TWO things I want to say this morning. I want to speak about a historical episode and I want to ask one question. The episode concerns what is, I think, the very first attested moment in this country when the tensions surrounding culture and the federal government became most vividly apparent—the extensive and extraordinary congressional debate in 1814 over the offer by Thomas Jefferson to sell his personal library to the government for the sum of $25,000. Neil Harris has recently pointed out how suggestively this debate forecast contemporary issues in defining the relationship between government and culture in our country. Opponents produced five basic arguments why the Jefferson library should not be bought. And every one of these are still with us. These books were held to be dangerous and subversive, particularly to morals. Secondly, they were seen as esoteric, unnecessary, and socially irrelevant. And third, most of them were pronounced to be unreadable, particularly by members of Congress. Fourth, it was protested that they were very costly, requiring an expenditure of taxpayer monies inflated by an unholy conspiracy of pedants and dealers. And fifth, there were far better and more appropriate things to do with public money, if any at all were available. To capture just a bit of the flavor of the opposition, I quote one, tiny bit of the actual debate. An opponent of the purchase, Cyrus King of Massachusetts, a leading Federalist, complained that the library assembled by Jefferson contained "irreligious and immoral works of the French philosophers who caused and influenced the volcano of the French Revolution." King was able simultaneously to combine these charges of subversion with the other charges of pedantry. These books, he continued, were in languages which many cannot read and most ought not to. So to sum up this overall observation, subversive, useless, obscure, costly, and low on the national agenda of needs. Here is a quintet of objections familiar to all of us who have struggled to get public funds in support of culture. The simple purchase of a magnificent library was sufficient to arouse all of these anxieties and stimulated a series of overstatements and exaggerations which form a tradition that continues to haunt these discussions today. In the end, of course, the great collection was acquired but the final vote in the House was close, 81 to 71.

Now, to get to my question. It takes a tiny bit of time to set it up. It seems to me that implicit in what you have to say are two models of the federal government as a sponsor of cultural activities, a strong and a weak model. The strong model is something like a ministry of culture with a highly centralized structure of agencies under it, with a highly articulated agenda for national cultural policy. The United States has effectively rejected this strong model as being out of keeping with our pluralistic and federalist tradition. But there is a weaker model, and with the creation of the NEH and NEA in 1965, we have embraced it. Legislation establishing the two endowments speaks "of a broadly conceived, national policy of support for the humanities and arts." So we've adopted this weaker model, but it seems to me there are additional features of it that nationally benefit culture. First, as you mention, the tax deductibility for gifts to charity, including cultural institutions, began as early as 1918. Less often, notices in these discussions is another fiscal feature that benefits culture. It is national policy not to tax philanthropic foundations. We legally require only that they give away 5 percent of their assets each year. This amounts to significant tax revenue loss. U.S. foundations made an estimated 19.5 billion dollars in contributions and grants in 1998 to non-profit groups—up from 16 billion in 1997. To be sure, the foundation gifts flowing to arts, humanities, and culture is a very modest percentage of total giving. And as an aside I might note that the national failure of any body to collect and categorize data of such giving for culture is exasperating for all who seek to study trends. The Foundation Center in New York does not have a clear, working definition of humanities, and humanities sometimes bleeds into culture, and culture and humanities themselves into arts. But, and here at last is my question: When the federal government as a matter of policy explicitly foregoes this tax revenue and thereby encourages more foundation giving, is it not strengthening its support of culture? To put the question another way, where along the spectrum of the weak to the strong models of cultural policy do we situate the national commitment such as we have to exempting most foundations from tax requirements?

Index